THIRD MAN BOOKS

D1605636

THIRD MAN BOOKS

For more information:
Third Man Books, LLC
623 7th Ave S
Nashville, Tennessee 37203

A CIP record is on file with the Library of Congress.

FIRST EDITION

Cover design by Caitlin Parker
Art direction by Jordan Williams and Amin Qutteineh
Layout by Amin Qutteineh

ISBN: 979-8-98661-457-1

DYNAMITE NASHVILLE

UNMASKING THE FBI, THE KKK, AND THE BOMBERS BEYOND THEIR CONTROL

Betsy Phillips

What's been done in the dark will be brought to the light.
You can run on for a long time,
Run on for a long time.
You can run on for a long time,
But sooner or later . . .

Traditional folk song

For Z. Alexander Looby, who deserved justice.

Contents

USEFUL MAPS

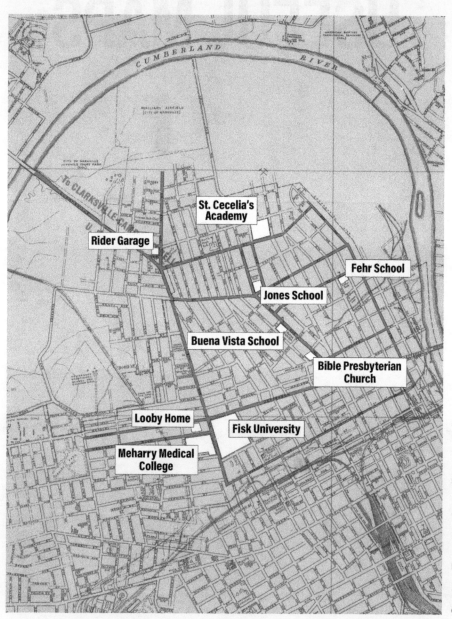

St. Cecelia's Academy

Rider Garage

Fehr School

Jones School

Buena Vista School

Bible Presbyterian Church

Looby Home

Fisk University

Meharry Medical College

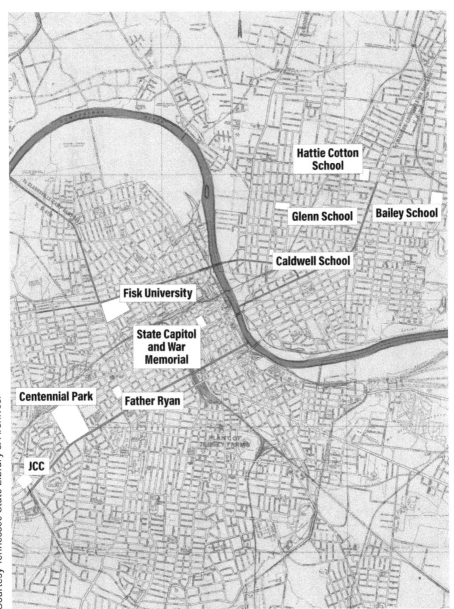

Hattie Cotton School

Glenn School

Bailey School

Caldwell School

Fisk University

State Capitol and War Memorial

Centennial Park

Father Ryan

JCC

TIMELINE

(Text in bold refers to Nashville-specific events)

May 17, 1954

US Supreme Court rules in the case of *Brown v. Board of Education*, declaring public school segregation unconstitutional.

September 1954

Two Nashville Catholic schools desegregate: Cathedral High School and Father Ryan High School.

August 28, 1955

Fourteen-year-old Emmett Till is murdered while visiting relatives in Mississippi.

September 1, 1955

Robert Kelly attempts to enroll in Nashville's East High School. He is turned away because he is Black. His father hires Z. Alexander Looby and Avon Williams to sue the school board.

September 3, 1955

Emmett Till's open-casket funeral is held in Chicago and covered extensively by the national Black press.

September 6, 1955

Oak Ridge High School in Oak Ridge, Tennessee, desegregates.

December 1, 1955

Rosa Parks is arrested for not giving up her seat on a Montgomery, Alabama, bus.

December 5, 1955

Martin Luther King Jr. leads the Montgomery bus boycott.

January 30, 1956

Dr. King's home in Montgomery is bombed.

September 1, 1956

Clinton, Tennessee's eponymous high school is desegregated by twelve students. John Kasper instigates a riot in retaliation, and the National Guard is called in.

January 10–11, 1957

Black pastors and civil rights leaders meet in Atlanta and begin planning nonviolent protests against racial discrimination. They form the Southern Christian Leadership Conference (SCLC).

September 4, 1957

Nine Black students desegregate Little Rock Central High School, sparking a dramatic confrontation between Arkansas governor Orval Faubus and President Eisenhower.

September 10, 1957

Hattie Cotton School in Nashville is bombed.

March 16, 1958

The Nashville Jewish Community Center is bombed.

March 26-28, 1958

The Nashville Christian Leadership Conference (NCLC), led by Rev. Kelly Miller Smith, holds its first workshop.

Fall Semester, 1958

James Lawson enrolls at Vanderbilt Divinity School and begins leading workshops in nonviolent protest at Clark Memorial Methodist Church.

October 5, 1958

Clinton High School is bombed.

February 1, 1960

The sit-in movement begins in Greensboro, North Carolina.

February 13, 1960

The Nashville Sit-Ins begin.

February 19, 1960

Chattanooga high-school students from Howard High begin their lunch counter protests.

March 3, 1960

James Lawson is expelled from Vanderbilt Divinity School because of his civil rights work.

April 16-17, 1960

The Student Nonviolent Coordinating Committee (SNCC) is founded.

April 19, 1960

Z. Alexander Looby's Nashville home is bombed. Protesters lead a silent march downtown to confront Mayor Ben West. Diane Nash gets the mayor to admit that segregation is wrong.

May 10, 1960

Nashville lunch counters begin to desegregate.

November 14, 1960

Ruby Bridges desegregates New Orleans public schools.

May 4, 1961

The Freedom Rides begin.

April 3, 1963

Activists launch a series of massive demonstrations in Birmingham.

April 12, 1963

Martin Luther King Jr. is arrested in Birmingham.

May 2, 1963

The Children's Crusade begins in Birmingham.

May 3, 1963

Birmingham commissioner of public safety Bull Connor turns fire hoses and dogs on the child activists.

June 11, 1963

Governor George Wallace blocks Black students from attending the University of Alabama.

August 28, 1963

The March on Washington for economic and civil rights for African Americans, Martin Luther King Jr. delivers his "I have a dream" speech.

September 15, 1963

Racial terrorists blow up the 16th Street Baptist Church in Birmingham, killing Addie Mae Collins (14), Carole Denise McNair (11), Carole Robertson (14), and Cynthia Wesley (14). More than twenty others injured.

THE LIMITS OF THIS BOOK AND MY HOPES FOR IT

A few months before the sixtieth anniversary of the bombing of Hattie Cotton Elementary School in 2017, I thought I would write something for the *Nashville Scene* about the bombing and who had committed it and why it remains unsolved. Five years later, I'm still working to answer those questions and more.

Who committed Nashville's three unsolved integration-era bombings—Hattie Cotton Elementary School in 1957, the Jewish Community Center in 1958, and Councilman Z. Alexander Looby's house in 1960?

The two most prevalent theories were either that racist agitator John Kasper did it or that the local Ku Klux Klan did it. But these "solutions" only raised more questions. John Kasper was in jail at the time of two of the bombings. Are we supposed to believe he had a batch of such devoted followers that he could order an assassination attempt from jail—and that people would keep quiet about it for sixty years? If it was the Klan, why did the bombings stop? They had successfully terrified the city and nearly derailed school integration, and no one had been caught. Why would they abandon such an effective tool? And again, we're supposed to believe that a rabble of local racists tried to assassinate a politician and then kept quiet about it for half a century? It didn't ring true. How could three bombings—one of which, I reiterate, was an assassination attempt on a sitting US politician—remain so thoroughly unsolved?

I set about to see if I could solve them.

What I soon discovered is that Nashville's local violence of the 1950s was a precursor to the violence that would grip the South in the 1960s and 1970s, an early version of what we would come to know and fear.

This contradicts the myth of Nashville's peaceful integration. To hear the story, you'd think civil rights organizer and sit-in leader Diane Nash gathered some friends for a stroll one day, happened across Mayor Ben West downtown, and, during a pleasant chat, convinced him of the injustice of segregation, which he ended then and there without incident.

The truth was uglier. It's true that no one was killed here. There aren't iconic photos of people suffering (actually there are, but the papers

AP Photo

didn't run them).[1] But African Americans who were in Nashville during this era have always spoken plainly about its brutality. The rest of the city hasn't made a habit of listening.

Which means we don't know our own stories. Worse, it means we've been conditioned to not look too hard at what we don't know.

Just as these were the early, formative years for the people who would go on to lead the Student Nonviolent Coordinating Committee (SNCC) and head up the Freedom Rides, these were the early, formative years of their organized enemies. Just as Nashville was full of young people who would go on to be American civil rights heroes—Rev. James Lawson, Diane Nash, future congressman John Lewis, and so on—we had America's nightmare here in J.B. Stoner, Edward Fields, John Kasper, Robert Gentry, and so on. Their evil was still developing when they were in Nashville, so it's gone unrecognized.

But once you are able to see what you're looking at, Nashville's three unsolved integration-era bombings—Hattie Cotton Elementary School on September 10, 1957, the Jewish Community Center on March 16, 1958, and the home of Z. Alexander Looby on April 19, 1960—take on a new importance. It's not just that these are some of the earliest appearances of the racists who would go on to do so much damage to our country. Nashville is where they first worked out the best ways to do these terrible things without paying any price for it.

Much of this book focuses on the minutia of why these racial terrorists weren't caught—though most of us already know that the police weren't uniformly in disagreement with their goals, and that the FBI's agenda during this time was often at odds with solving these kinds of crimes. That lesson cost our nation dearly in the coming decades.

But another reason these bombings have never been solved is that the people who might have relevant information are still staying silent.

If you've ever seen photographs of little first graders integrating Nashville's schools or of stoic college students sitting at lunch counters, then you've seen mobs of furious white people holding signs, throwing rocks, and hurling epithets. The captions of these photos always identify the Black people risking their safety for justice; they very rarely identify anyone in the angry mobs.

These events happened only sixty years ago. Most of the first graders who integrated Nashville's schools in 1957 are still alive. When white Nashville natives go into the Civil Rights Room at the downtown branch of the Nashville Public Library and see those pictures enlarged on the walls, some of them must know some of the people in the mobs. They must know the names of the managers at the lunch counters. Someone knows who bombed Hattie Cotton Elementary School, the Jewish Community Center, and Z. Alexander Looby's home. Yet the community at large has been denied that knowledge.

My focus is small: I want to know who did those bombings. If I can't know that, I want to know why not. I want to know who made the decision that protecting white racist terrorists was more important than telling Nashville the truth.

This book is therefore not directly about school integration or the civil rights movement in Nashville. That work has already been done—you can read *The Nashville Way* by Benjamin Houston, *Making the Unequal Metropolis* by Ansley Erickson, Congressman John Lewis's *March*, or David Halberstam's *The Children*, among others, for yourself. It is also not a biography of Z. Alexander Looby or Avon Williams or other Black Nashvillians who deserve considered examinations of their lives and accomplishments. I'll be dealing with the ugly underside, the white supremacist side, which, until now, no one has tried to piece together.

To be clear, I have not solved these bombings. Admittedly, this makes for a strange premise for a book: here are three unsolved crimes that, even after we spend eighty thousand words together, will remain unsolved.

Why, then, this book?

I'll level with you: my answer to that question has changed over the course of writing it. I finished the first draft in 2017, fueled by outrage that someone had tried to kill Z. Alexander Looby—a sitting city councilman, an elected representative of Nashville—and that the would-be murderer was never caught. We can all shrug and say, "Well, it was 1960, what do you expect? They didn't care about crimes against Black men." But, folks, it was only 1960 for one year. What has prevented Nashville from investigating the crime in any of the six decades since?

The answer to that last question is why I've not chucked this project into a deep hole. When I started writing, I thought the answer was laziness or disinterest. And while I'm sure there's some of that, what I discovered over the course of writing is that it's very hard to get answers to these old unsolved cases.

The files of the Tennessee Bureau of Investigation and its precursor organization, the Tennessee Bureau of Criminal Identification, are sealed by state law. No one who isn't in law enforcement can see those files, except under very narrow and specific instances when state legislators might be able to. Even the governor's ability to see those files is severely limited. This means that, for all practical purposes, the TBI operates without citizen oversight. There is no way for the media to look into a TBI investigation. Families of victims in cold cases can't review the files on their loved ones to see if the TBI discovered something that is meaningful to the family—a name, a location, something that might give them a clue.

FBI files are theoretically subject to Freedom of Information Act (FOIA) requests. I had very little luck actually getting files. Most of what I asked for they claimed they'd destroyed. The files they hadn't destroyed (or hadn't lied about destroying, but we'll get to that) are at the National Archives. I have standing FOIA requests in at the National Archives, but I have lost hope that those will be filled before I am old or dead, whichever comes first. And, frankly, I did almost die while writing this book.[2] People I would have liked to interview—like Kwame Lillard—died before I got the chance. The longer I wait, the more people who deserve the truth pass away without at least some part of it.

I have a lot going for me. I have the support of the *Nashville Scene*.

I've had help from former congressman Jim Cooper getting the FBI to admit that they had not destroyed the Looby bombing file. I've spoken with a retired US attorney, a working federal defense lawyer, a terrorist, the DA's office, and witnesses. And I have had all the time I need to write this book (thanks, Third Man Books).

I could not get the information I need to definitively tell you what happened.

This is what motivates me now. Nashville has the right to know the truth about itself. As we struggle to overcome our history and traditions of racism, we need to know the truth about our history. And it's being kept from us.

That makes me angry. I hope it will also make you angry.

My hope is that this won't be the last word on these bombings, but the first effort to get the truth.

I believe these crimes are solvable and that someone out there has the missing pieces that will give us definitive answers. I'm hoping that me saying, "This is what we know," might spur an old memory or make sense of an overheard conversation. It might put other facts known to scholars of this era into context.

I also hope it will spur historians to look more closely at Tennessee during this era. For instance, it's clear that the Chattanooga Klan was working closely with the Nashville Klan. Like Nashville, Chattanooga had a school bombing, a religious recreational center bombing, and a bombing of the home of a Black civil rights lawyer. The Chattanooga Klan was targeting Martin Luther King Jr. Same as Nashville.

As little work has been done on racist violence in Nashville during this era, it makes for a mountain of research compared to Chattanooga. Two of the most important racial terrorists of the era—J.B. Stoner and the head of the Dixie Knights, Jack Brown—came out of Chattanooga, and no one's gotten the facts from this part of Chattanooga's history nailed down. I rely heavily on FBI files, because the Nashville police files from this era were destroyed decades ago (any police files I did find came from other sources—the FBI files, personal collections, and other police departments' files), and while I suspect the files from the Tennessee Bureau of Criminal Identification (the precursor to the TBI) must still exist somewhere, it is against the law for the TBI to let me see them.[3]

So, one of the big challenges was that there was just so very little information from some obvious channels to be found. Police records are missing. Participants are long dead. Family members are reluctant to talk. No one's yet done the necessary research in other cities.

But the other big challenge is that there's too much information from the FBI. The files available through the National Archives are enormous. J.B. Stoner's file is three thousand pages long. The file on the Dixie Knights is around thirty thousand pages long. And there's no way to browse files to see what might be relevant. In order to get any of them, they have to be vetted to make sure no classified information is released. For less than 500 pages, that vetting is at least a two-year process; vetting more than 500 pages takes more than a decade. Both require a per-page reproduction fee.

I love Nashville, and I believe people here deserve a firm answer about what happened and why, but I don't have that kind of time or money. So, there are answers, better answers than I've been able to piece together here, sitting in the FBI's files—technically available, but not actually available.

As anyone who has studied the 1960s knows, the FBI ended up doing some very shady, evil things to the people involved in the civil rights movement. We don't know for sure when the FBI began looking the other way when their Klan informants threatened and harmed Black people, but it's a matter of public record that they did.

This, sadly, means that we must take everything in their files with a grain of salt. We must balance the information in those files with what scant information we can find elsewhere. We must not assume that the FBI's end goal with these cases was bringing the perpetrators to justice. In fact, they may have had other goals that directly conflicted with justice.

But, as deeply flawed as the FBI files may be, they're the most comprehensive primary sources we have on these bombings. This is why I've included so many long quotes from these files and other documents; they amount to our first and only opportunities to hear what happened from people who were there.

I also want to make clear one self-imposed limit on the scope of this work. I have a list of about three hundred people tied to Nashville's racist violence—some only very loosely, some pretty directly. I put together the list so that I could see if the same people recurred in the background of these incidents; or what areas of town might have housed large groups of active racists; or whether there might be family connections from incident to incident, connections that would only be apparent if I realized last names were repeating.

I haven't thoroughly researched everyone on that list. Some folks only went to Rev. Fred Stroud's Bible Presbyterian Church in North Nashville, a renegade racist congregation Stroud formed after he got kicked out of the Presbyterian church in the '30s. Others were only on John Kasper's witness list at his trial for inciting a riot during his Nashville activities. Their names came up once and never again, so I didn't look into them.

In that list of three hundred people, not all of whom I've looked at closely, I've found three cases of patricide—two successful, one not. I know a lot of people, but don't know anyone who's tried to kill their father. A one percent father-murder rate seems worth noting.

I've looked into these patricides, and these cases have left me with deep sympathy for the killers or attempted killers. Our inability to investigate the Nashville bombings and deal with the violent racists in our midst has come at a steep cost, and it was often the children in the orbits of these racists who paid the direct price.

Choices we made as a city cost these children dearly.

I'm not going to name those children or tell those stories. I want to assure any family members who might be reading of that. But I think it's important for us to know that our "no harm, no foul" attitude toward these bombings and the violent politics behind them meant we outsourced dealing with these violent, dangerous people to children.

If we don't like how they handled their situations, we need to remember that, by failing to deal with this head on, we put them there.

These bombings did harm people. They were traumatizing to the people whose buildings were bombed. They were traumatizing to the people in our city who worried that they would be next. Leaving the bombings unsolved further eroded trust in law enforcement. And the kinds of people who are willing to hurt people often remain willing to hurt people, their own children in some cases. Not chasing them down when we had the chance left them in positions to hurt their loved ones, and it forced those loved ones into desperate actions to keep themselves safe.

Some of the bombers in the big terrorist network that got part of its start here went on to other cities and continued their evil. These bombers did have victims. As a city, we've just avoided facing them or their families.

CHAPTER 1

IN WHICH WE DISCUSS NASHVILLE'S LONG HISTORY OF RACIST VIOLENCE IN RESPONSE TO BLACK EDUCATION AND WE MEET Z. ALEXANDER LOOBY

White opposition to Black education in Nashville, including terrorist violence, has a long history. Alphonso Sumner, a free Black barber, secretly opened a school for Black children in 1833. By 1836, he had 200 students, some of them enslaved. After he was accused of aiding runaway slaves—though this may have been a pretense—a white mob nearly whipped him to death. He fled to Cincinnati. His school closed.

In 1838, Nashville free Black people opened a school for free Black children. This was allowed as long as they hired a white teacher. They brought in John Yandle. He lasted two years before the white threats of violence caused him to quit. Black educators kept going until 1856 when the city council closed the schools and enacted an ordinance that fined white people $50 for teaching Black children.[4]

That was the end of formal schooling for Black children in Nashville until after the Civil War.

The postwar era brought with it an influx of white missionaries determined to provide educations for Black Nashvillians. As well intentioned as these do-gooders were, their actions often had the effect of reinforcing the idea that white people set the agenda for what Black children in Nashville should learn. That caveat aside, black schools—religious and public—opened across town. Black universities and Black trade schools flourished.

Fisk University is the best known of these historically Black colleges, but another was Roger Williams University. The earliest iteration of the school was founded in 1864 by Baptist minister Daniel Phillips. It grew steadily and moved locations a few times. In 1874, Phillips bought a plantation on Hillsboro Pike near Vanderbilt University to transform into a permanent home for the college.

Historian Bill Carey shares:

> Even though not everyone in the surrounding area was thrilled about the presence of an African-American college, the relationship with Vanderbilt was cordial, at least

according to one Roger Williams professor. "Vanderbilt football coaches coached the Negro team," he recalled in the 1930s. "Roger Williams students went to games at Vanderbilt and sat with the others on the bleachers—a practice which would not be allowed today. Individual students, white and black, formed friendships that outlasted school days."[5]

In 1903, someone shot at the college chapel. In 1904, someone shot the college president's wife through a window of her own home (she was not killed). A month later, at the start of 1905, someone burned down the campus's Centennial Hall. In May of the same year, another building on campus burned down. The terrorism had its effect, and Roger Williams got the message that it was no longer welcome on that plot of land. The school began efforts to sell off the property and twenty-five acres of the campus was sold to the trustees of Peabody College in 1910. The other acres were subdivided for homes, and the deeds to those homes all forbade them from ever being sold to Black people.

In 1913, the United Daughters of the Confederacy began raising money to put a building on Peabody's new campus. This would be Confederate Memorial Hall.

Z. Alexander Looby and the Columbia Riots

In 1914, fifteen-year-old Z. Alexander Looby arrived in the United States from the British West Indies. Black education was central to Looby's life's work. He attended Howard University and Columbia University. He eventually received his law degree from NYU before settling in Nashville in 1926, where he worked as a professor at Fisk and where he helped found a law school that Black people could attend. He lived in Memphis for a few years, worked as an attorney, got married, and moved back to Nashville, where he worked as a lawyer for decades before the events in this book took place.

Okay, listen, I know it's kind of corny to use a Black guy's education as evidence of his support for Black education, but what I'm trying to get at is that he believed in the importance of established Black institutions— Howard and Fisk, for example—and establishing more Black institutions. His life trajectory is also important for understanding the philosophical conflict he felt with the sit-in protestors. He'd gotten an advanced degree from Columbia University. He'd come to Tennessee and won court victory after court victory that slowly advanced the cause of Black people. For him, it was obvious that you could make the system work for you and, when it didn't, you could make your own institutions that would meet your needs. The generation gap between him and the students he represented was enormous. He was 58 in 1957. Diane Nash was 19. But a thing I deeply respect about Looby is that he represented the sit-in protesters even though he didn't agree with their tactics. He went to court and stood up for them, because they needed him. He didn't withhold help just because they weren't doing things the way he thought they should.

Even though Looby is not very well known in Nashville anymore, and certainly doesn't have the statewide stature he deserves, there is no more important a figure in Tennessee history in the first half of the twentieth century (with the exception of Ida B. Wells, who straddled the turn of the century). Every single legal advancement Black Tennesseans were able to make in that time period happened either directly because of Looby or because of things Looby was involved in.

The fact that he loomed so large on the Tennessee landscape and was so important for most of his life and yet has faded so thoroughly from a large swath of the public's imagination is a troubling testament to how entrenched is the racist habit of disregarding Black accomplishments.

It also skews our ability to understand these bombings. If we don't realize how famous Looby was, how widely known he was as a decades-long adversary of segregation, not just among Black people but among white people as well, we're missing an important component of what linked these bombings to other racial terrorism in Tennessee.

The incident that first put Looby squarely in the public's focus was the Columbia Riot of 1946. Black members of the armed services had come home after liberating Europe from racist oppressors during World War II and began pushing for the United States to be liberated from racist oppressors as well.

In February 1946, Navy veteran James Stephenson defended his mother from an aggressive white clerk in a Columbia, Tennessee store. (Columbia is about an hour's drive from Nashville, the last big town you hit going south on Highway 31 before you reach Pulaski, Tennessee—birthplace of the Ku Klux Klan.) Stephenson and his mother were arrested. After they posted bond, white people began gathering at the courthouse to form a lynch mob.

But now the Black section of town was filled with men with guns and military training. They set up armed patrols, positioned snipers, and kept the lynch mob out of their neighborhood. It was a mitigated success. Two Black "rioters" ended up dead. Columbia law enforcement looted Black businesses. More than one hundred Black people were arrested.

But the NAACP's legal team, Thurgood Marshall (who later became a US Supreme Court justice), Nashville's Z. Alexander Looby, and white Chattanoogan Maurice Weaver kept all but one "rioter" out of prison.

Contrast this with the Memphis riot of 1866, where a white police officer tried to arrest a Black Civil War veteran and was stopped by a Black crowd. White mobs swarmed Black Memphis and targeted Black veterans and their families. The mobs burned down houses, churches, and schools. Five women were raped, and forty-six Black people were killed. No one was ever arrested.

It doesn't necessarily seem like it in retrospect, but the outcome of the Columbia riots was an enormous paradigm shift. In Tennessee, even if an activity—like burning someone's home down—was a crime, the law was rarely applied if white people committed it against Black people. Black people simply could not count on having legal protection; in cases where it seemed like they might, white people formed angry mobs and terrorized and killed them.

But in Columbia, Black people did have access to the legal system; they were afforded trials; and there was national disgust and outrage over the fact that they were attacked and then tried for defending themselves. Plus, the lynch mob failed.

At the end of the trial, when the NAACP's legal team was leaving town for the last time, the story goes that a convoy of police officers followed them, pulling them over repeatedly for whatever nonsense reason they could come up with.[6] The last time the police pulled the legal team's cars over, they arrested Thurgood Marshall for drunk driving. He was placed in the back seat of a police car and driven away into the night.

Only six years before, in west Tennessee, Haywood County police had come to Brownsville NAACP officer Elbert Williams's house and taken him away. He was lynched. Looby and Weaver knew that police taking Marshall away for trumped-up reasons was not going to end well. They turned around and followed the police, who took Marshall out into the countryside and drove him around long enough, I would guess, to realize that if they were going to kill Marshall, they'd have to kill Looby and Weaver too. And, if they did that, they couldn't be sure there wouldn't be terrible repercussions for them—especially since Weaver was white.

Marshall was released. Charges were never filed.

Let that soak in. Not six years before, police officers in Tennessee could take part in killing NAACP leaders with no fear of negative repercussions. In 1946, they couldn't be sure they'd get away with it.

Most of the retellings of the Columbia riots have focused on Marshall's role, because it's cool to know we had such an important figure and such a brilliant legal mind here working for justice. But if we want to understand what happened in Nashville a decade later, we need to keep our eye on Looby.

Looby made sure those Black Columbians had access to the legal system, made the legal system work for them, and saved Marshall from being murdered by police. Looby wasn't leaving Tennessee when this was all over. Looby was Tennessee's most prominent and often only civil rights lawyer. A massive change had come to Tennessee—Black people did have access to the legal system; the legal system didn't reflexively rule the way whites wanted it to; and lynch mobs could be thwarted. At the center of that change was Z. Alexander Looby.

Looby was already a prominent lawyer—obviously, or he wouldn't have been brought in on the Columbia case—but this victory established his legend. The story was that he only took Black clients, and that he never lost a case. As far as I can tell, the first part of that is true. I don't think this is surprising, since his practice was focused on civil rights. He did lose cases, though, as he was quick to point out when asked about the myth growing around him. That said, in an interview he did with John Britton in 1967 for the Civil Rights Documentation Project, Looby comes across as proud and flattered that people believed he was undefeatable.

In 1951, Looby was elected to the Nashville city council, which meant that he became even more of a public figure. Now he was someone white Nashville heard about all the time, instead of someone briefly mentioned in news stories that ran deep in the paper, if the white media deigned to run those stories at all. Take the story that appeared on page 19 of the *Tennessean*, on March 29, 1951, a few months before his election. A five-and-a-half-foot-tall cross had been set ablaze at the intersection of Acklen Avenue and Grove Avenue[7] on the south side of town near Belmont University. The paper reported, "A note, apparently written by an ignorant person, was found at the foot of the cross, [police lieutenant] McDaniel said. Written on rough paper it was a warning to Z. Alexander Looby, Negro attorney. Many words in the note were incorrectly spelled."[8]

A small story, buried at the top of page 19, with no mention of the threat against Looby until the end. The lede was that someone had burned a cross, not that someone had threatened Looby. Obviously, he was on the radar of segregationists, but until he was elected to the city

8

council, Looby didn't occupy a lot of white civic space. After he was elected, stories about him, no matter how minor, were front page news.

In the wake of the US Supreme Court's decision in *Brown v. Board of Education* declaring segregation in public schools unconstitutional in 1954, Looby filed suit against the Nashville public school system on behalf of Alfred Z. Kelly and his son, Robert. That case would lead directly to the desegregation of Nashville's public schools' first grade in 1957.

But because Nashville desegregated one year at a time beginning with first grade, under a court order and with court supervision, lawsuits went on for years. Looby didn't win the Kelly case and wash his hands of school segregation; he remained involved in integrating Nashville's schools until well after 1960—the year his house was bombed. In every story about Nashville school integration throughout the era, you are likely to see two names: Z. Alexander Looby and Judge William E. Miller (who we'll get to).

The way the story has come down to us is that Looby's house was bombed because he was providing legal representation to the students protesting Nashville's segregated downtown through sit-ins (which he was). But it's actually not clear that this is why he was attacked. The groups that had been threatening him from 1954 until the bombing had been threatening him in the context of school desegregation.

There's also one more controversy that Looby was involved in that hangs over every other facet of this era, even if it doesn't seem directly related to integration. Nashville was trying to move from a city government—one that presided over a city that sat like the yolk of an egg in the middle of a more rural Davidson County—to a metro government that would, after 1963, preside over almost all of Davidson County (Goodlettsville, Berry Hill, and Belle Meade being among the few exceptions).

Looby supported these efforts.[9] He was a vote on the city council in favor of metro-fication. White racists were opposed.

In response to growing Black social power in Nashville, whites had moved to the non-Nashville parts of Davidson County. This meant that Nashville provided a place for white people to work and shop, but their property taxes no longer came to the city. But if Nashville was going to provide the urban amenities people wanted, it needed that tax base. The plan was to annex as much of the county as the city could in order to get it.

At the time of the bombings, there were two school systems—Nashville and Davidson County. If Nashville schools desegregated and all of Davidson County became Nashville, the folks who had moved out into the county to avoid having to participate in civic life with Black people would be out of luck. Their public school children would have to attend desegregated schools.

But let's take a moment to appreciate the giant loophole the law enforcement situation created for the bombers. Like the twin school systems, there were two police departments—Nashville PD and the Davidson County Sheriff's Department. The Davidson County sheriff was the most powerful person in rural Davidson County. The sheriff had traditionally been a typical political machine boss, doling out favors to friends, swaying elections, and conducting himself with a level of amiable corruption.[10]

Nashville didn't want a second law enforcement entity with the same duties and powers as the Nashville Police Department, so everyone knew that metro-fication would massively disempower the sheriff. This, in fact, is why the Davidson County sheriff now runs the jail and picks up bulk trash and doesn't do much more. The position has been defanged precisely because of how powerful it was at the time we're looking at. Obviously, the sheriff didn't want to lose this power.

How eager do you think the sheriff would have been to help solve bombings that happened in Nashville—bombings whose perpetrators might have lived in or escaped to rural Davidson County? Why would the sheriff have made it easier for Nashville to prove it had a competent police department that could also investigate crimes outside city limits? It was in his best interest to stay uninvolved. Let the Nashville police sink or swim on their own. Without his help, it seemed likely they would, indeed, sink.

CHAPTER 2

1949–1954, A BRIEF HISTORY OF LOCAL NON-KLAN RACISTS AND OF NASHVILLIANS BLOWING UP THINGS

Guide to the Racists in this Chapter

Donald Davidson Acclaimed Poet and Head of the Tennesseans for Constitutional Government
Frank Houchin No One, Yet
Jack Kershaw Davidson's Righthand Man
Rev. Fred Stroud Leader of the Bible Presbyterian Church

The Tennessee Federation for Constitutional Government

The most influential organized racist group in Nashville was the Tennessee Federation for Constitutional Government. As popular as the Klan was, upper-crust white Nashvillians certainly weren't going to join. How gauche! No, they needed civilized, erudite hate groups filled with people of the richest social classes to belong to. Poet and beloved Vanderbilt professor, Donald Davidson, stepped in to fill the need.

It would be hard to overstate the cultural capital Davidson had in Nashville. He was literally one of Nashville's most famous intellectuals. He enrolled in Vanderbilt University in 1909, earning both a bachelor's degree and a master's degree, before he became an English professor. He was one of the founding members of the Fugitives, a group of Vanderbilt students and professors who wrote poetry and got together to discuss it in the 1920s. Other members of the Fugitives included John Crowe Ransom, Allen Tate, Andrew Lytle, Frank Owsley, Robert Penn Warren, Ridley Wills, Cleanth Brooks, and Laura Riding.[11]

After the Fugitives drifted apart, Davidson became a founding member of the Agrarians, a similar group of Vanderbilt-affiliated people who met informally to, as Paul Murphy puts it, "discuss ideas."[12] The Agrarians consisted of Vanderbilt professors John Crowe Ransom, Lyle Lanier, Herman Nixon, Frank Owsley, and John Donald Wade, along with Allen Tate, Henry Kline, Andrew Lytle, and Robert Penn Warren, among others. This must have been when Davidson came to know Vanderbilt student Jack Kershaw, most famous nationally for defending James Earl Ray, most famous locally for building a large, hideous sculpture of Nathan Bedford Forrest that until recently sat along the interstate south of town.

Kershaw's obituary claims that Kershaw "became associated with a group of intellectuals who called themselves the Fugitive Poets of Vanderbilt in the 1920s. This group of students would go on to make a great impact regarding how the history of the South would be told."[13] Except that Kershaw was born in 1913, which means about the earliest he could have been at Vanderbilt was 1930—after the Fugitives had moved on. This doesn't especially matter. He was clearly in with the Agrarians and met Donald Davidson at this time, but it's indicative of the kind of largesse with which Kershaw regarded the truth, his willingness to heap a good story on top of it just to spruce it up a little.[14]

The Agrarians were deeply racist.[15]

Toward the end of the "Donald Davidson" entry in the *Tennessee Encyclopedia of History and Culture*, Paul Murphy writes, "Davidson, who considered African Americans racially inferior, defended segregation as a social institution developed by white southerners to preserve their culture and identity. In the 1950s he headed the pro-segregation Tennessee Federation for Constitutional Government, the state's generally ineffective version of a White Citizens Council."[16]

As hilarious as "generally ineffective" is, I wonder if that's really true. Sure, the Tennessee Federation for Constitutional Government did, on its surface, seem to exist only to give Davidson and his buddies a feeling they were doing something to stop the social changes they opposed without them actually having to go outside and interact with ordinary people. They didn't stop desegregation. So, it does seem like they failed, like they were "ineffective."

But let's take a step back and look at the bigger picture.

White Citizens Councils sprang up in response to the *Brown v.*

16

Board of Education ruling in 1954. These groups were supposed to be a more respectable alternative to the Klan. Unlike the Klan, they would work within the system to prevent integration and they would be made up of middle-class people and community leaders. Nashville didn't have a White Citizens Council for a very simple reason: our Klan was plenty respectable, made up of middle-class people and community leaders who were working within the system. There was no shame in being a Klansperson in Nashville in the 1950s. The papers regularly ran front page stories about Klan activities with the Klan members barefaced and happily identified. Also, if, for some reason, you didn't want to join the Klan, you could just join Rev. Fred Stroud's Bible Presbyterian Church and do your organized segregationist activities with your fellow congregants.[17]

Davidson's group, the Tennessee Federation for Constitutional Government, wasn't trying to be Tennessee's equivalent of the White Citizens Council. It was trying to be for segregationists what the Fugitives and the Agrarians were for poetry and Southern mythologizing—a small, elite group who met and discussed ideas and held influence. They wanted to set the tone and guide the discourse, to be influencers. They didn't want and never had a large membership of ordinary people.

Even when the TFCG decided a group of ordinary people was needed, they founded the Parents Preference Committee, which was full of white parents who opposed integrating Nashville schools. I don't find any indication that they increased their own membership.

The 1955 roster of the TFCG is fascinating. It lists Donald Davidson as chairman. His first qualification is "Professor of English, Vanderbilt University." Next is Jack Kershaw, vice-chairman, "Nashville real estate developer, widely known as a Southern painter and sculptor." L.V. DuBose, also vice chairman, "is in the Production Control department of the Crosley Division of the A.V.C.O. Corporation of Nashville."[18] Robert F. Lee, secretary, is described as "Assistant Business Manager of Vanderbilt University and also Instructor in English at the same institution." Dudley Gale, treasurer, "Chairman of the Greater Nashville

Committee of the Chamber of Commerce and has been a trustee of the Nashville Children's Museum since its organization." The list continues with Lambeth Mayes, corresponding secretary; Ward S. Allen, bursar; and Paul Manchester, director of public relations, head of the romance languages department at Vanderbilt.

And then there's Paul F. Bumpus, who served as counsel for the TFCG. His biography reads, "Has practiced law in Nashville since 1950. A native of Maury County, he served as District Attorney-General for Maury, Wayne, Lawrence, and Giles counties. While serving as Attorney-General, he handled the so-called 'racial cases' in Columbia, Tennessee."[19]

Let's be clear what this means: Bumpus was the guy who lost to Looby in the Columbia riots cases. And here he was serving as council for the group Davidson created in response to *Brown v. Board of Education* and the lawsuit Looby had filed on behalf of the Kelly family to desegregate Nashville schools.

Donald Davidson, who wanted to give Southern whites a myth of Southern whiteness they could draw on in order to be great, seems clearly to have been using the Tennessee Federation for Constitutional Government as part of his aesthetic project. It's hard for me to read Bumpus's prominence in the TFCG as anything but an acknowledgment that a large hurdle to white supremacy was Z. Alexander Looby. To effectively fight integration, you needed someone who had experience fighting Looby.

When word came down that Clinton, Tennessee was going to desegregate in 1956, the TFCG asked the state supreme court for an injunction. Davidson sent Kershaw to Clinton to address the community. After the Clinton riots, Davidson sent Kershaw to bail out most of the segregationist rioters. We're going to see Kershaw show up again to advocate for the Hattie Cotton bombing suspects.

Kershaw and Davidson were close. They had worked together on behalf of Strom Thurmond's Dixiecrat Party in the '40s. Davidson scholar Mark Royden Winchell writes, "Davidson formed a close friendship with

Kershaw during the latter half of the 1950s. This was a time when he was estranged from most of his former colleagues in the Fugitive and Agrarian movements."[20]

Kershaw seems to have taken the lessons he learned working with Davidson to heart. Davidson was using the money and the social standing of the Tennessee Federation for Constitutional Government to help the more violent racists of the lower classes get out of the jams their activism got them in.[21] Kershaw went on to found the League of the South in 1994, a racist group that, like the Tennessee Federation for Constitutional Government, offers a less trashy alternative to the Klan. Like the TFCG, the League of the South often provides organizational help and material support to more violent racists.[22] Also, like Davidson's group, the League of the South has been able to hide in plain sight, with a remarkable number of whites acting like they're just some anachronistic social club whose members aren't hurting anyone with their old-fashioned views.

Kershaw also set up the Mary Noel Kershaw Foundation, in honor of his wife. This was a slush fund for the League of the South.

In 2017, the League of the South aided white supremacists at Charlottesville. Also in 2017, Rev. David O. Jones collected money from the men in his suburban Nashville Bible study, including retired federal judge Robert Echols, and funneled it through the Mary Noel Kershaw Foundation to his organization, Heritage Covenant Schools, which provides resources for conservative Christian homeschoolers. The men in his Bible study claimed not to know anything about Rev. Jones's racist beliefs or that he was the past state chair for the League of the South.

So, was Davidson's group "ineffective," really? Davidson and Kershaw perfected a blueprint for supporting and funding racist activists while keeping their own group mostly free from the taint of the violence they facilitated. Kershaw took that blueprint and created a really effective group that still does that work successfully today, a group with ties to prominent judges, politicians, and attorneys—even though they may deny those ties when it becomes inconvenient.

I, too, would like to dismiss Davidson's racist work as "ineffective," but the truth is that it's been very influential and continues to be an important component of racist terrorism today.

The other thing about "ineffective" is that it lets Vanderbilt off the hook. If Donald Davidson was a racist, but not very good at it, then it was relatively harmless that they kept him as faculty and let him have access to hundreds of young people. But if he was good at it, if his activism was successful, then keeping Donald Davidson around at the very same time they were expelling Vanderbilt Divinity School student James Lawson for his work organizing the sit-in movement, it starts to suggest something morally careless about Vanderbilt's approach that, for all its good work in acknowledging some racial sins of its past, it has not begun to reckon with. It's one thing—and an ugly thing—to not allow Black students to attend, then to create an oppressive, miserable atmosphere for them once they were there (and then to punish them, even expel them, for working to change it); it's another, even uglier thing to do all this while one of your professors is running an effective and highly influential racist organization out of your English department.

The First Racist Bombings

The bombings we're discussing weren't the first racist bombings of the modern era in Nashville. On April 6, 1949, someone stuck a 15-foot cross on the train trestle that crosses Antioch Pike and set said cross on fire. Law enforcement believed it was a warning to Dr. Needham Roberts, a Black dentist who had bought a bunch of land along the road, within sight of that trestle, and who intended to develop it into housing for Black people. Needham sold the land to white developers, but that didn't stop racists from blowing up two houses in the development in December of the same year. The development was changed to white. This bombing also remains unsolved.

This incident highlights something that is crucial for us to understand as we move forward: Nashville was very institutionally segregated. Black and white kids went to different schools. Black and white people shopped in entirely different ways (for instance, Black people couldn't try on clothes in department stores). They ate in segregated restaurants. They buried their dead in different cemeteries. But they lived in the same neighborhoods, even on the same blocks.

The era of neighborhood segregation was brought about by the carving up of the city with interstates in the 1970s. Mixed-race neighborhoods dissolved. The shock is to us, whose Nashville has "always" had Black neighborhoods and white neighborhoods. We're the ones who project our own experience of the city back into the past and ask, "Where were the Black neighborhoods in 1880? In 1920?" We get answers we don't question because they line up with how we experience the city now. But in order for anything I'm about to tell you to make sense, I need you to understand that Nashville didn't have all-Black neighborhoods and very few all-white neighborhoods until the interstates went in fifty years ago, a decade after the Looby bombing.

The reasons Black people wanted to integrate Nashville's schools was not because white schools were so great (white schools were better resourced, but Black schools expected their teachers to have master's degrees, at least) but because it was stupid for any kid to have to walk by his neighborhood school in order to go to a Black school.

This is the kind of revelation that is so obvious once you hear it that it seems like the kind of thing you must have already known; but in my case, at least, I'm still having a hard time accepting it because it's so contrary to what I've been taught. The neighborhood schools Black families wanted to attend were, indeed, that: their neighborhood schools. Their mixed-race neighborhood schools.

Between 1949 and 1960, there were more than fifty cross burnings in Davidson County. I had initially thought that these were racist intimidation tactics to keep Black people from moving into white neighborhoods. But what I understand now is that this was an early effort to create white neighborhoods—to run off people who already lived there. The police chalked most of these cross burnings up to pranks by teens, but as we'll get into in the next chapter, that doesn't preclude them from also being racist plots. Some teens were arrested for cross burning. Once. The only other arrest I could find related to cross burnings was that of Joe Baker, a Black man who found a cross burning in his yard up in Madison (a northern Nashville suburb) on April 23, 1950. According to the *Tennessean*, Baker grabbed the burning cross in one hand, his shotgun in the other, and proceeded to stop every car driven by white people that came by, demanding, "Did you do it?" He was eventually charged with public drunkenness, but he said he hadn't been drinking. Apparently, he was just pissed. The paper never reported the disposition of his case. Somehow, we don't have a statue of this hero.

Dynamite was Cheap, Easy to Acquire, and Fun to Use

I had initially thought that, in the cases I'm looking at, the fact that the bombers were using dynamite would be helpful. Dynamite was traceable, right? But it turns out that dynamite violence in Nashville in the 1950s was very, very common. Dynamite was readily available. You could buy a stick at your local hardware store for a quarter, and newspapers from the time make it seem like construction sites just left dynamite lying around for the taking by anyone willing to sneak onto the site and steal it.

There were a number of newspaper stories about teenagers who would steal dynamite or blasting caps and then leave those items near elementary schools where young children would find them, play with them, and lose an eye or some fingers. You'd think that this would be a cause for great alarm, but the media treated it as a "boys will be boys" thing. You have teenagers literally leaving explosives for smaller kids to find and hurt themselves with. If that's not explicitly on the list of "your kid may be on the path to being a serial killer" traits, it's certainly covered by "harms small animals." But the term "serial killer" hadn't been coined in the 1950s. America was worried about rebellious teenagers, but more the kids who wore T-shirts and tight skirts and listened to R&B (and, at the end of the decade, rock & roll) than the kids putting dynamite out for grade-schoolers to find.

Adults were also blowing things up. People liked to fish with dynamite. People used dynamite to blow wells and clear cesspools. Union troubles in Nashville were often punctuated with dynamite, and barbershops were blown up on a regular basis during the 1950s, usually because of labor disputes and union activities.

Focusing on people able to get their hands on dynamite narrows our suspect pool to "everyone." Looking at people willing to blow up things important to other people gives us "too many teenagers" and "barbers" among others. Still a really broad list.

Jesse Wilson, The Man Who Never Met a Problem Dynamite Couldn't Fix

But if these three integration-era bombings were connected, was there any suspect who fit that pattern? Was there a person in Nashville who was already known for blowing up government buildings and who was willing to bomb Nashville politicians?

Yes. Starting in 1952.

Was that person ever a suspect in these bombings?

As far as I can tell, no.

Why not?

Welcome to the first of many mysteries.

Forty-seven-year-old Jesse Wilson was the president of the trucking company Tennessee Motor Lines, which had a terminal downtown on 3rd Avenue South and a terminal in Chattanooga. Wilson ran his trucks heavy, which became a problem for him first when Kentucky put truck scales on Highway 31-E in Hodgenville (a little more than halfway between Nashville and Louisville) and then when Tennessee put scales on Highway 31-W at Goodlettsville. Both scales were blown up. Wilson appears to have been the only suspect.

Two years later, in January 1954, Wilson had two of his employees beat up two former employees down in Chattanooga. It was all over the papers here.

On March 18, 1954, a man hired by Wilson bombed the yard of attorney and former mayor of Nashville, Thomas L. Cummings, who was representing the two men Wilson had ordered beaten. This man was also supposed to bomb the home of *Tennessean* publisher Silliman Evans, because Wilson was angry about the amount and kind of coverage the paper had given those earlier bombings and the beatings. This bombing didn't happen; before it could, Wilson was involved in another bombing, and the would-be bomber testified that Wilson had taken him to Evans's home to scope out the best place to put the explosives.

On March 20, Wilson and some men who were loyal to him filled the floor of Wilson's 3rd Avenue Tennessee Motor Lines terminal with sawdust, soaked the sawdust in oil, moved trucks into the terminal, and blew the whole thing up. This bombing was intended to be an insurance scam, and Wilson blamed union strife for it, even claiming the union had bombed the building.

Carl Stokes, one of Wilson's bombers, testified at trial that some of the trucks didn't run, so the men had to push them. Here's how Stokes described the bombing, according to the *Tennessean*:

> "He [Wilson] went to his office. He had a desk with a top
> that rolled up. He raised it and got six sticks of dynamite.
> He got out some black kid gloves and taped the dynamite,
> three sticks together with black tape. He took a pencil and
> punched a hole in the dynamite and put a fuse in and took
> a pair of pliers and mashed it so it would not come off."
> He [Stokes] said Wilson then placed the dynamite
> in two trucks, on one cross-member and under a hood.

Wilson then crammed an electric heater with paper, Stokes said, and tested the time it required for the paper to ignite after the heater was turned on. "It took three or four minutes," Stokes recalled.

The heater, he said, was placed near one of the dynamite-laden trucks, and a long extension cord run outside. Herrod has testified he returned later and plugged in the cord, setting off the fire.[23]

Stokes also testified that Wilson had ordered him to do a series of bombings in Chattanooga, but Stokes refused. Lest you think that being arrested for a series of bombings would be enough to keep Wilson on the straight and narrow, Wilson paid a man, Jack Jones, to kill Stokes and two other witnesses. Fortunately, the would-be hitman alerted authorities.

But get this! After all that, Wilson only served twenty-eight months. He was released from prison in January 1958. He didn't reform. In 1961, he was charged with a series of burglaries in the Carthage area, about an hour east of Nashville. He was out of money because he'd lost his trucking company.

Here we have a guy willing to bomb people, who knows how to case a building looking for the best place to bomb it, who blows up government facilities, and who was behind the bombing of a Nashville politician. A guy who was, by 1958, desperate for money. And here we have three unsolved bombings—including a government building and the home of a Nashville politician. Wilson couldn't have bombed Hattie Cotton in 1957 because he was in jail, but why wasn't he the first person the police talked to in the other two cases? How did they not look at our bombings and Wilson's bombings and see similar targets? I also don't think Wilson did any of our bombings, but I have sixty years' worth of hindsight. How did the police and the FBI decide in 1958 or 1960 that Wilson wasn't worth talking to?

The answer to that may be Frank Houchin. While Wilson was on trial for blowing up his own terminal, part of his defense was that Jack Jones and an old friend of Jack's, Frank Houchin, were framing him and trying to blackmail him about it.[24]

While Frank Houchin's middle name wasn't literally Trouble, it should have been. He had a string of arrests going back at least a decade for robbing liquor stores and hardware stores. Clear back in 1936, when he was twenty-one, Frank was busted as part of an "alleged gang of thieves" that annoyed the city for at least six months.[25] In 1949, he was caught up in a scandal with a crooked ex-cop. Frank was in and out of jail repeatedly and he was looking at serious legal problems with the Wilson mess.

And in late 1957, Frank joined the Klan.

CHAPTER 3

1956, THE BEGINNINGS OF RACIST ATTACKS ON TENNESSEE SCHOOLS

SOUTHERN WHITES ARE
THE NEGROES' BEST
FRIENDS . . . BUT
NO INTEGRATION

Guide to the Racists in this Chapter

Emmett Carr Middle Tennessee Klan Leader and Pro-Southerners Leader
Asa Carter Renegade Klansman from Birmingham
Donald Davidson Local Racist Poet
Dr. Edward Fields Stoner's Partner in Crime
John Kasper Segregationist from New Jersey
Jack Kershaw Davidson's Lackey
Ezra Pound Non-Local Racist Poet
J.B. Stoner Chattanooga and Atlanta Klansman

The First Schools in the State to Desegregate

In 1954, Nashville had the first schools in the state to desegregate—
Father Ryan High School (a boy's school) and Cathedral Elementary and
High School (the elementary school was mixed gender, the high school
was for girls).

The desegregation of these two Catholic schools is really fascinating.
The Catholic Church had already been pressuring Catholic dioceses in the
American South to desegregate.[26] With the *Brown v. Board of Education*
decision, the Nashville diocese saw the writing on the wall and decided
to act of their own volition and on their own terms instead of waiting for
either the larger Church or the federal government to force the issue.

The Nashville diocese informed parents that the Black Catholic
schools were in need of major maintenance and renovations; when they
were inspected, they would likely not pass (though the Black schools
stayed open, so whether this was true or, maybe, would be true in the near
future, is unclear). These Black students could either be moved into more
well-repaired schools with white students or Catholic families were going
to have to pony up the money to fix the Black Catholic schools. The diocese framed integration as the less expensive of two options. It also told
Catholic parents that they were no longer required to send their kids to

Catholic schools, so if they were really opposed to their children going to school with children of other races, they could put them in public school.

As good a case as the diocese presented for integration, this still must have been outrageous to some parents. Yet, though the diocese must have been having these discussions at least throughout the summer of 1954 to give parents time to withdraw their kids and get them registered in public school, if need be, no one breathed a word of this to the media. The first day of integrated enrollment in Tennessee came and went without broad notice. It wasn't until two weeks later that the *Tennessean* became aware of it. On September 5, on an inside page, the *Tennessean* ran a short story, "Catholics Enroll Negro Students: Father Ryan, Cathedral Admit Unannounced Total."

The story read, in part:

> This is the first year in which Negroes have been admitted to Catholic schools on a non-segregated basis. Bishop William L. Adrian announced the change in school policy following the U.S. Supreme Court's ruling that segregation was illegal.
>
> Father Frank Shea, assistant superintendent at Father Ryan high school said yesterday 293 students had registered.
>
> "We don't keep track of the number of Negro students we have," he said, "so I can't give you any figures."[27]

There's a story, I don't know how true it is, but I like it so I'm going to tell you, that Shea's actual quote was something more like, "We don't have white students and Negro students. We have Catholic students. We don't keep track of the number of Negro students we have, so I can't give you any figures."

No media were present for the first integrated day of school in Nashville. But this quiet, massive change did not go unnoticed by racist terrorists.

The Plot Against Father Ryan

By January 1956, the headquarters of the Pro-Southerners had moved to Memphis and Nashville's own Emmett Carr, age 45, had formed a Nashville branch. Carr was best known for his leadership of the Middle Tennessee Klan, but interestingly, the local papers all noted that Carr was ex-Klan at this point and that he intended the Pro-Southerners to be nothing like the Klan, being more devoted to protecting segregation through voting and legislation than violence. In this way, they were similar to Donald Davidson's group. But like the Tennessee Federation for Constitutional Government, what the Pro-Southerners' public position was and what they were actually plotting were two different things.

Here was Carr's plot:

> On February 7, 1956, Memphis Confidential Informant T-5, who has furnished reliable information in the past, advised that EMMETT CARR and the Pro-Southerners were organizing white high school students in the underprivileged sections in Nashville, Tennessee. Informant stated that this organization was being done in order to get the students to go to Father Ryan High School, an integrated Catholic boys' school in Nashville, some Saturday night during a basketball game and start a riot. Informant stated the organization had picked Father Ryan High School because of the fact that this is a Catholic high school and because of the fact Negroes have been admitted to it as students.[28]

The FBI file also reveals that this informant got his information from a Catholic guy "who had been in personal contact with EMMETT CARR."

This tells us a few things—that the desegregation of Father Ryan and Cathedral did send at least some racist Catholics to organized anti-Catholic racists who accepted them; that white teenagers could be enlisted in racial violence; and that integrated sports was especially alarming to racists.

But the fact that this riot never happened also tells us something. I asked Frederick Strobel, a Catholic historian in Nashville, about Catholic school desegregation and whether the Church knew about this plot. He didn't think they had known, but he pointed out that one reason the riot may not have come off is that there were hardly ever, if ever, any Black students at basketball games in the early days of desegregation. They weren't yet allowed on the Father Ryan team and Black students didn't, as far as he knew, attend many evening activities at the school. So, it's very likely that even if the rioters had shown up, they would have found a gym full of white people. That would have sucked the wind right out of the rioters' sails.

The lesson here? Racial violence needed to be directly linked to the presence of Black people in formerly white spaces or you couldn't count on your foot soldiers to go through with it.

By March 1956, the Pro-Southerners were falling apart, and Emmett Carr was back with the Klan. By September, he was totally done with the Pro-Southerners.

One interesting thing the FBI file notes is that in May 1956, Carr may have taken several carloads of Nashville Pro-Southerners to a Klan rally in Chattanooga.

John Kasper, Ezra Pound's Biggest Fan

John Kasper has long been most people's main suspect in the Nashville bombings, since the bombings started after he arrived in Nashville in

1957 and they concluded after he got tired of going to prison for being a racist activist in the early '60s. The problem with Kasper as a suspect is that while he could rile a crowd, he wasn't very good at actually committing terrorist acts. The plots we know he headed up fizzled out.

Also, a lot of other racists loathed him. If our bombings could have feasibly been pinned on him, it's very likely that some other racist, possibly even Emmett Carr, would have told the world that Kasper did it. Still, it's also obvious that Kasper was an important part of the mix that led to Nashville's bombings; Kasper wasn't the mastermind behind our bombings, but it's unlikely our bombings would have happened without him.

Kasper was born in 1929 in Camden, New Jersey. His parents were very conservative Protestants, and by the time Kasper came to Nashville, his mother was attending a Bible Presbyterian Church in New Jersey, the same small sect Nashville's Rev. Fred Stroud belonged to.[29] As Kasper put it in a letter to his mentor, poet Ezra Pound, "Now der Gasp wuz borned at Camden, New Jersey and brung up in Pennsauken, N.J. Ma is a renegade Catholic, Pa was a Lutheran, and we wuz members of the 1st Presbyterian Church of Merchantville."[30] Call it a fake patois, call it baby talk, whatever this way of writing was, it certainly illustrates the strange relationship that developed over the years between Pound and Kasper.

Kasper attended Columbia University, which was where he became a fan of Pound's and began corresponding with him. At Pound's request, Kasper started a small publishing company in 1951—Square Dollar Press—which published Pound. During his time in New York City, Kasper also ran a bookshop in Greenwich Village. At this point, Kasper was already a raging anti-Semite, but he was also holding integrated dance parties at the shop, dating a Black woman, and, according to the FBI, sometimes sleeping with a Black man.

Kasper's anti-Black attitudes seemed to more fully form once he moved to Washington, D.C., to be closer to Ezra Pound, who was imprisoned at St. Elizabeth's Hospital in the city on charges of treason for his fascist activities during World War II. Pound and Kasper corresponded extensively. Luckily for Pound defenders, Kasper destroyed the letters he received from the poet, so we don't know what kinds of direction and encouragement Pound was giving Kasper. The letters Pound kept from Kasper, though, make it clear that Kasper was keeping Pound up to date on his activities and that Kasper felt his activities would please Pound.

I think—and this is peak nerdy—that Pound has benefited from so few scholars looking at him and Donald Davidson together. As long as Pound defenders can say, "Come on! How could a brilliant poet be a dangerous and virulent racist providing support and inspiration to racial terrorists? Point to one other example!" there's always doubt.

But what we in Nashville know, or should now know, is that there was one other very prominent example: Donald Davidson. And if a deeply beloved, well-regarded professor at the city's elite university could do this, why couldn't a guy hiding from treason charges in a hospital room do the same?

Oddly enough, considering all they had in common, Davidson and Kasper didn't work together much. Pound scholar and Kasper biographer Alec Marsh writes, "Davidson was an ideologue whose vocation as a poet, agrarian philosopher, Jeffersonian principles, and Southern orientation overlapped Pounds in several ways, and might have been a natural ally, even a moderating influence on Kasper."[31] Kasper may have been a dynamic, charismatic, persuasive white supremacist who was out in the streets calling for violence, but he was a carpetbagger, and it's not surprising that Davidson—and Carr—wanted little part of him.

In direct response to *Brown v. Board of Education*, Kasper founded the Seaboard White Citizens Council in the Washington, D.C., area. This put him fully on the FBI's radar, and they were tracking him as his little band of racists burned crosses and picketed the White House. Kasper was also a leader in the Tennessee White Citizens Council, though, since Nashville already had Davidson and company, Tennessee wasn't desperate for another group of ostensibly "decent" racists, especially because Kasper was so openly aligned with the Klan—at least at first.

The Clinton, Tennessee, Riots

Kasper came to national prominence as a segregationist leader in the fall of 1956, when Clinton High School, in Clinton, Tennessee, just north of Knoxville, desegregated. (This probably goes without saying, but I'll say it anyway, Looby was one of the lawyers on the case that led to Clinton desegregating.) Kasper came to town shortly before the start of school and called for pro-segregationists to meet up and picket. The first day of school, Monday, August 26, was okay. Not great, but there were no major incidents.

But the next day white people were pissed, and John Kasper ran around giving fiery speeches that only stoked their anger. On Wednesday, the federal judge who had ordered Clinton desegregated issued a temporary restraining order against Kasper and his followers. Kasper turned around and held a rally of 1,000 to 1,500 people, where he called the restraining order meaningless. The judge had him arrested on contempt charges.

This did nothing to calm the racists. Asa Carter, a 31-year-old Klansman from Birmingham, Alabama, came up to join the protest efforts.[32] Carter's presence in Clinton should have been alarming. He had recently been fired from his job as a syndicated radio host for his inflammatory rhetoric and had to part ways with the Alabama Citizens Council as a result. Yes, that's right, he was too racist for the "respectable" racists of Alabama. Let that sink in. And he was welcome in Clinton. Over Labor Day weekend, the racists rioted. They overturned cars, smashed windows, and threw dynamite in Black neighborhoods. They threatened to dynamite the mayor's house, the newspaper plant, and the courthouse. Governor Frank G. Clement sent in the National Guard to keep order.

In the wake of this, some racist whites were arrested. Donald Davidson sent Jack Kershaw over from Nashville to bail out those he could, except John Kasper.[33]

This didn't end racist violence. Throughout the fall, white Clinton residents burned crosses on the lawns of high-school teachers and civic leaders who supported integration. Someone fired shots at the home of two of the Black students.

Kasper, who was out on appeal for his contempt charge, came back to Clinton in November to organize a Junior White Citizens Council in the high school. If you see pictures of the Clinton Junior White Citizens Council, you won't fail to notice that, in addition to forming a group willing to serve his racist ends in the halls of a school he couldn't legally enter, Kasper had found a way to surround himself with cute girls who adored him.

But an interesting thing started happening in Clinton, a crack that would only widen once Kasper got to Nashville. Word of Kasper's life in New York City got out. People learned he had dated a Black woman and thrown those cool dance parties. Some racists were like "Dude, what?" and in the wake of that question, a conspiracy theory began to develop. Kasper, the theory went, was not actually a white supremacist, but was an *agent provocateur* sent by the FBI or the Jews or both to make Southern white supremacists look like unhinged, violent lunatics who other white people should not support, but be afraid of.

But, in fact, Kasper's behavior is easily understood by his own stupid conspiracy theory that Black people, when left alone, didn't want integration in the South, but were, instead, being led astray by the wily Jews who convinced them to be unhappy in their lot. If Kasper wholeheartedly believed this while he lived in NYC—and all evidence is that he did—then why couldn't he befriend and even be romantically involved with Black people, who, if kept free from Jewish influence, were fine people who just weren't as good as him? Then, when he came south and found an insufficient number of Jews in East Tennessee to sustain such a level of trickery, he could have come to believe that Black people weren't just the unwitting pawns of Jewish people, but were, instead, working hand-in-hand with them. He then became more straightforwardly anti-Black, while still being a raging anti-Semite.

But Clinton racists began to suspect Kasper's motives. So, they (yes, the racists) bombed Kasper's Clinton headquarters to try to get rid of him.

Kasper came to Nashville not just because we had a fight over desegregation brewing here, but also because he had worn out his welcome in Clinton—not with the integrationists, but with his fellow segregationists.

J.B. Stoner, Chattanooga Klavern No. 317, and the Rise of the Dixie Knights

Before we can turn our attention fully to Nashville, we need to spend a little time looking at some of the segregationists from Chattanooga. I wish we were spending more than a little time, but I haven't been able to find out much about this era in Chattanooga's racist history.

J.B. Stoner was born in 1924 and grew up in Chattanooga and its suburbs. By the time he was sixteen, he was corresponding with Nazi propagandist Fred "Lord Haw Haw" Kaltenbach. In 1940, the *Chattanooga Times* reported that Lord Haw Haw had called out a sixteen-year-old Stoner specifically by name on his radio show: "Young Mr. Stoner, you are a brave lad. I will try to see to it that you get the services of a German surgeon when the war is over."[34][35] Stoner had been stricken with polio when he was a toddler and one of his legs was considerably shorter than the other. Stoner assured the *Times*, "I am not in sympathy with the German cause. I am against Jews, and Hitlerism." During the 1940s, Stoner started the "Stoner Anti-Jewish Party," a political party that was . . . well, you can read. It's through this organization and their shared loathing of Jews that he and Ed Fields, out of Louisville, would become lifelong friends. It seems likely that his antisemitism accounts for his liking of John Kasper.

When he was eighteen, in 1942, Stoner re-chartered a chapter of the Klan. This Klan chapter, we know from Stoner's FBI file, was part of the Associated Klans of America, which had chapters in Atlanta and Knoxville, among other places, and we know that Stoner travelled to Knoxville and Atlanta to meet with those chapters.

Stoner told the FBI that after a fight with Klan leader Dr. Samuel Greene (apparently over Stoner's anti-Jewish activism) Stoner resigned from the Klan. But by 1949, Stoner's name was on the membership list of Klavern no. 317. I haven't been able to suss out if Klavern no. 317 was the chapter that Stoner chartered in 1942, but it is clear that the goals of Klavern no. 317 and Stoner's personal goals were closely aligned. Klavern no. 317 was kicked out of the Klan—yes, the whole Klavern—in, it seems, 1950, for their anti-Jewish activity. Once Stoner moved to Atlanta, Klavern no. 317 was able to rejoin the Klan. In Atlanta, Stoner met in person the handsome racist, Ed Fields (born in 1932), who had been a member of the Nazi organization known as the Black Front, in addition to other groups like the Columbians, and the Christian Anti-Jewish Party. Fields was one of the founders of the National States Rights Party. They became close friends.

There are a few reasons I think it's important for us to keep an eye on Klavern no. 317 in relation to our bombings, even though there is so little information about them available:

One—these are the Tennessee assholes Stoner knew best and with whom he had long-term friendships. When Stoner told people that he had a "man in Chattanooga" who would do bombings for him, the most likely place to look for that man would be Klavern no. 317.

Two—when the Birmingham, Alabama, authorities were trying to figure out how all the dynamite was coming into their city, since much of it was a brand not sold in Alabama, they reached out to cities across the South for information. Memphis told Birmingham that the dynamite was coming out of East Tennessee, being stolen out of the mines and moved through some network throughout the South.[36] The most obvious network of people was the Klan, and Klavern no. 317 sat right at the nexus of the most violent parts of that network.

CHAPTER 4

AUGUST 1957, WHEN THE KLAN TELLS THE FBI THEY WON'T HAVE ANYTHING TO DO WITH JOHN KASPER, SO THE FBI IGNORES JOHN KASPER FOR A WHOLE MONTH

KEEP OUR
WHITE SCHOOLS WHITE

<u>HEAR SEGREGATION LEADERS:</u>

Ace Carter   Rev. John Mercurio
Bill Hendrix   Dr. Ed Fields
Rev. Fred Stroud   John Kasper
                    and Others

TELL WHY Nashville has been
sacrificed as the first major Southern city
to mix White and Nigra children in public
schools.

FIND OUT what can be done to stop
the horrors of race mixing and the race
riots, murders, hangings and race hatred
that is certain to come if the School Board,
Ben West, Frank Clement, and the Federal
Courts go through with their evil plans to
destroy all races in Nashville.

<u>ALL CHRISTIANS</u> <u>Bring</u> <u>Your</u> <u>Friends.</u>

TIME: 2:00 P.M., Sunday, August 11th

PLACE: Robertson Road and Croley Drive
        (In West Nashville, off Charlotte Ave.)

SPONSOR: TENNESSEE WHITE CITIZENS COUNCILS.

HONOR---PRIDE--FIGHT
SAVE THE WHITES

Guide to the Racists in this Chapter

Emmett Carr Nashville Klan leader
Asa Carter Birmingham renegade Klansman
Dr. Edward Fields J.B. Stoner's friend and member of any racist group that will have him
Bill Hendrix Florida Klan leader
John Kasper New Jersey racist and instigator of mob violence in Clinton, Tennessee
Thomas Norvell FBI informant
Charles Reed Kasper supporter, FBI informant, and friend of Thomas Norvell
J.B. Stoner Chattanooga Klansman who moved to Atlanta
Rev. Fred Stroud Leader of the Bible Presbyterian Church
Robert and Carrie Wray Nashville Kasper supporters

A Series of Segregationist Rallies

By August 1957, John Kasper had decamped from East Tennessee and made Nashville something of a permanent headquarters. Locals who had been following the nightmare at Clinton were understandably nervous—Nashville was now, thanks to Z. Alexander Looby, under court order to desegregate in September.

On Thursday, August 1, the *Tennessean* ran a short but jam-packed story about the beginning of Kasper's war on Nashville. He was going to hold a summit for white supremacist groups at Centennial Park at 2 p.m. on Sunday. He had a who's who of segregationists scheduled to appear, including Asa Carter, who had been at Clinton with him; Florida Klan leader Bill Hendrix; and Kentucky White Citizens Council official Dr. Edward Fields, who was J.B. Stoner's dear friend.

The story was quick to note, however, that Emmett Carr and his Klan would not be there.

"Understand, I'm not fighting with the man," [Carr] told a reporter, "but he's got such a bad background and such a bad reputation that we'd just rather not associate with him."[37]

The Park Board had hoped to find a way to stop Kasper's gathering. By Saturday, they had decided that if Kasper didn't have a permit for a rally, he couldn't hold one in Centennial Park. Kasper, who was already in hot water for his willingness to defy a federal judge, was not about to let a city park board stop him.

At 1:30 in the afternoon, he and his crowd showed up at the West End entrance to Centennial Park. Park Superintendent F.W. Pickens and the police met them.

"You must have a permit," said Pickens.

"All right, what do I have to do to get a permit?" Kasper said.

"The park board is the only one who can grant a permit," Pickens answered.

Turning to the crowd, Kasper said: "We didn't apply for a permit because we thought the right to free speech was guaranteed by the first amendment to the constitution. Any law or ordinance or regulation that abridges it is unconstitutional."

Pickens interrupted: "Kasper, you're making a speech and I told you you can't make a speech here without a permit."[38]

The caravan of hate packed up and moved to a field out west of town in Croleywood. Kasper called for a race riot and railed against the Jews. Other speakers denounced various politicians. But as the hot afternoon wore on, the crowd dwindled. In his speech, Kasper accused Emmett

Carr of skimming money off of Klan members. Carr told the *Tennessean*, "There's one or all of three things about Kasper. One, he's probably an integrationist working backwards; two, he's an agent for the government; and three, he just hasn't got all his marbles."[39]

Listen, this stuff is hilarious. Especially Pickens being all "you're making a speech when I just told you you can't make a speech without a permit." But it's also very funny that Kasper's been in town all of two seconds and his great mission to prevent Nashville's schools from desegregating is already being undermined by a public fight he's having with another racist. So much for presenting a united front of segregationists. That dream didn't even last through the first meeting.

I'm telling you this, because I, too, am laughing. I think laughter is an appropriate response to these dumbasses.

But I think Nashville made a crucial mistake because the situation was so funny: because these were so clearly a bunch of doofuses who could barely get their acts together without descending into squabbling, Kasper's arrival wasn't the giant red flag it should have been. Even with the troubles at Clinton, the Clinton racists hadn't started shooting at people yet. The Clinton High School wouldn't be bombed until the next year. The threat Kasper presented, as far as Nashville knew, was that he might instigate a riot. And yet here he was, being peacefully turned away from a rally in a park. Maybe Nashville would just be better able to contain him than Clinton was.

That belief—that this was kind of a containable joke—was a crucial mistake.

But it was a mistake we as a city weren't alone in making. The FBI already had a substantial file on Kasper, following his cross burnings in D.C. and in Florida. They had also paid close attention to him while he was in Clinton. Yet, on July 25, Special Agent in Charge Francis Norwood sent a memo to J. Edgar Hoover, the director of the FBI, saying that after calling around to Klansmen in Nashville and hearing that they weren't going to be associating with Kasper, and then reading in the papers that the

Tennessee Federation for Constitutional Government was avoiding him, "no investigation or inquiry concerning Kasper will be made in Nashville UACB [Unless Advised to the Contrary by the Bureau]."[40]

The next item in Kasper's file is dated "8-30-57." The FBI had let Kasper operate in Nashville for a month without keeping track of him.

The other mistake law enforcement officials made was not recognizing what the presence of Dr. Edward Fields at the rally meant—that J.B. Stoner was tied up in this. Maybe that's understandable in the summer of 1957. Stoner had revitalized the Chattanooga Klan by then, yes, and he and Fields already had a club devoted to their mutual hatred of Jewish people. But his willingness to bomb and his ties to other bombers hadn't fully developed at this point.

Still, when Stoner's name started popping up repeatedly in relation to the string of anti-Semitic bombings throughout the South—including Nashville's JCC—you'd have thought that someone, anyone, might have been curious about how early Stoner had been sniffing around Nashville. And here we have Fields in Nashville at the beginning of August 1957. You don't get Fields without Stoner. Not in 1957, that's for sure. Fields was Robin to Stoner's Batman. If you see one involved, you can safely assume the other one is as well.

What John Kasper Was Doing while the FBI Wasn't Watching

Anyway, back to our story. If Dr. Fields was in town, then Stoner was somewhere close by, skulking around, watching, and gathering information. This is both a safe assumption we can make based on what's known of Stoner and Fields's activities and on the fact that the FBI found a note Kasper had made saying that Stoner was in Nashville in August of 1957.[41] Stoner later said he was here.

On August 8, Kasper and other racists attended a school board meeting, demanding board members find a way to defy the federal court order to desegregate. William Keel in the *Tennessean* recorded the names of other segregationists who spoke—R.E. McKenzie, E.S. Dollar, Rev. Fred Stroud, L.V. DuBose (vice chairman of the Tennessee Federation for Constitutional Government), W.C. Orman, Betty Stephens, and Carey Hambrick.[42] What this tells us is that, in spite of Emmett Carr's insistence that the local Klan wanted nothing to do with Kasper, Carr's own sect, even the guy right below him in the pecking order—E.S. Dollar—was fine working with and appearing with Kasper. Same could be said to be true for the Tennessee Federation for Constitutional Government.

According to the school board minutes,

> The citizens, speaking as individuals, in addition to protesting the plan, feared violence and for the safety of their children. Reverend Fred Stroud stated that "Almighty God, down through the years has been the greatest segregationist of them all; that we must put some courage in the backs, hearts and minds of the people of Tennessee and not integrate."[43]

On August 10, Kasper told the *Tennessean* that he was looking to form a segregationist political party. But a rally he had that weekend was filled with a less than enthusiastic crowd and neither Asa Carter nor Bill Hendrix bothered to show up. Conventional wisdom had it that they were still sore that Kasper had held integrated dance parties in his younger days. Kasper said he was going to lay low for a couple of weeks. In actuality, when he wasn't in Nashville, he was over in East Tennessee dealing with his legal troubles from Clinton.

One of the homes he laid low in while in Nashville was that of Robert and Carrie Wray. Thirty-seven-year-old Robert worked at AVCO, which had been the famous Vultee Aircraft factory during World War II,[44] before a series of mergers and buyouts. Thirty-year-old Carrie was a stay-at-home mother of three. They lived on Jay Street, in Woodbine, south of downtown. During Kasper's downtime, Carrie Wray wrote Governor Frank Clement a letter, which he received August 23, and passed along to the Department of Education on August 26. There's no indication it was shared with police. The letter reads:

Dear Sir,

As a housewife and mother born and raised in the state of Tennessee I feel compelled to write you and ask you to please intervene in this segregation issue before the streets of Nashville and Davidson county are filled with blood. I am very much concerned with the talk going around about dynamite and shotguns and you could hear it too 'tho most of it is whispered.

The talk is on the city busses [SIC], in department and grocery stores in any and all public places and the South is beginning to hate the negro. I am afraid for our little children and I for one am not going to send mine to an integrated school and endanger their very life. We are actually sitting on a powder keg which will be lit in September. Couldn't you go to the Supreme court and tell them it just won't work in Tennessee?

Georgia, Alabama and Mississippi are standing together, why is Tennessee doing nothing. At least make a report to the newspapers or on television etc. and let the people know where you stand on this vital matter. I beg you before it is too late.

Sincerely,

Mrs. R.W. Wray[45]

While it's true that Governor Clement received a lot of angry letters from people opposing integration, he only received one from a woman living with a segregationist known for inciting violence. Not that Clement knew that, of course. But what a missed opportunity. If only someone would have asked Mrs. Wray who it was she heard talking about "dynamite and shotguns."

There's one other bit of the letter that gives me pause. She says, "I am afraid for our little children and I for one am not going to send mine to an integrated school and endanger their very life." Why does Carrie think that sending her kids to an integrated school would endanger them? After all, there are a lot of things white supremacists could do to thwart integration that wouldn't put white children at risk. That wouldn't put schools at risk. Carrie seemed to have known that kids in integrated schools were in danger. It's possible to read this letter as a genuine expression of fear, but I suspect that Carrie is actually making a veiled threat, like a mafioso remarking about how lovely your home is and how it would be a shame if something happened to it.

On August 25, Kasper held another rally at the Robertson Road and Croley Drive location in Crowleywood, west of town. Asa Carter was there, complaining about Black people, as one does at a segregationist rally. He also had complaints about music.[46]

> Carter said in Birmingham high schools, children don't even recognize the names of great Confederate heroes, except for Lee. He said they think "they're the names of rock 'n' roll singers or something."[47]

Oh, kids today with their rock 'n' roll music.

The newspaper story on the event contains one bit that backs up Carrie Wray's warning that things were going to turn violent.

Most of the cars were decorated with Confederate flags

and signs reading "Keep Our Schools White." One carried
an American flag. Another sported a model of a gallows
from which a doll was hanging by the neck. The doll was
painted black.[48]

Kasper appears to have held rallies every night that week, but because Nashville was still treating him like a joke, neither the *Tennessean*
nor the *Banner* covered them.

This is a shame because Klan leaders from all over the South were in
town. On August 21, for instance, Kasper held a meeting where Asa Carter,
Bill Hendrix, and Rev. Stroud gave speeches. Since there was no media
coverage, we don't know what was said. A Nashville detective, John Nolan,
was said by the FBI to have reported that on August 23, "KASPER stated
he had discussed dynamiting a public school with 'certain people.'"[49]

School Registration

On August 27, Nashville schools held registration. Black parents registered first graders at five formerly all-white Nashville schools. On the
28th, the *Tennessean* ran a school-by-school breakdown of registration
at the desegregated schools. (Note that Hattie Cotton is not on this list.
Patricia Watson's parents did not register her until the first day of classes.
No one knew ahead of time that she'd be at Hattie Cotton.)

> Bailey—one Negro, 55 white.
> Buena Vista—three Negro, 40 white.
> Fehr—three Negro, 56 white.
> Glenn—two Negro, 71 white.
> Jones—four Negro, 50 white.[50]

The city was erupting over a dozen children in basically two neighborhoods. No one in South Nashville or West Nashville was yet going to

be sending their kids to school with kids of a different race. This was two parts of town desegregating and, by and large, segregationists focused their in-person protest efforts on the schools near Fred Stroud's church.

They also took to the phones. The assistant school superintendent, W.H. Oliver, received threatening phone calls, though he didn't reveal to the *Tennessean*'s reporter, Wallace Westfeldt, what those threats were. However, because the racists had called every W.H. Oliver in the phone book, another W.H. Oliver, a truck driver, told Westfeldt that "he had been receiving calls apparently intended for the assistant superintendent. One caller, when told the truck driver was asleep, replied, 'He may be asleep now but he'll be asleep for good later.'"[51]

The calls that went to the Black kids' houses were more straightforward in their threats. Mrs. Horace Guthrie, Patricia Guthrie's mother, told Westfeldt that she'd gotten a call from a woman saying, "You had better not send your child to a white school because we'll beat her to death and bomb your house." Mrs. Maud Baxter, Marvin Moor's mother, "said a caller threatened to throw acid on her child and burn a cross in front of her home."[52]

Men get most of the attention, but women were very heavily involved in the segregationist movement. Most of the people who confronted School Superintendent W.A. Bass at registration, pissed about integration, were women. The people demanding the names of parents trying to register their kids were women. At Glenn school, Westfeldt reported:

> A small knot of women stood in front of the walkway leading to the school's front door. They passed out "Keep Our White Schools White" buttons, Klan pamphlets stamped with a Tennessee White Citizens Council mark, anti-Semitic pamphlets published by Conde McGinley, a longtime professional anti-Semite in Union, N.J.; handbills announcing a Kasper meeting and citizens council membership applications.[53]

At some point on the day of school registration, John Kasper gave a speech and said, "We're going to talk to the 'niggers' and tell them if they want to avoid the shotgun, dynamite and rope they had better get out of the white schools."[54] (This language is very similar language to Carrie Wray's letter, which makes me wonder if she wasn't hearing some early version of this speech in her house.) That put him back on the FBI's radar.

Let me be clear, this language brought him back to the attention of the FBI on the day he gave the speech—August 27—not the day after, when papers reported it. The FBI heard about the speech from Thomas Norvell, 33, a World War II vet who worked as a mechanic, who called the FBI and told them that he and his friend, Charles Reed, 50, "had been attending KASPER's meetings chiefly because they were curious about his views on segregation."[55] Norvell had apparently grown very concerned about what he was hearing at these meetings and told the FBI that "he believed that KASPER's group would resort to violence." When he gave his full statement to the FBI on September 12, he told them, "Sometime late in August a meeting was held at which Asa Carter and others appeared. There was some talk about organizing a group which would practice violence."[56] In other words, once the out-of-town Klansmen showed up, some small part of the crowd around John Kasper began talking about forming a terrorist cell to attack a Nashville school.

The FBI does not appear to have shared this with the Nashville police.

Worse than that—and that's pretty dang bad—the FBI does not appear to have asked Norvell who all was talking about organizing this group. Norvell and Reed had both been with John Kasper all August, helping him hand out literature, making signs, and attending his meetings. Reed took down the names of people who attended the meetings. Norvell and Reed absolutely could have identified who was in the discussion about forming this group.

Nothing in the file indicates the FBI asked them to.

CHAPTER 5

THE HATTIE COTTON ELEMENTARY SCHOOL BOMBING

Guide to the Racists in this Chapter

Jack Brown Leader of Chattanooga Klavern 317
Emmett Carr Middle Tennessee Klan leader
John Dalton Member of Chattanooga Klavern 317
Bill Hendrix Florida Klan leader
Eldon Edwards Imperial Wizard of the US Klans
John Kasper Rabblerouser
Jack Kershaw Donald Davidson's errand boy
Thomas Norvell FBI informant
Charles Reed Kasper supporter and friend of Thomas Norvell

September Begins

John Kasper was over in North Carolina until late Thursday of the first week of September 1957. The *Tennessean* covered his return. This is the whole article:

> Kasper Returns, To Try Boycott
>
> Segregationist John Kasper returned to Nashville from North Carolina last night and addressed a gathering of segregationists in front of the War Memorial building.
>
> Kasper told the group that an effort will be made to organize a boycott of integrated schools here by white students. He said the organization would be attempted by the local White Citizens council and the Ku Klux Klan. Kasper spent last week in North Carolina speaking against integration there.
>
> Others addressing last night's meeting were the Rev. Fred Stroud and KKK leaders Emmett Carr and E.S. Dollar.[57]

There's a lot going on here that's worth noting. One, we see Kasper at the War Memorial building, which means he is, in essence, at the state capitol, which is right across the street. He's not at the site of Nashville's city government, which is only three blocks away. He's taking his mob right to the state. He'll be back in this location.

This "involving the students" thing is something we know Kasper did in the past—see, for instance, his cadre of cute girls over in Clinton. But as we know from Emmett Carr's Father Ryan plot, it's also a strategy Carr and the Klan had been wanting to use. A big problem with this strategy is that Nashville was just integrating its first grade. Who were these segregationist boycotters in the first grade going to be?

But the most crucial thing this story tells us is that whatever Carr's problems with Kasper were, by early September, he had set them aside and Kasper and Carr were now openly plotting to thwart integration. Kasper had the local Klan on his side.

The Hattie Cotton bombing took place just after midnight on Tuesday, September 10, 1957, the culmination of activities that took place all over town the preceding weekend and on the first day of school: Monday, September 9.

I'm going to relate the incidents of this weekend in chronological order, as best as I have been able to piece them together from newspaper stories and the FBI files I have available to me. If you feel like the things I've told you to this point might be particulars you hadn't heard of, but that none of it really conflicts with what you already knew about these bombings, here's where things are going to start to get weird for you. Honestly, things are about to get weird in general, but readers who don't know about the bombings already (especially non-Nashvillians) won't experience the dissonance of finding out that what they thought they knew was pretty wrong.

The FBI at this time was not interested in getting dragged into what they saw as local squabbles. They wanted to know what was going on, but that was the extent of it. Their goal was to preserve their access to information. So, if at any point in this next part, you're wondering, "Why didn't the FBI tell the police or arrest so-and-so themselves or do this or do that?" just consider whether doing so might have weakened their ability to collect information.

Also, consider that the police just wanted to keep order and restore calm. They wanted to arrest and run off the rabble rousers, and they wanted the mobs to be afraid to cause more chaos. This isn't exactly the same as finding and prosecuting the bombers, which would also be at odds with the FBI's goal of keeping information flowing.

Plus, remember that "good," "respectable" white people were segregationist activists. We don't know all the ways prominent white Nashvillians might have been tied into efforts to use violence to stop integration—not just the bombings, but the mobs that preceded them. I think it's fair to assume, based on what we know did happen, that the police were not eager to push too hard down paths that might jack things up for people they knew or people who were well connected.

Okay, all that being said, here we go.

Thursday, September 5

On Thursday, September 5, Kasper came back to Nashville and gave his speech calling for the school boycott. Klan leadership was present and approving. Meanwhile, FBI Special Agent Norwood talked in person with Thomas Norvell, who had contacted the FBI after being alarmed by the rhetoric of the crowd at other Kasper rallies. Norvell told Norwood that "he has never heard KASPER make any statement indicating that he adheres to violence in connection with the racial situation[58] and that to the contrary, KASPER has always made statements to the effect that he is opposed to violence. He stated that some of the people who have been at the KASPER meetings have talked of possible violence."[59]

Friday, September 6

On Friday, September 6, a last-ditch effort by segregationists to forestall integration failed in court and Judge William Miller ordered Nashville to begin desegregating first grade on Monday. Present in the courtroom was Z. Alexander Looby, who was the lawyer for the parents who brought suit to desegregate. So too was John Kasper, unsurprisingly, and Donald Davidson's sidekick, Jack Kershaw. Nellie Kenyon in the *Tennessean* reported:

> "Since Judge Miller admitted from the bench that he had already made up his mind before coming into court and didn't even read our brief (submitted by the Parents' Preference committee)," said Jack Kershaw, vice president of the Tennessee Federation for Constitutional Government, "if there is any way humanly possible to appeal the decision it should be done right away. We feel an appeal should be made immediately, because if it is not, we fear violence."[60]

Saturday, September 7

That Saturday, September 7 (according to what the FBI was hearing from Norvell), John Kasper had gone to the home of Charles Reed, a Klansman who had been collecting Kasper's mail for him. Kasper, according to Reed as recounted by Norvell, had "some sticks of dynamite and four quarter fruit jars of powder in his possession.[61] By innuendo, Kasper allegedly indicated to Reed that the dynamite and powder would be used on a school."[62] Kasper, according to Norvell, told Reed that the dynamite "came into Nashville from outside the city and had not been purchased locally."[63] Reed, though, was being less than cooperative. He denied everything Norvell told the FBI.

Sunday, September 8

On Sunday, Norvell called Agent Norwood again and "stated that he had learned from REED that KASPER had contacted REED and that the use of the dynamite would be delayed for a week or ten days."[64] Meanwhile, John Kasper and Bill Hendrix, Kasper's Florida Klan friend, held a rally in their favorite field in West Nashville. Two hundred people attended and listened as Kasper called for a student boycott and picketing at schools on Monday. After it started to rain, the mob caravanned to Bailey School in East Nashville and held another meeting there.

The Nashville police had officers attending Kasper's rallies, collecting information on what he was telling his followers. According to the FBI, the police chief and the DA intended that these officers would then testify in court as to what they'd heard Kasper saying, should the need arise. Since the police files are missing, we don't know much about the scope of this plan, just that it pissed the FBI off. We'll get to why the FBI might have been so angry.

Monday, September 9, The First Day of School

Monday, the first day of school, was a complete shit show. The schools that desegregated first grade that day were Glenn, Jones, Buena Vista, Fehr, Hattie Cotton, and Clemons—though these were not all the same schools where Black students had preregistered. The Black students who tried to go to Caldwell were turned away for technical reasons, and the little girl who was supposed to go to Bailey was transferred to a Black school by her parents at the last minute. No one knew Patricia Watson would be attending Hattie Cotton until she showed up and registered that morning. No protesters knew to be waiting for her there. No angry mobs thronged outside. John Kasper did not visit Hattie Cotton.

Angry crowds of racists did gather at most of the other schools. John Kasper and Rev. Fred Stroud spoke to those crowds at Glenn, Caldwell,

Fehr, Jones, and Buena Vista. Kasper was photographed at Bailey. Kasper threatened violence and urged the gathered white people to come to his rally that evening on the steps of War Memorial Auditorium. At Glenn, a group of fifteen to twenty people harangued parents and tried to block them from bringing their children into the school. This group (of adults!) surrounded the little Black six-year-olds and jeered at them. The situation was tense enough that many parents, white and Black, came and got their kids. Some in the crowds threw rocks and bottles—the bottles being doubly terrifying because of the threat of an acid attack.

The *Tennessean* reported that Kasper told the Glenn crowd, "Keep your children at home. Some of you men who want something to do, go over to Bailey school. Some of you go over to Jones and Caldwell. We aren't ever going to give up. They don't have enough jails for all of us."[65]

That evening, Kasper had his largest, angriest rally on the step of War Memorial Auditorium. John Egerton, in his article, "Walking into History: The Beginning of School Desegregation in Nashville," recounts how it went:

> With what seemed like a mixture of confidence and desperation, Kasper stood before his audience that Monday evening and slowly heated his rhetoric to the boiling point. Using language laced with dehumanizing epithets and images of violence, he pressed once again the emotional buttons of defiance and menace that had always seemed to work for him in the past: communism, atheism, mongrelization, rape, mayhem. The crowd was on his leash, waiting to be led. He told them they had a constitutional right to carry weapons, and the time had come for them to arm themselves and get into the fight.
>
> They moved across Charlotte Avenue to the steps of the State Capitol, with Kasper in the lead. "We say no peace!" he shouted. "We say, attack, attack, attack!"

Then, brandishing a rope, the Jersey racist with his newly-acquired Southern accent closed with a final flourish: "This is Dixie! Who do they think they're playing with? We're the greatest race on the face of the earth! Let's for once show what a white man can do!" Standing gaunt and grim-faced, Kasper absorbed the frenzied crowd's deafening roar of approval. He looked for all the world like the leader of a lynch mob.[66]

If it looked like a lynch mob, that was in part because Kasper seemed to have a victim in mind. The *Tennessean* reported that a policeman testified that Kasper had taken that rope, formed it into a noose, and "remarked that it would 'fit' the neck of City Councilman Z. Alexander Looby, a Negro."[67] Meanwhile, police were stationed at each of the schools where demonstrators had been active that day. Hattie Cotton was apparently not considered an active site.

According to the FBI, when Charles Reed came home Monday night at about 11:00, he "found Kasper waiting for him in a distraught emotional state. Kasper asked him 'where the hell' he had been when he needed him. Kasper indicated he wanted Reed to go with him, but Reed refused, saying he was all wet from the rain."[68] Kasper left.

The Explosion

Egerton reports that white people were rioting in pockets all over town—mostly young, angry men. "From their midst came a whispered rumor that Fehr would be blown up at midnight."[69] But police were guarding Fehr. Instead, at 12:33 A.M. on September 10, Hattie Cotton exploded.

The bomb went off at the east end of the main hallway, between the library and a classroom. Walls crumbled. Ceilings fell. Every window was knocked out.

The *Tennessean* described the authorities' theory of the bombing:

> The investigators believe approximately a case of dynamite, possibly still in its box, was placed outside the building in the porchway of the entrance on the east side of the school.
>
> The detonator was probably an electric cap connected to wires, rather than a dry fuse set by fire, investigators said. They believe this because police found detonating wires near the school.
>
> [. . .]
>
> O.O. Lee, state fire marshal whose office is investigating the explosion, said "We estimate that approximately 100 sticks of dynamite caused this explosion."
>
> [. . .]
>
> He said that investigators agree that whoever set off this dynamite either was very professional and was informed as to his margin of danger—or he was very lucky. From the effect of the blast it would seem that he "knew just what he was doing," Lee said.
>
> To successfully set off the charge and escape injury it was probably necessary to string wires some 50 feet from the place the dynamite was placed. From this point the charge could have been exploded by a battery. The explosion would have been immediate and the dynamiter would have been able to escape in a waiting car driven by a confederate.[70]

Within ten minutes of the blast, police were rousing John Kasper out of bed at his new East Nashville address on Scott Avenue. He had apparently been asleep. The noise hadn't woken him, even though people as far away as Donelson reported hearing it.

From our perspective, sixty years on, we know the police were wrong about the size of the bomb. It wasn't one hundred sticks of dynamite—which probably would have leveled the school. Hattie Cotton's west wing was undamaged and students were back in the building a week later. The east wing was repaired and reopened by February 1958. It seems fairly clear now that there was just one bomb and that it was substantially smaller than the police initially thought it was.

But at that moment, it must have seemed to the FBI that the bomb that blew up Hattie Cotton was not the bomb they'd been told John Kasper had. The size was wrong, plus Norvell had said Kasper's plot had been pushed back. Based on the facts available at that time, it must have seemed like John Kasper had a plot to bomb a Nashville school with the small bomb he had shown Reed, which had been pushed to the second week of school.

When Hattie Cotton exploded and everyone thought that bomb was huge, the only conclusion the FBI could have drawn was that Nashville still had a bomb in play, that another plot—Kasper's plot—was ongoing. Also note: the FBI hadn't yet told the Nashville police about Reed and Norvell.[71] We don't know when or if the Nashville authorities were warned that Kasper's crowd had a bomb plot baking, but the FBI clearly had heard that segregationists were actively planning to bomb a school and had explosives.

So, as you read this next section, keep in mind that this is all happening while the FBI had information that strongly suggested there was another bomb out there and another plot possibly in motion.

FBI Weirdness and Witness Hiding

On Tuesday, September 10, the FBI interviewed Norvell and Reed together. Norvell told the agents, in front of Reed, what Reed had told him. Reed denied saying it. The FBI believed Norvell.

At 3:37 P.M., J. Edgar Hoover sent a memo to his closest confidants at the FBI: Clyde Tolson, Leland V. Boardman, Alex P. Rosen, and Lou Nichols. In it, Hoover brought them up to speed on what'd happened in Nashville and said they had an informant who said he saw Kasper with dynamite. Hoover wrote, "Our Agent was also told to advise the Chief of Police and the Sheriff of this matter," meaning the matter of them having an informant who had seen Kasper with dynamite.[72] This pretty clearly suggests that before the bombing, no Nashville law enforcement knew specifics about Kasper's alleged bomb plot.

At 4 P.M. in Washington, D.C., J. Edgar Hoover sent another memo to Tolson, Boardman, Rosen, and Nichols. In it, he complained about the attorney general asking Nashville's mayor to get affidavits from the police officers who were at Kasper's meetings, since he wanted the Bureau to secure affidavits. Both the police and the FBI were trying to find a way to get Kasper's bond from his arrest over in Clinton revoked. But they were at cross-purposes over who should be doing what.

Hoover also spent a paragraph discussing the Reed and Kasper bomb plot, such as it was, and whether they could find someone who could corroborate Norvell's version of Reed's statements. And then there's this interesting bit:

```
The Attorney General has told me he learned
from Fred Mullen that Kasper had been
arrested by the Nashville police. I stated
that he was probably taken into custody for
questioning regarding this matter since
affidavits had been requested of the police
```

by the Mayor. I told the Attorney General
that the police did not know the identities
of Norvell and Reed because we did not want
their identities disclosed.[73]

This sounds like Hoover had had a discussion with the attorney general in the twenty minutes since he composed his last memo, and that the situation in Nashville had changed. Now the police know the FBI had heard of a bomb plot by Kasper before Hattie Cotton was blown up (and that the FBI did not tell the Nashville police about it), but the FBI was keeping the identities of their informants secret.

Then, there's a strange memo dated September 10, 1957—though someone had handwritten September 11, 1957, on it. This memo states: "This information was furnished to the Chief of Police of Nashville and the Sheriff of Davidson County, Tennessee, on September 9, 1957."[74]

This unsigned memo seems to directly contradict what Hoover wrote. Hoover made it sound like no law enforcement in Nashville knew about what the FBI had heard until after the bombing. This memo makes it sound like the FBI warned Nashville authorities that a plot was afoot, but Nashville failed to act in time to stop it.

Both scenarios are troubling. Unfortunately for the FBI, all we as a city have to help us judge which scenario is more likely is the FBI's behavior in other instances and what the FBI wrote in later reports.

The specific later report I'm talking about was a huge one Special Agent Richard Lavin wrote on April 24, 1959. Deep within it, Agent Lavin describes exactly what happened during the Hattie Cotton bombing from the FBI's end. I'm including the whole section devoted to the school bombing, because I think it clarifies the timeline, illuminates Norvell's relationship with the FBI, and clearly shows that the FBI withheld information from the Nashville police. Since this report was typed in standard typewriter font, the identities of the people whose names have been redacted are fairly obvious. Norvell has a bigger white box than Reed. I'm putting my educated guesses in brackets based on the earlier information in the file.

5. POSSIBLE CONNECTIONS WITH BOMBINGS

A. Hattie Cotton School Nashville, Tennessee

W.E. HOPTEN, Director, Tennessee Bureau of Criminal Identification, on September 10, 1957, advised that the Hattie Cotton School, Nashville, Tennessee, had been bombed. HOPTEN advised that it was estimated that several cases of dynamite had been used.

On August 27, 1957, [Thomas Norvell] contacted SE JOHN D. JONES telephonically. [Norvell] advised that he had been attending meetings held by JOHN KASPER and that he and [Charles Reed] had been attending KASPER's meetings chiefly because they were curious about his views on segregation. [Norvell] stated he was not in agreement with KASPER's ideas and he believed that KASPER's group would resort to violence.

On September 5, 1957, [Norvell] was contacted by SA FRANCIS W. NORWOOD and he advised that he never heard KASPER make any statement indicating that he adhered to violence and on the contrary had always made statements to the effect that he is opposed to violence. He stated that some of the people who have been at the KASPER meetings have talked of possible violence.

On September 7, 1957, [Norvell] contacted SA NORWOOD and furnished the following information which he stated he had gotten from [Charles Reed. Reed was] approached on the morning of September 7, 1957, by JOHN KASPER, who asked [Reed] if he could use dynamite. KASPER explained to [Reed] that he had several sticks of dynamite, which came into Nashville from outside the city and had not been purchased locally. He also said he had four quart fruit jars full of gun powder or an explosive of some sort.

On September 8, 1957 [Norvell] again contacted SA NORWOOD and stated he had learned from [Reed] that KASPER had contacted [Reed] and that the use of dynamite would be delayed for a week or ten days. He stated that he understood that it would be used at a school REDACTED.

[Reed] was interviewed by SAs WILLIAM L. SHEETS and EDWARD T. STEELE at his residence on the afternoon of September 10, 1957. [Reed] denied that he had had any conversation with KASPER or [Norvell] or anyone else pertaining to dynamite, gun powder, or other explosives.

[Thomas Norvell and Charles Reed] interviewed together at REDACTED on September 10,
1957, by SAs NORWOOD, STEELE, and SHEETS.
At this time [Norvell] in the presence of
[Reed] repeated the information previously
furnished. Again [Reed] denied any knowledge
and stated in the presence of [Norvell] that
he did not know where [Norvell] got such
ideas.

On the morning of September 11, 1957,
[Reed] telephonically contacted SA STEELE
at the Nashville Resident Agency Office and
again denied he had any information about
the dynamite and stated that he felt that
if JOHN KASPER were released from jail, he
would come to [Reed's] house and that possibly [Reed] could get some information.
He then stated that he could sure use some
money as he was not employed and was unable
to pay his debts.

On September 12, 1957, [Reed] again
telephoned the Nashville Resident Agency
Office and advises SA NORWOOD that he had
been lying and that he did have information
about the dynamite. He stated that he had
actually seen the dynamite in KASPER's
possession. [Reed] then voluntarily came
to the Nashville Resident Agency Office and
furnished a signed statement [Reed] set
forth that KASPER had come to his house on

September 7, 1957, with a box of dynamite.
According to [Reed], KASPER asked him to
keep the dynamite, but [Reed] refused.
[Reed] also stated that a day or two before
KASPER brought the dynamite to his house
KASPER and [Reed] had ridden around in
the car a little. KASPER stated he wanted
to look at the schools and see which one
would be the easiest. [Reed] understood
him to mean the easiest school to dynamite.
[Reed] stated on Monday, September 9, 1957,
he arrived home at 11 P.M. KASPER was on
[Reed's] porch and as he walked up he put
a flashlight in [Reed's] face and stated,
"[Reed] where in the Hell have you been?"
According to [Reed] KASPER was acting like
a maniac the way he talked and waved his
hands. Later that night [Reed] heard a dull
thud and immediately thought that KASPER had
used the dynamite.

On September 12, 1957, [Norvell] furnished a
written statement to SAs NORWOOD and STEELE,
in which he set forth that on Monday night,
September 9, 1957, he went to the residence
of [Reed] at about 9:00 P.M. After he had
been there a little while KASPER came in and
asked for [Reed]. Told him that [Reed] was
not there. According to [Norvell] KASPER was
very nervous and paced up and down on the
porch. He stayed at the house about an hour
and a half and stated several times that

he was very anxious to see [Reed]. KASPER
stated, "Tonight of all nights I wish he
would get here."

On September 13, 1957, SAC JULIUS M. LOPEZ,
JR., and SA JAMES B. ANDERSON presented
to FRED ELLEDGE, United States Attorney,
Nashville the statements made by [Thomas
Norvell] and [Charles Reed]. Mr. ELLEDGE,
after discussing the matter with Mr. MC
CLEAN of the Department of Justice, advised
that even if the allegations were true, such
allegations related to a state matter and in
no way constituted an offense within federal
jurisdiction.

On September 13, 1957, SAC LOPEZ furnished
DOUGLAS E. HOSSE, Chief, Police Department,
Nashville, the information secured from
[Norvell] and [Reed].[75]

This version of events has clearly been polished up to make the FBI
look a little less bad. But it does clarify that Norvell was someone the
FBI knew and trusted and that the FBI didn't tell the Nashville police
about Reed until three days after the bombing.

What Charles Reed Actually Told the FBI

It's worth looking at the statement Charles Reed gave the FBI on September 12, because what he said in his own words was a little different
than what the FBI attributed to him.

On Saturday, Sept. 7, 1957 about 3:30 PM, Kasper came to my house at 1715 Nassau Street, Nashville, Tenn. Tom Norvell was the only other person at my house when Kasper came. Kasper parked his car, a Plymouth wine colored convertible, in front of my home. I saw him take a pasteboard box out of his car. He came in my bedroom with the box and put in [sic] on the floor at the foot of my bed. The box was about 18 inches long, 12 inches wide, and 28 inches deep. He pulled out some soiled shirts and then removed a little cardboard box about 10 inches deep and put it on the floor. Kasper said, "Reed, what am I going to do with this stuff?" I said "What's that?" and he said "Dynamite." I told him he could not leave it at my house as it was too dangerous. He acted mad and jittery and said "We gotta put it somewhere." He asked me to put it under the floor of my house, but I refused. Then I happened to think of an abandoned house on Delta Street and I told Kasper to come with me. That I had thought of a better place. [. . .] We went around the [abandoned] house to the back and set the box down, opened the top and raised up some excelsior. He pulled up a quart fruit jar. He told me that was loose dynamite. Then he picked up a stick of dynamite and handed it to me. He told me to feel of it. I saw three sticks of dynamite, one that I held in my hand, and two in the

box laying in the excelsior. There could
have been more in the box. Kasper pulled
out a piece of wire about two and one half
feet long. He said that was a fuse and that
it would burn one foot per minute, or two
and one half minutes. This wire was black
and looked to me like it was insulated. Also
looked like it had a thread of white running
through it—made into the insulation—not
wrapped around it. The quart jar contained
a yellowish orange looking substance in the
form of something like grape nut flakes—in
other words, not fine like sand or powder,
and not coarse like a corn flake. More like
you would take a hand full of corn flakes
and mash them in your hand. The substance
did not lay close together. The stick of
dynamite I held in my hand was wrapped with
brown oily looking paper. It looked like it
was greasy, but did not feel greasy to my
hand. I never examined dynamite before, but I
believe what I held in my hand was dynamite.[76]

Almost as soon as the FBI decided that it was going to have to tell
the Nashville police about Reed, they were coming up with reasons
to disregard Reed's statement: he wanted the reward money, he had a
head injury, he was a drunk. And while it's hard to know if the changes
to the description of what Reed said he saw were deliberate or just the
result of drift as things were repeated second and third hand, Reed's own
statement is much more exact and descriptive than "Reed saw Kasper
with some dynamite." Reed was able to describe the components of a
bomb. Most compelling to me is that he seems to be describing a jar full

of flake TNT without knowing it. Anybody would recognize a stick of dynamite (or at worst confuse it with a roadside flare), but Reed seems to have seen something he didn't recognize and was able to describe it well enough that, more than half a century later, I can give a pretty good guess as to what he saw. That says to me that he saw something—that he wasn't just making stuff up for the reward.

There are a couple more things to add to our FBI timeline.

Klavern No. 317 Appears in Nashville

On September 11, A.E. Shockley, principal of the all-Black Head School, received a call at the school "from an individual who identified himself as 'Dalton, (phonetic) with the Ku Klux Klan.'"[77] This Dalton said he was going to blow up Head School at 10:30 that night. This did not happen, fortunately.

The FBI checked its files to see if they might have known who this Dalton was. "The one possibility developed was a John Dalton of Rossville, Ga.,[78] who according to various file references was active in the Chattanooga, Tennessee, Klavern 317 from 1950 to 1956, present status not known."[79] At the time of the Hattie Cotton bombing, Klavern 317 was headed up by Jack Brown. According to the FBI, "STONER was formerly a member of the Chattanooga Klavern No. 317 and was banished from the Klavern in 1944. He stated he rejoined Klavern No. 317 in December 1949, and was expelled in January 1950, for making a motion at a Klan meeting to throw all Jews out of Chattanooga."[80]

Unbeknownst to authorities in Nashville, the same month that Hattie Cotton blew up, Imperial Wizard of the US Klans, Eldon Edwards, kicked Klavern No. 317 out of the Klan (yes, again) for—wait for it—its "alleged uncontrollable proclivity for violence."[81]

But what, exactly, had Klavern No. 317 done that was so violent? The last big thing they'd done in Chattanooga was to blow up the porch of civil rights attorney R.H. Craig, in early August 1957. Nothing happened in Chattanooga in September that would warrant Edwards's action.

But there had been violence *against white people* in Nashville. White children, even, since they were the vast majority of students at Hattie Cotton. And that violence sure seems like it had Chattanooga ties—Dalton and Stoner.

Remember the part where Norvell told Agent Norwood that Kasper had told Reed that the dynamite had been purchased outside the city and brought in? This is a thing J.B. Stoner was going to go on to do repeatedly in the late 1950s and 1960s. He's alleged to have done it for the Atlanta synagogue bombing in 1958. He's alleged to have done it for the 16th Street Baptist Church bombing in Birmingham in 1963.

And lo and behold, the FBI learned in 1958 that J.B. Stoner was bragging around Birmingham about having bought the dynamite that blew up Hattie Cotton. From whom? It seems pretty likely from Klavern No. 317, members of which may have even come to town to help with the job.

FBI files not only eventually give us a pretty good idea of what happened in the Hattie Cotton bombing, they also make utterly clear that the FBI at the time of the bombing—even knowing that the school had been blown up and that Kasper and his followers likely had more explosives—were not being completely forthcoming with the Nashville police about what they knew, when they knew it, and who they knew it from.

This seems outrageous. What if there was a second bomb out there? Remember, Head School had received a bomb threat. The police needed to speak with Reed immediately to try to discern Kasper's plans for the dynamite he had (if that story was true). If they thought this bomb was the only bomb, Reed saw it in Kasper's hands. If the goal was to get Kasper put in jail and kept there, an eyewitness is pretty damn important.

What the heck was the FBI doing?

Well, let's see what happened to the people the Nashville police did get their hands on.

CHAPTER 6

THE AFTERMATH, THE BEATINGS, AND THE MAN IN THE GARAGE

Guide to the Racists in this Chapter

J.B. Blackwell Bombing suspect and seemingly fake person
Robert Bromley Wallace Rider's tenant and fellow fraudster
Emmett Carr Nashville's highest-ranking Klan leader
Asa Carter Renegade Alabama Klan leader
Carroll Crimmons Bombing suspect
Vincent Crimmons Bombing suspect
James R. Harris Bombing suspect
W.D. Hodge Bombing suspect
Frank Houchin Local criminal who was somehow tied into the truck depot bombings back in 1952
John Kasper Lead troublemaker in Nashville at this time
Jack Kershaw Donald Davidson's compatriot
Thomas Norvell FBI informant
Charles Reed Thomas Norvell's friend
Wallace Rider Nashville Klansman and insurance fraudster
James McKinley "Slim" Thompson An Alabama associate of Rider's
J.B. Stoner All-around racist and terrorism facilitator
William Arnold Wilkins Inconsequential suspect
Carrie Wray Kasper supporter

On the morning of September 10, 1957, rioters were back out at the schools early. This time, the police were not messing around. They arrested protesters left and right and, among them, folks driving blue-and-white Hudsons. Such a car had been seen driving away from Hattie Cotton at the time of the bombing.

William Arnold Wilkins, a twenty-year-old from the Bordeaux area, was the first to be picked up. He, like other segregationists, was back out on the second day of school to be part of whatever might happen, and he was driving such a car. Police told the *Tennessean* that "wire found at Wilkins' home was 'generally of the same type'" used by the bombers.[82]

The Crew from Whites Creek

Next, the police arrested James R. Harris, J.B. Blackwell, and Vincent Albert Crimmons, who were also in a blue-and-white Hudson, decorated with KKK signs and other segregationist slogans.[83] They were picked up near Fehr School first thing in the morning. The police found a Billy club, a bolo knife, and mallets in their car.

Sources told the *Tennessean* that Harris, Blackwell, and Crimmons made statements that seemed to indicate they knew something about the bombing. Whatever those statements were, they caused the police to go arrest Vincent's brother, Carroll Crimmons, and W.D. Hodge, who, like the other three, lived out along or near Whites Creek Pike just outside the city limits.

The police said they found fragments of wire in the car with Harris, Blackwell, and Vincent Crimmons, and that Blackwell and V. Crimmons had experience using dynamite to clear cess pools. The picture of the police with these wire fragments shows a substantial length of wire, which seemed to fit with their theory that the bombers would have run a long length of fuse.

The story the *Tennessean* was getting from police diverges wildly from the story the FBI was getting from police. Early on the morning of September 13, Special Agent in Charge Lopez called FBI headquarters and told them the *Tennessean* had a story saying there was a witness to the bombing, a woman who had been in the car when the dynamite was acquired and had told the police who did the bombing. Lopez told Headquarters that he thought this was Betty Jean Moore, who had told police "that one William Wilkins had stated to her some time ago that he had three sticks of dynamite in his 1949 Hudson. According to information available to Lopez, there is no indication that Wilkins is implicated in this bombing."[84] Lopez thought the police had released the tale of the squealing witness to "keep the story alive."

Wilkins was trying to impress a girl and got briefly caught up in the biggest local news story of the day.

What happened to the Whites Creek Pike guys is much more troubling.

These men, as far as I can tell, had indeed been hanging around Kasper rallies and at least some of them had Klan ties. But, in most ways, they were very much outside the mainstream of the charismatic, middle-class racists who seem to have been involved with the planning of this bombing. William Hodge left almost no trail. I can say for certain that he was born. I think he may be the W.D. Hodge that died in the 1970s and is buried out west of town, but I don't know that for sure. The FBI had nothing to say about him in the files I've seen. The FBI has a little information about James Harris. He was a veteran in his late forties with a prosthetic left leg. He had, according to the FBI, eight children and a sixth-grade education. He was unemployed.

Vincent and Carroll Crimmons, we know a little more about. Vincent had a juvenile criminal record but seemed to have gotten his life together prior to the bombing. Carroll did not have an easy life after this arrest. He spent the rest of his life in and out of trouble for crimes ranging from DUI to child abuse.

Vincent was married to a Blackwell. The stringer for *Life* magazine sent word to his editors that J.B. Blackwell was Vincent's brother-in-law. On the one hand, the only Blackwells living out along Whites Creek Pike were Vincent's in-laws, so since J.B. reportedly lived out that way, he had to be related to that family. But if he was Vincent's brother-in-law, he could not have been 42, as the papers reported, because Vincent's mother-in-law was only 44 in 1957 and his father-in-law was not much older. No Blackwells who I could find had those initials. I'm going to continue to call him J.B. Blackwell, because I don't have a better, more accurate way to identify this individual, but I want to be clear that either this is not his name, or he is not Vincent's brother-in-law. "J.B. Blackwell" is, I think, an unintentional pseudonym bestowed by confused media.

The Crimmonses were, according to the *Tennessean*, dues-paying members of the Ku Klux Klan. But they were weird people to be Klansmen. First off, the Crimmons brothers' parents are buried in Calvary Cemetery, which means their parents were Catholic, which suggests the Crimmonses were at least raised Catholic. That isn't to say that they couldn't have been racial terrorists—we know Emmett Carr had been working with Catholics—but if the Crimmonses were so outraged about school desegregation that they were willing to bomb a school, why wouldn't they have bombed Father Ryan or Cathedral? Why wait years and bomb a public school?

The other odd thing is that Vincent Crimmons's mother-in-law, Amanda Blackwell, supposed mother of the mysterious J.B. Blackwell, was a Collins from Bells Bend in rural Davidson County; her mother's maiden name was Barnes, also from Bells Bend. The Barnes family and the Collins family are two of the Melungeon families that settled out in the bend in the 1800s. Tennessee Melungeon history is complicated, but what you need to know is that they weren't always considered exactly white, and they faced persecution because of it.[85] Both the Barnes and Collins families have marked as their race either a *W* over an *M* in the 1910 census—meaning they had first been classified as Mulatto and then the census taker decided to classify them as white—or visa versa. Next to their names, the census taker has written either "Portuguese" or "Portuguese Indians," as if he wanted to have some explanation for his bosses as to his confusion.

It's not too hard to imagine why people living in a segregated society that haven't always had all the benefits afforded to the average white person might become racists—as a way of proving their whiteness. And consider in particular how important being white would have been for someone in Bells Bend. There was a county school for white children in Scottsboro at the north end of the bend. The closest school for black children was clear in Bordeaux. Being perceived as white in rural Davidson County often literally meant your children could go to school and your family had easy access to public services. The extended families of these men had good motivation for being unimpeachably white.

On the other hand, people who leave no trace usually leave no trace because they were too poor or too poorly connected. Guys like this make good scapegoats. Who cares what happens to them?

Larry Brinton, who was on the police beat for the *Nashville Banner* that day, saw the police arrive at the jail with two suspects who he thought were brothers. He couldn't say for sure if this was Vincent Crimmons and J.B. Blackwell, but as far as I can tell from newspaper reports, they were the only two men brought in together.

Brinton says he was standing near the entrance where the paddy wagons were brought into the jail, talking to a couple of police officers, when these men were brought in. Brinton recounts that a police officer asked the men, "Would you be willing to take a lie detector test?" This confused Brinton, because "I'm standing there, thinking what the hell's going on? They don't have no damn lie detector test here."

The two men, not knowing this, agreed to take the test.

A half an hour or so after the men were taken inside for the "test," Brinton followed. He made his way to where the men were being questioned. "They had this long table and they had this guy up on the table and officers had his legs and officers at the front of him were holding him down and paddling him."[86] That was the test. Brinton says they passed.

The police also allegedly—though they never denied it—took a wooden board to Carroll Crimmons when they brought him in later.

FBI files confirm Brinton's story of police brutality. The files also make clear that the police knew these guys were poor suspects almost as soon as they brought them into custody. Late in the evening of September 10, the special agent in charge (probably Lopez) sent an urgent teletype to headquarters explaining the situation in Nashville in the wake of the bombing. In part, it read:

```
Nashville papers today recited arrest five
individuals by local police as possible
suspects instant explosion, stating suspects
car contained detonator and wire similar
to explosive wire and also weapons and KKK
lettering. In this connection Nashville PD
arrested following individuals for refusing
to move along from vicinity of Nashville
school—Vensen Albert Crimmons, age thirty-
two, James R. Harris, age forty-seven, J. B.
Blackwell, age forty-two, Carol Crimmons,
brother of Venson Crimmons, and W. D. Hodge.
First three charged with unlawful possession
of weapons in that two heavy wooden mallets
and machete knife bearing "US Navy" were
found in car. Last two individuals were
charged with vagrancy. Suspects car did not
contain detonators or explosive, and wire
found therein is radio wire and not type
used for detonation purposes. Nashville PD
advises does not consider these individuals
good suspects instant explosions.[87]
```

Without the police files, it's hard to nail down the exact timeline here, but what we're left with seems to indicate that the beatings of these suspects (to try to get confessions) was taking place even as the police considered them poor suspects.

This is inexcusable. It borders on inexplicable, except that in our whole long history of racialized violence over education in Nashville, no white racist did anything that would intentionally hurt an innocent white bystander. For all John Kasper's talk, I am certain that when he talked about shotguns and dynamite, most people—with the possible exception of Carrie Wray—thought he was talking about terrorizing Black people. Blowing up their houses, their schools. The police didn't haul the Whites Creek guys in and beat them because the police were anti-racist. The police were shocked and pissed that anyone would dare bomb a white school, would dare scare white families, and would dare risk hurting white children. Literally, until that moment, Nashville thought racial terrorism harmed Black people and sometimes their white allies. Period. It had never dawned on white Nashville that segregation-ists or white people who hadn't picked a side could be targeted.

These guys made great suspects because they were marginalized in so many ways—dirt poor, a couple Catholics, one not quite white, and probably new to the Klan.[88] They didn't have the kinds of broader social support networks that would signal to the police that these were folks you should follow the rules for. And Nashville cops had more leeway with how rough they could get with suspects back then. But there was still a line, and beating someone with a piece of lumber was probably across it.

Beating someone with rich and powerful friends, friends tied into the national scene, tied into Vanderbilt's prestige, was definitely way, way over the line. The Whites Creek gang did not appear to know they had such a friend, but when the Tennessee Federation for Constitutional Government caught wind of the police brutality, Jack Kershaw went down to the police station to look into things, then he went to the media to complain about the men's treatment. The DA, Harry Nichol, did his best to keep Kershaw away from the alleged bombers, saying, according to the *Tennessean*, "They are strangers to you, Mr. Kershaw. You don't have anything to do with this case."[89] But Kershaw's interest alone was too much heat for the DA to handle.

Kershaw's accusations of police brutality hit the papers on September 20. On September 21, DA Nichol released Harris and the Crimmonses without bond. Nichol told the *Tennessean* this was because, "We want to see what a jury thinks is justice for Mr. Kasper. I think he should be tried before these men."[90]

They were never charged for the bombings.

During Kasper's trial for inciting a riot, Vincent Crimmons claimed he never even heard Kasper advocating violence, even though Crimmons had attended Kasper's rallies.

And that was that. As far as Nashville knew, those Whites Creek guys were the bombers, at the behest of John Kasper. The fact that the police never really considered them good suspects never made its way into the public consciousness. The bombing was never solved, but most everyone thought they knew what had happened.

The simple overlooked truth here is that John Kasper was a thorn in the side of the city, and he had few prominent friends. Emmett Carr, Nashville's highest-ranking Klan leader, didn't trust him. Donald Davidson loathed him. Until Hattie Cotton was bombed, it had not occurred to white Nashville that racists would endanger white children to get their way. The city was outraged and terrified. Kasper wasn't a local, he wasn't widely liked even by people who shared his goals, and he didn't have any powerful local allies. If there had been an iota of evidence that Kasper bombed Hattie Cotton, he would have been tried for it.[91]

Other Potential Suspects in the Hattie Cotton Bombing

If we're asking ourselves who would target a school and could easily recruit folks to bomb it, Carr's the guy with the track record and the known connections. If Carr had appealed to Klavern No. 317 for help with the bombing of a school and then it ended up being a predominately white school, it explains why Klavern No. 317 was kicked out of the Klan that same month. It also explains why the police never really had any good suspects. It's possible some or all (though I lean toward "some," for reasons we'll get into in a second) of the bombers came in from Chattanooga, with Chattanoogan dynamite that J.B. Stoner had paid for.

So, why does the idea persist that Kasper alone was responsible? First, it lets Nashville off the hook. Some "outside agitator" came into our peaceful town and ruined it. It wasn't something neighbors did to each other, or would have even dreamed of doing to each other, until this charlatan started putting ideas into foolish heads.

But second, it seems obvious that whoever did this was someone who had been at Kasper's rallies or on his mailing lists or hanging out with him. The circumstantial evidence points in Kasper's direction because the bomber is someone near Kasper.

So, who was near Kasper?

Here's who Judge Miller issued a restraining order against in the wake of the bombing: John Kasper's pastor friend, Fred Stroud; John Mercurio, a racist pastor from out west who had preached at Kasper rallies; Wilson Lee Brown, who had been arrested at Fehr the night of the bombing; James Jarrell, who doesn't seem to have existed, at least not by that name; Emmett Carr; Vincent Crimmons; Margaret Conquest, a white woman who had led the disturbances at Glenn School; J.A. Stinson and his wife, Mary, who led the demonstrations at Jones School and who were hosting John Mercurio; James Harris; and Paul McConnell.[92]

McConnell, as far as I can tell, never comes back up. But there's only one Paul McConnell in the city directories at this time—living on Delta Avenue in North Nashville, a block away from Buena Vista School and just a few blocks away from Jones School. This nonexistent James Jarrell character is curious. While it's true that the courts decided he wasn't a real person, or at least not a real person by this name, there were James Jarrells living in Nashville. None of them had connections to Kasper, though, as far as I can tell. But there was a Henry Jarrell, sometimes known as H.A. Jarrell, who ran for vice-mayor of Nashville in 1959 with Bessie Williams at the top of the ticket. John Kasper ran their campaign. And on September 15, 1957, Thomas Norvell called FBI agent Norwood and told him he had just remembered that his wife had been talking to a Mrs. Jarrell and a Mrs. Orman at a Kasper rally on September 5. "Mrs. ORMAN told them that she had seem some dynamite that had been brought into town and knew who had it. She did not say who had the dynamite or where she had seen it."[93]

Though Kasper primarily stayed with the Wrays that August, he had also spent some nights at the Ormans. Mrs. Orman would have been in a position to know what Kasper was up to, and here Norvell is handing the FBI the names of two witnesses with close ties to Kasper. Nothing in the file suggests the FBI talked to Mrs. Orman or Mrs. Jarrell.

Out of everyone in this story, Norvell appears to be the closest thing we have to a hero. He heard of a bomb plot, and he alerted authorities. But I suspect the answer to why he was never publicly given credit can be found in the fact that he knew what Klan members were up to and how to contact the FBI. If the FBI had a good source, they weren't going to publicly out him and risk him being the victim of police violence. This might explain why the FBI was reluctant to tell the police about Reed and Norvell all along. If you need willing informants, turning them over to a police force known for beating people is not in your best interest.

But if you don't tell the police when you know about a bomb plot against a school in their district, you're going to make the police very angry. My guess is that the Nashville police were deeply pissed that the FBI had kept Reed and Norvell from them, and that, whether or not the FBI realized it, the force lost interest in working with the FBI on this case in any meaningful way after that.

The Confession the FBI Got

I think this explains why, when the FBI got a solid lead on the actual bomber at the end of 1957, the Nashville police blew them off. This is the memo about that good lead, dated January 8, 1958:

```
On December 30, 1957, Memphis Confidential
Informant T-1 furnished the following
information to SA FRANCIS W. NORWOOD at
Nashville, Tennessee:
```

The informant advised that REDACTED talks freely about the use of dynamite. REDACTED states that he has some in his possession and exploded a dynamite cap in his garage on Thursday night, December 26, 1957, but did not explode any dynamite. He exploded the cap to demonstrate his ability to use dynamite equipment safely. REDACTED spoke of the Hattie Cotton School explosion and stated only thirteen sticks of dynamite were used on that particular job.

REDACTED further explained that in order to do so much damage with thirteen sticks of dynamite, bags of cement were used to cover the explosives. He stated further that if the authorities had looked closed enough they would have found dry cement all over the place. REDACTED had in his garage some bags of cement and stated they were like the ones used at the school. He claimed to have a small battery with a button on top for purposes of exploding dynamite which he kept in his truck. He stated that there were only three men on the Hattie Cotton School job, and that this particular school was picked because it was the school in Nashville which was not being watched closely. He stated that there was one Negro going to that school, the rest of the students being white.

REDACTED failed to state whether he had been

paid for the job. He stated that he could
do a job like that without being blown up
himself because he had considerable leader
wire and indicated that he had approximately
300 yards of this particular type of wire.
He stated all that is done to set up a
job is to roll out the wire and touch the
battery. When asked if that is the way he
did the job on the Hattie Cotton School,
REDACTED laughed and said "you know I
wouldn't do anything like that."

The informant pointed out that he could not
tell whether REDACTED was lying or not. He
also pointed out that REDACTED was drinking
at the time that he made the above statements.

This information was furnished
immediately to Lt. REX WHITE, Nashville
Police Department, who is handling the
investigation of the Hattie Cotton School
explosion for that organization, Mr. TOMMIE
KERKELES, Chief Investigator, Sheriff's
Office, Nashville, and Mr. WINFRED E. HOPTON,
Director, Tennessee Bureau of Criminal
Identification, Nashville.

Lt. WHITE, who conducted a crime scene
search at the Hattie Cotton School at the
time of the explosion, stated that he is
sure that there was no dry cement at the
school, nor were there any fragments of

cement sacks at the scene of the explosion.
He further stated that there was some doubt
that the wire found at the scene of the
explosion was dynamite wire as it may have
been used by the telephone company or the
intercommunications system at the school.[94]

It appears, from a teletype sent to headquarters immediately after Norwood received this information, that it came to Norwood in the form of a letter. The letter isn't in the file, but Norwood's teletype includes a lengthy quote from it:

He demonstrated his ability to safely use
it after I told him I was afraid of any
explosive material. I suggested that he
should contact the parties who desire the
destruction of schools. He spoke of the
Hattie Cotton school explosion and explained
that only thirteen sticks of dynamite was
used on the job. He further explained in
order to do so much damage with thirteen
sticks of dynamite, bags of cement was used
to cover explosives, further stating that
if the authorities had looked close enough
they would have found dry cement all over
the place, and pointing to some bags of
cement under a work bench in his garage, he
said just like that stuff there. He claims to
have a small battery with a button on top for
that purpose, in his truck. I asked how many
it took for a job like that, and why they
picked Hattie Cotton school, which was in

East Nashville. He said there was only three
men on that job, and that was the only school
in Nashville not being watched so close.

[. . .]

I ask REDACTED if they got a good price for
job on school. He did not answer. I said it
had to be for money or practice for there
was no niggers going to that school. Yes
there was REDACTED said; ther [sic] was one
nigger going there. I said just the same
I don't understand how you do a job like
that without getting blown up yourself.
Hell I got enough leader wire to reach to
Eighteenth and Buchanan he said. All you
do is set up the job and roll out wire and
touch the battery. I asked if that is why he
did job on school—he laughed and said you
know I wouldn't do anything like that.[95]

So, there's a lot here. First, let me note that the cover letter that accompanied the memo seems to indicate that the letter writer and guy claiming to be the bomber were in the Klan: "Memphis Confidential Informant T-1 is REDACTED. He has not furnished sufficient information, which can be verified concerning the activities of REDACTED or the US Klans, Knights of the Ku Klux Klan, Inc., for a determination to be made as to his reliability."

Next, is he providing information only the bomber could know? This is really hard to discern. We do know that Patricia Watson, who desegregated Hattie Cotton, registered on the first day of school. No one but her family knew she was going to be there until she was. After the school was bombed, her parents put her in an all-Black school. It is very possible that, even after the bombing, many racists in town weren't really aware of why Hattie Cotton in particular was targeted. Certainly, by now, it is widely understood that Hattie Cotton was targeted because the police were guarding the schools where protesters had gathered that day and, since there had been few, if any, protesters at Hattie Cotton, there weren't police there. But how widely was that understood at the time? I just can't say for certain.

Then there's the bit about the bomb—thirteen sticks of dynamite under bags of dry concrete. Lieutenant White's claim that he found no evidence of dry concrete at the school makes no sense. Every picture of the entrance after the bombing shows an enormous amount of dust and debris. Those photos also show that, while the outside of the school was brick, the interior walls (at least the interior of the outside walls) were made of concrete blocks, many of which were destroyed in the blast. It wouldn't have been unreasonable for White to say he couldn't tell if there was evidence of dry concrete aside from the dust of the damaged bricks, but saying there was none when pictures show concrete dust is very strange. I don't know what to make of it. It sure seems like White lied to the FBI, but it's a lie that doesn't make any sense. Pictures would have proven him wrong. Anyone who learned the school was constructed, in part, of concrete blocks would know there was concrete dust. So, I also think it's plausible that this isn't exactly what White told the FBI. He may have just said that he didn't find any remnants of bags.

But I suspect what's actually going on here is this: Nashville police were now withholding information from the FBI. And they had a lot of information.

The Confession the Fire Marshal Heard

On the night of January 10, 1958, there was a fire at 2103 and 2105 18th Avenue North, right across from the Jewish cemetery, right outside

Photo by Betsy Phillips

the city limits. A man named Wallace L. Rider owned the properties and Robert Bromley lived there. This was right next door to the Rider-Justin Garage, located at 1700 McDaniel Street, which was a known Klan hangout. The State Fire Marshal, perhaps the only competent investigative body in the state, was suspicious of the fires and suspected they were set in order to collect insurance on the buildings. On January 11, Chief Deputy State Fire Marshal O.O. Lee interviewed a witness, Frank Houchin.

Cast your mind way back to the first bombings we talked about, the destroyed truck scales. They seemed not to be related in any way, but it was still weird that the man convicted of them, Jesse Wilson, was never asked about these later bombings. Remember how part of Wilson's defense was that Jack Jones and his friend were framing him, and that the friend, Frank Houchin, was blackmailing him? And remember how the bombing of his downtown terminal was linked to insurance fraud? Well, here's Frank again, wrapped up in another fire that might be linked to insurance fraud.

Fire Marshal Lee asks Houchin how long he's known the property owner, Wallace Rider, who Lee suspected was involved with the fires on his properties. Frank replies, "Let's see, he says he was there when I was initiated into the KKK." Frank then tells the fire marshal that Rider later came to Frank's house to bring him all this Klan literature because Rider was quitting the Klan.

> Q. Where did you get those pieces of [Klan] literature?
>
> A. Rider brought them out to my house and turned them over to me telling me he was out, he had quit. He said he called [Lloyd] Dowdy, the Secretary, and told him he was bringing the stuff to me.

Q. He was mad because they wouldn't be any
more active and take any more drastic steps
than they were taking, was he not?

A. Yes, sir. He claimed he was financing all
the activities and even furnishing lumber to
build the crosses and pay for the literature
to have it printed.

Frank told the fire marshal that the day after Christmas, he and
Rider hung out at the Rider-Justin Garage and drank. They talked about
how to commit insurance fraud and Rider said he had a buddy named
Slim who helped him do it. "Slim" was the nickname of James McKinley
Thompson, a man who lived down in Alabama. Rider said, "he could
drive about 120 miles and get him and bring him up here, let him do
a job—dynamite or whatever—let him do the job and in six hours he
could have him back in Alabama."

Q. And it was on that occasion that [Rider]
discussed the dynamiting of the Hattie
Cotton School over in East Nashville?

A. That is right.

Q. And did he tell you that he and anybody
else did that?

A. Let's see exactly the way he put it now—
he told me—

Q. Just a minute. After you mentioned this
in your report about the school, you said he

used 13 sticks, etc. You have got that in the report?

A. Yes, sir.

Q. Did he tell you anybody else was with him?

A. He gave reference to Slim, James McKinley Thompson, as being with him. I tried to draw out of him who the other fellow was. At that point he told me: "You know I didn't dynamite the Hattie Cotton School" and I said "Just about like you didn't fake those robberies if that is what you mean" and he laughed and I said "I thought you did a pretty good job of it." I asked him how he did all that damage with 13 sticks of dynamite and he said "If the authorities had looked close they would have found dry powdered cement all over the place because they had put that on the dynamite to hold the impact and make it do more damage by having the cement on it" and he pointed on the bench where there were four sacks.

[. . .]

Q. Did he mention anybody else other than Slim?

A. I asked how many and he said there were three of them.

Q. But he never did call the other fellow's
name?

A. No, sir.

Q. Did he say anything about having any wire
that was used to explode dynamite with?

A. I asked him how he did a job like that
without getting hurt himself and he said he
had enough wire to reach to 18th and Buchanan from his garage which was about two good
city blocks and he had a battery in his truck
with a button on top for that purpose.[96]

We can gather a few things from this. One is that Houchin was Memphis Confidential Informant T-1 for the FBI. Two, Houchin was working with the fire marshal in some similar capacity, since they make mention of him writing up reports. Three, the bomb crew had three people on it—Wallace Rider, Slim Thompson, and an unnamed man (possibly Stoner?). Four, even after Rider left the Klan for it not being violent enough, Houchin kept hanging out with him. He was not put off by Rider's thirst for violence.

From what I've been able to find, Wallace Rider kept a low profile. He was arrested in 1952 for robbing a liquor store and a service station. But otherwise, there's not much in the papers about him. There's some indication, which I could not verify, that at some point he started going by William Rider instead of Wallace. If this is so, then his body was donated to Meharry Medical College when he died in 1998, which might be cosmic justice—if the man who terrorized Nashville's Black community benefitted Nashville's Black medical school in death.

Slim Thompson is interesting. He lived down in North Alabama,

just outside of Florence, but he had family here in Nashville. The memo that accompanies the fire marshal's interview with Houchin describes Thompson: "Height: 6': Weight about 150 lbs; complexion – Red; Eyes – Blue; Hair – Brown; is of thin build, has his left thumb; left index and middle fingers missing or amputated as the result of a dynamite cap explosion when he was 10 years of age."[97]

Sound familiar? Take a look at the hand of the guy holding the flyer (you can see his face in the image at the top of the Preface). It's not his left hand, but what are the chances of there being two guys in Nashville on the day of the Hattie Cotton bombing missing three fingers?

Piecing Together the Truth

If this history is a puzzle with many pieces missing, I think the FBI files and media reports fill in enough gaps that we can make some reasonable guesses as to what happened here.

We know, thanks to the letter from Carrie Wray and media reports of Kasper's speeches, that Kasper had been talking about the use of dynamite. We know from Norvell and FBI reports that (once out-of-town Klansmen started to arrive) people began discussing forming a terror cell and blowing up a school. We know that two people in Kasper's circle said they saw dynamite—Reed said he saw Kasper with it and Mrs. Orman, one of Kasper's hosts, said she saw it. Mrs. Orman also said the dynamite had been "brought into town," and we know that J.B. Stoner said he was responsible for getting the dynamite here. It seems a Chattanooga Klansman was in town making a bomb threat right after the Hattie Cotton bombing, which suggests that Stoner made arrangements for the dynamite to come into town with a Chattanooga Klansman/men. The other thing that suggests the involvement of the Chattanooga Klan is that we know they did *something* bad enough to get them kicked out of the Klan in September 1957—but there was no Klan violence in Chattanooga in September 1957. The only place in Tennessee that had any violence that might have caused Klan leaders to freak out was here in Nashville.

About that freak-out, though, there was one other factor we need to consider: the presence of Asa Carter. At the time of the Hattie Cotton bombing, Asa Carter was leading a Klan splinter group, Original Ku Klux Klan of the Confederacy. Before that, he had been the head of a splinter White Citizens' Council group most famous for attacking and trying to kill singer Nat King Cole when he was on stage. Carter's Klan was very violent, to put it mildly. In the short time it existed, between 1956 and 1958, Klan members shot at each other numerous times and they gruesomely attacked a Black man, Judge Edward Aaron, on September 2, 1957.[98] Carter was not present for the attempted murder, likely because he was here in Nashville helping to organize a school bombing. But he was the leader of the group. Aaron's assault would not have happened without Carter's knowledge and permission.[99]

If I had to make an informed guess about why the US Klan started kicking out Klaverns in September 1957, I would say it's likely that it was not just the targeting of a vastly predominately white elementary school, but the targeting of that school with the help of Asa Carter, the leader of a group of violent renegades who had the authorities breathing down their necks.

This leaves us with Kasper calling for bombings, but not quite knowing how to make one happen. But Stoner knows. He makes arrangements to get dynamite here and, I think it's likely, gets Carr on board to provide some bombers, possibly an experienced Chattanooga bomber.

But, since Kasper was run out of town by the end of September and no more schools were bombed, well, no harm, no foul, right?

Oh, wait . . .

The FBI and the Ku Klux Klan.
Best Friends Forever?

OLENT ACT OF ANTI-SEMITISM IN TH

mbing wrecks a synagogue in Atlanta as a new party of racists carries on

rces of bigotry in the South, which have grown bolder and uglier the long fight over segregation, struck last week at another target. week after the bombing of the Clinton, Tenn. high school (LIFE,), an explosion rocked a synagogue in Atlanta and focused the s attention on a violent and well-organized wave of anti-Semitism, n style. After a series of arrests, five men were indicted by an grand jury. All of them are reportedly connected with a new ousing organization known as the National States Rights Party ge). Two of the five have shown up before in Chattanooga as nts in an anti-Semitic demonstration (*above*). "We believe,"

says the platform of their new party, "in White Folk Community."

Many southerners were quick to conde which was the fourth similar bombing in "It is the harvest," wrote Atlanta *Constitu* defiance of courts and the encouragement part of many southern politicians." Mone temple came pouring in from southerners o holding its next services in the da maged san text was taken from Micah 4:1: "And ne

TO SYNAGOGUE, CALLED "THE TEMPLE," IS ESTIMATED AT $200,000. BOMB LEFT GAPING HOLE IN THE WALL AND

Guide to the Racists in this Chapter

Kenneth Adams Klansman from Anniston, Alabama

Raymond Anderson United Klans Tennessee Grand Dragon in the early 1960s

Richard and Robert Bowling Brothers who bombed things for Stoner

W.H. Brough Leader of Florida's Knights of the Ku Klux Klan; friend of Roper, enemy of Hendrix

Emmett Carr Middle Tennessee Grand Titan and Pro-Southerners

Asa Carter Alabama renegade Klansman

Robert "Dynamite Bob" Chambliss One of the 16th Street Baptist Church bombers in Birmingham

E.S. Dollar Nashville Grand Titan

Eldon Edwards Leader of the United Klans, Knights of the Ku Klux Klan

Vernon Doyle Ellington United Klans Tennessee Grand Dragon in the late 1960s

Ed Fields Stoner's sidekick

Thomas Hamilton Leader of the Association of Carolina Klans

Bill Hendrix Leader of Florida's Southern Knights of the Ku Klux Klan and enemy of Samuel Roper

J. Edgar Hoover Head of FBI

William Hugh Morris Leader of the Federated Klans of Alabama

Thomas Norvell FBI informant during the Hattie Cotton case

Harry William Pyle Memphis Pro-Southerners

Charles Reed Thomas Norvell's friend

Samuel Roper Leader of the Association of Georgia Klans and nemesis of Bill Hendrix

Gary Rowe FBI informant and Klan infiltrator

M.B. Sherrill Florida White Circle League, Pro-Southerners, and Grand Titan for the eastern coast territory of the Association of Florida Klans

J.B. Stoner Klan, Christian Anti-Jewish Party, National States Rights Party

At the metaphorical heart of this book is a question: Why was the FBI so unhelpful? So, I thought here, at the physical heart of the book, we should take a stab at answering it.

Here, in the months between the Hattie Cotton bombing and the JCC bombing, is when the FBI would have you believe that something fundamental shifted in the approach of these terrorists. When J. Edgar Hoover briefed the National Security Council and the president on November 6, 1958, he told them,

> Since January 1, 1957, there have been over 90 bombings, or attempted bombings, in the United States, of these, at least 69 have involved Negro victims and at least eight, Jewish religious and educational facilities. [That part was typed. The next part was handwritten.] [Illegible, possibly "Past"] 3 weeks—90 bomb threats: [Illegible again, and again perhaps "Past"] week—[illegible] Nov 1–4 were 16 such threats. Waves of hysteria allowing actual bombings in Georgia & Tenn [typed] In the early bombings [handwritten] prior to 1958 [typed] there was no evidence to show that these bombings could be attributed to specific organizations. Rather, they were individual acts of terror strictly within the jurisdiction of local authorities. When these outrages occurred, we in the FBI have made immediately available to local authorities our laboratory and finger print facilities here in Washington.

> As the bombings directed toward religious and educational facilities continued, the FBI extended its cooperation to cover out-of-state [handwritten] investigative [typed] leads which local authorities could not handle. We extended such assistance to the Jacksonville, Florida, and Birmingham, Alabama, Police Departments in connection with the bombings of a Jewish center and a Negro high school in Jacksonville on April 28, 1958, and the attempted bombing of a Jewish temple in Birmingham on the same day.
>
> Recently, however, there has been some indication of a general interstate pattern to these bombings.[100]

This is not how local law enforcement felt. We're going to talk about this at length later, but the FBI was so unhelpful that law enforcement officials in Southern states had to hold a conference themselves to share information on bombings. It's also obviously not true that the bombings before 1958 were all somehow only local events. We had racists from all over the country in town before Hattie Cotton exploded. Our Klan had ties with Klan groups throughout the South.

Now is probably a good time to talk about those Klan groups.

Detangling The Ku Klux Klan

The Ku Klux Klan had been somewhat dormant in Nashville and Middle Tennessee during the war years. This may be surprising if you assume every bad thing in the pre-1963 South was done by hooded men by the light of a burning cross. But it's also important to remember that in a racist society where the justice system can be counted on to keep minorities "in their place," racists don't need groups like the Klan. The system does the work the Klan would do.

As we talked about with the Columbia Riots, racists saw growing evidence that the system was not necessarily going to continue to serve racist ends. This "failure" of the system to oppress Black people and keep them "in their place" indicated to white racists that Tennessee once again needed people working outside the system to do what the system would not—keep Black people separate from and in lower social standing to white people.

We needed, they thought, masked vigilantes with secret identities to act outside the law to keep regular folks safe. The fact that the Klan and Batman are motivated by the same impulses is troubling, but it should also help us understand how Klan members saw themselves and the seductive story they told themselves about why their activities were important and necessary. They were superheroes in their own minds.[101]

If some "bad guys" got hurt along the way? Well, who weeps for the Joker?

An important thing to keep in mind when we're discussing the Klan of the 1950s is that there wasn't "The" Klan. Just like we see on the far right today, these groups were constantly beset with infighting and people breaking off to form new, "truer" groups and then rejoining old groups or not doing anything official, but still hanging out with people from the old groups. Obviously, people who found crosses burning in their yards didn't run out and grab the nearest white-hooded figure and ask him specifically *which* racist group he belonged to, they just referred to The Klan. But it might be more clarifying to think of "A Klan," since not everybody who was a Klan member belonged to the same organization or even recognized other Klans as legitimate.

But by the mid-1950s, we had an active Klan in Davidson County, led by Middle Tennessee Grand Titan Emmett Carr. The news coverage at the time indicates that right below Carr in that Klan was E.S. Dollar, the Nashville Grand Titan. When crosses were burned at Fort Negley—the site of a Union Civil War fort that sits on a hill just south of downtown—these were probably the guys who organized it. Figuring out the structures above them is difficult. Klansmen were petty and liked to bicker and there was infighting and convoluted feuds. A great deal of this next part could be reduced to "Boo-hoo-hoo. You hurt my racist feelings and I'm not going to be in the Klan with you," but I think it's important to try to understand.

At the start of the 1950s, there were four main Klans in the Southeast—Thomas Hamilton's Association of Carolina Klans, Bill Hendrix's Southern Knights of the Ku Klux Klan out of Florida, William Hugh Morris's Federated Klans of Alabama, and Samuel Roper's Association of Georgia Klans. The first three had an alliance, of sorts, but newspaper reports make it clear that Roper and Hendrix never could get on the same page and, thus, the Association of Georgia Klans was perceived as being in some state of exile because they were too violent or their approach and philosophies were too radical. There may be some hint of truth there, but I think it's also important to note that this is mostly mythologizing to give a petty, personal fight some outsized importance.

The Klan mentioned in Nashville in the early 1950s was the Federated Ku Klux Klan, Inc., which (based again on news stories) seemed to be at least loosely affiliated with the Federated Klans of Alabama. In 1950, William Hugh Morris (of the Federated Klans of Alabama) was claiming he had a Klavern here in Nashville, though he refused to believe they could be involved with a rash of cross burnings in town.[102]

In 1951, the Florida Klan split. Hendrix continued to lead the Southern Knights of the Ku Klux Klan and W.H. Brough started the Knights of the Ku Klux Klan. Brough's group aligned with the Association of Georgia Klans—the Klan of Samuel Roper, Hendrix's nemesis.[103]

On Christmas Day, 1951, a bomb exploded under the house of Harry and Harriett Moore, Florida NAACP leaders who lived in Mims, just sound of Jacksonville and east of Orlando. The Moores died. Four

Klansmen were implicated in their deaths: Earl Brooklyn—who had been kicked out of the Georgia Klan for "being too violent"—Tillman Belvin, Joseph Cox, and Edward Spivey. They were never convicted, and Brooklyn, Belvin, and Cox died shortly after the bombing. There's still some controversy about whether they were in Hendrix's group or Brough's. Frankly, I don't understand enough about the Florida situation to say with certainty. For our purposes, it's worth noting that by 1951, Florida Klansmen had figured out how to blow things up and kill people with dynamite and get away with it, and that our Klan had meaningful ties to Florida Klansmen (and may have had opinions on and chosen sides in the Hendrix-Brough feud).

In 1952, Hendrix and Hamilton had a falling out and the Southern Knights of the Ku Klux Klan and the Association of Carolina Klans broke their alliance. Meanwhile, Hendrix and Morris seemed to be getting buddy-buddy.[104]

In 1953, Hendrix and other Klan leaders started the United Klans, intending to bring all the small Klans they weren't fighting with together into a group that would focus on segregation-related activism and avoid worrying about religion.[105] This group quickly morphed into the United Klans, Knights of the Ku Klux Klan[106] with Eldon Edwards from Atlanta heading it up.[107] From newspaper coverage, it's clear that this is the same group as the US Klans, Knights of the Ku Klux Klan, which, by the end of the era we're looking at, would be headed up by Alabaman Robert Shelton.[108]

In the middle of May 1954, M.B. Sherrill was passing out racist literature in Florida that came from the White Circle League of America, a segregationist outfit out of Chicago devoted to keeping white neighborhoods white. An informant told the FBI that Sherrill had been fighting with the Northern leaders of the League, so he broke away from them and was forming an organization known as the Pro-Southerners. This would be just like the White Circle League, but Sherrill "felt it would be more successful in the south inasmuch as it would be an all

Southern organization rather than an organization with headquarters in the north."[109] Sherrill's partner in this venture was Harry William Pyle, from Memphis, Tennessee.

In July 1954, the Pro-Southerners in Florida had reached out to at least one member of the Southern Knights of the Ku Klux Klan and asked him to join, but Bill Hendrix told the Klansman not to go.

Hendrix and Sherrill had been in the Southern Knights of the Ku Klux Klan together, but after the big break-up back in 1951 Hendrix stayed with the Southern Knights and Sherrill, as well as starting up the Pro-Southerners, became the Grand Titan for the eastern coast territory of Florida for the Association of Florida Klans, a group that included the aforementioned Knights of the Ku Klux Klan.[110]

When Emmett Carr was waffling about whether he still wanted to be in the Tennessee Klan in the mid-1950s, he was the leader of the Pro-Southerners group here in Nashville.

Atlanta Journal-Constitution via AP

The Christian Anti-Jewish Party

On October 27, 1958, *Life* ran a photo (photo pg. 108) that had been taken in Chattanooga in December 1954. The picture shows a rally thrown by the Christian Anti-Jewish Party—Stoner and Fields's first foray into publicly hating Jews together. Neither one of them lived in Chattanooga at the time. The original photo was destroyed when the *Chattanooga Times* and the *Chattanooga Free-Press* merged, so other than Stoner (who is instantly recognizable in his bowtie) and the two Bowling brothers (who are identified in the caption), the identities of the other people on the stage are still something of a mystery.

115

But many of Stoner and Fields's associates are known. After Stoner and Fields folded the Christian Anti-Jewish Party, but before they started the National States Rights Party, they briefly organized the United White Party in 1957. Since it quickly morphed into the National States Rights Party the next year, it's barely worth remarking on, except that it has a known founding membership list: Emory Burke, Dan Kurtz (member of the Chris-

AP Photo/Horace Court

tian Front in New York, and the National Renaissance Party, later active in the NSRP), Wallace Allen, John Kasper, Ned Dupes (a Knoxville businessman and supporter of John Kasper), Matt Koehl (member of the National Renaissance Party, worked on one of Admiral Crommelin's political campaigns, member and eventual leader of the American Nazi Party), Ed Fields, and J.B. Stoner.

I imagine some of these men are in that 1954 picture. I am confident I recognize two of them. I think that's Asa Carter in the middle (compare with his photo in Chapter 3) and Kenneth Adams on the right of the group on the right.

We've already talked some about Carter, since he was in Nashville in the weeks leading up to the Hattie Cotton bombing, but we've not talked about his friend and fellow Anniston, Alabama, Klansman—Kenneth Adams. As far as I can tell, Kenneth Adams is only tangentially related to our story. However, it is one hell of a tangent. H. Brant Ayers, the publisher of the *Anniston Star*, Adams's hometown paper, described Adams as "a personable psychopath," and said Adams was responsible for a lot of racial violence that happened in Anniston.[111] Adams was one of the men arrested for attacking Nat King Cole during a performance. He

AP Photo/Horace Court

was among the men who organized the attack on the Freedom Riders in Anniston in 1961. According to the *Anniston Star*, "these episodes were only two of the more than a dozen brutal shootings and beatings he inflicted upon black residents in and around Anniston over a fifteen-year rampage."[112] You will be unsurprised to learn that a few years ago the *Anniston Star* discovered in FBI files that Adams had (back in the 1960s) been plotting to bomb the paper as well as the home of an integrationist pastor. The FBI had not communicated word of those plots at the time. And Adams was affiliated with the Dixie Knights.

Here, then, is the core of the network I've been looking at. Men who facilitated and perpetrated some of the worst crimes of the civil rights era and got away with it. And they're not hiding—not their faces, not that they knew each other.

If I'm right about that being Asa Carter and Kenneth Adams, then five of the ten men on that stage in 1954 went on to be racist bombers—the Bowling brothers, Stoner, Carter, and Adams. And we're likely looking at three faces I *know* were in town in the weeks before the Hattie Cotton bombing: J.B. Stoner, Ed Fields, and Asa Carter. Stoner was already a known Klansman, a known pen pal of a Nazi, and a known supporter of the white nationalist group the Columbians, as well as leading the Christian Anti-Jewish Party, by the time he got to Nashville. He'd already been kicked out of the Chattanooga Klan twice for being "too violent." Ed Fields had already been a Columbian. He was already Stoner's partner in crime. Carter's men had already attacked Nat King Cole. Carter had already become a national figure with his rants about the evils of rock 'n' roll. He'd already started his renegade Klan group. All that before Hattie Cotton exploded.

Three incredibly violent men with a known track record for inciting others to violence with ties to incredibly violent Klan groups that had either splintered off or were on the verge of splintering off from the larger Klan, men who knew each other and had organized together in the past, men who were all in town in the weeks before the Hattie Cotton bombing—and yet, as far as the public knew, the police could not find any decent bombing suspects.

Throughout the writing of this book, I have thought, "If only people had seen that these weren't isolated incidents, that there was an association of terrorists who all knew and helped each other, they could have stopped them before all of the murders in the '60s." But this picture ran in *LIFE* in 1958. People knew.

But in that great American way of ours, we deliberately chose to not know it. Our ability to forget our past (almost as soon as it happens) cost us, and continues to cost us, dearly.

The FBI Joins the Klan

That great American Unknowing was in this case facilitated by the myth the FBI was making up. Are you going to trust this photo from 1954, which appears to show that many of the worst of the worst violent racists knew each other and organized together, or are you going to trust the FBI, who claimed that we didn't see interstate planning until 1958?

Elsewhere in the FBI file, there's a memo from Hoover dated September 2, 1965,[113] addressed to the attorney general, stating,

> As you know, this Bureau has solved a number of cases involving racial violence in the South. In this regard, public attention particularly was focused on the FBI's role in the solution of the brutal murders of Mrs. Viola Liuzzo, Lieutenant Colonel Lemuel A. Penn, and the three civil rights workers in Mississippi. However, we have achieved a number of other tangible accomplishments, most of which are not publicly known, and I thought you might be interested in them.[114]

He goes on: "Particularly significant has been the high-level penetration we have achieved of Klan organizations. At the present time, there are 14 Klan groups in existence. We have penetrated every one of them through informants and currently are operating informants in top-level positions of leadership in seven of them." One of those men penetrating the Klan was Gary Rowe. At the FBI's behest, Rowe infiltrated Eastview Klavern 13 (one of the most violent Klan groups in Alabama) and was involved in attacking the Freedom Riders, probably bombing Martin Luther King Jr.'s motel room, and possibly murdering civil rights activist Viola Liuzzo (he was at least in the car with the person who shot her).[115]

Robert Chambliss claimed Rowe actually planted the dynamite at the 16th Street Baptist Church. Much later, Rowe told authorities he'd shot and killed a Black man in a Birmingham riot in 1963 and that the FBI had covered it up.[116]

This whole thing is pretty bad—from the FBI protecting violent racist informants to bragging that it has control of half of the Klans in the nation in 1965—but it's about to get worse. Hoover says,

> In one southern state, for example, the gov-
> ernor, on one occasion, expressed his great
> concern and fear of an outbreak of racial
> violence because of the tense situation. But
> the head of the Klan organization in that
> state is our informant, and we have had him
> warn every member of his organization that
> he will not tolerate violence in any form.
> As a result, we have been successful to date
> in holding Klan violence in the entire state
> to an absolute minimum.[117]

Do I even have to tell you what state he's talking about?

In 1967, Hoover put out a secret report titled "Ku Klux Klan Investigations FBI Accomplishments." In it he gives more detail about how things worked in Tennessee:

> In the early stages of Klan growth in the
> State of Tennessee, we were able to devel-
> op as a Bureau informant the Grand Dragon of
> the United Klans of America, Realm of Ten-
> nessee. Through this high-level source we
> were able to control the expansion of the
> Klan. More importantly, we were able to dis-

```
courage violence throughout the state. The
Klan in Tennessee has not expanded to the
proportions it has in other states and its
lack of success can be attributed to our
highly placed informant.[118]
```

For as long as I've been working on this project, I've heard rumors that the FBI ran the West Tennessee Klan. Until I saw this file, though, I was unable to substantiate it.

Toward the end of his *Counterpoint* article, "The Troubling Legacy of Martin Luther King Jr.," historian David Garrow names who he thinks this Grand Dragon is: "The evidence points to ME 313-E being former UKA Grand Dragon V. Doyle Ellington, now aged 80, who lives in Brownsville and is on Facebook."[119]

I don't think this is right.

Here's my reasoning: the early stages of Klan growth in Tennessee were the 1950s. Vernon Doyle Ellington was 20 in 1958. And we know that at that point the Grand Dragon of Tennessee was George Compton of Maryville. He would have been a member of the United Klans of America. In August 1963, Highlander Center leader Aimee Horton wrote a letter to the editor of the *Knoxville Journal* about a Klan rally in the area:

> The meeting was attended not only by local citizenry and the curious, but by various outside higher officers in the Ku Klux movement, including certain higher officials from Georgia. As a result of this meeting, it was determined that one Raymond Anderson, who acted as master of ceremonies at the meetings, was the apparent local president or grand dragon of the klan.[120]

I didn't find a lot of information about Anderson other than that he was a private detective.[121] In August 1965, the *Commercial Appeal* reported that "Raymond Anderson of Maryville, the Ku Klux Klan's grand dragon for Tennessee claims that much of the credit for the fact that a mass civil rights demonstration at Brownsville on Saturday of last week went off without incident is due to the klan." That takes some hutzpah, but it's actually what Grand Dragon Anderson told the *Commercial Appeal* that I find more interesting: "And a number of state Highway Patrol members, sheriff's officers and FBI agents came up and told me they appreciated what we did to keep down trouble."[122]

It makes sense that FBI agents were at a big civil rights demonstration. But would they really have been advertising that they were FBI agents? Were they wearing big FBI emblazoned jackets? If not, if they were just there in "random law enforcement bureaucrat" get up, how did Anderson, a guy from East Tennessee, know who the FBI agents in West Tennessee were?

It gets a little weirder. In October 1965, news started coming out about the findings of an investigation the House Un-American Activities Committee had been making into the Ku Klux Klan. A story ran in the *Knoxville News-Sentinel* stating that HUAC had heard testimony that there were only five major Klan organizations in Tennessee at the time—Klaverns of the United Klans of America. Those Klaverns were in Knoxville, Maryville, Sevierville, Etowah, and Harriman. The investigation found, "no evidence of organized Klaverns in Middle and West Tennessee" and the paper reported that "Raymond R. Anderson of Maryville was named as Grand Dragon for Tennessee and Maryville as the state KKK headquarters."[123]

If the FBI was controlling the Grand Dragon of the KKK in 1965, that was Raymond Anderson. But you want further proof? Even though late 1965 was full of news stories about the HUAC investigation into the Klan (and what they were finding out about the Klan here in Tennessee), in February, the *Commercial Appeal* reported that the HUAC had decided not to call Anderson to testify. The chair of the committee, Edwin Willis, "was told Anderson's group is small, weak, and under close watch by state and local law enforcement agencies."[124] It goes without saying that this is not how Anderson's group had been portrayed until this point. It seems more likely that the FBI didn't want Anderson under oath in front of Congress, for fear of what might come out.

A year later, in February 1967, Anderson had quit being Grand Dragon. The *Commercial Appeal* reported that "V. Doyle Ellington, Brownsville café owner, told The Commercial Appeal he was elected Grand Dragon of Tennessee for the United Klans of America recently after Raymond Anderson of Maryville resigned for 'personal reasons.'"[125] Being discovered as an FBI informant is a pretty personal reason to want to flee the Klan. Just saying.

I feel fairly confident about this, with two caveats. Hoover was still bragging about the FBI running the Klan in Tennessee way into 1967, months after Anderson resigned. That and Garrow knows what he's talking about. If Garrow thinks it was Ellington, he likely has good reasons I'm not privy to. But it sure seems like it was Anderson.

Which raises another possibility: What if the FBI didn't have control of the man, but of the position? What if every man going back to whenever the FBI took control of the Tennessee UKA was expected to be an informant when he rose to power? We just don't know enough about what the FBI's relationship with the Tennessee Klan looked like, but it's clear to me that it was somewhat different than the kinds of infiltration they did in other areas and was unique in the web of informants they used.

Hoover said in 1967 that the FBI had developed the Grand Dragon as an informant back "in the early stages of Klan growth in the State of Tennessee."[126] Unfortunately, there's just not a lot of context clues about when Hoover considered these "early stages" to have been. If the FBI only had control over Anderson, then Hoover is fudging the timeframe and it was not in the actual early stages (the timeframe we're discussing in this book) but in the early 1960s.

But if the FBI is being honest and they took over United Klan in Tennessee during the rise of the Klan (which would mean they controlled the office of Grand Dragon, not just the man in the office), that had to be in the mid-50s, because that's when that was. If that's true, it sure explains a lot that's been weird in this story up until now. This is how the FBI had someone in the Klan who could tell them that the Klan wasn't planning on palling around with John Kasper. This is how the FBI knew that Thomas Norvell could be trusted, even when Charles Reed claimed he was lying. This is why the FBI hid Reed and Norvell from the Nashville police. The Klansmen were their boys.

If I'm right about this, then the FBI's conflict of interest here is so big you can probably see it from Mars. If an FBI informant is running the Klan that the bombers of Hattie Cotton may have belonged to, the FBI cannot let the police's investigation go far enough to involve, and potentially implicate, their informant. They have to hobble the investigation.

After Hoover told the president of the United States that the FBI's running the Klan had resulted in Tennessee's Klan being practically nonviolent, there's just no way the FBI was ever going to find Klansmen tied to Tennessee bombings. Or, for that matter, tied to Dr. King's assassination.

A Great Disappointment

Finding out that the FBI was running some Klans has shaken me in ways I honestly don't know how to process. I think I'm pretty aware of America's shortcomings and I know we've done a lot of evil and lied to ourselves until we believed it was good. I moved around a lot when I was a kid and I have first-hand experience with the ways small towns become corrupt and how dangerous it can be for the people who are not under the protection of those systems.

But I have also had a very core and fundamental belief—one so core that I didn't even realize I had it until this knowledge violated it—that there is help, that, if you can just hold on and shout loud enough and get word to the good people, they will come to your aid.

But who was coming to help Black people in America in the 1950s and 1960s when the FBI ran the Klan? When the law enforcement arm of the federal government was leading the lawless racists terrorizing them? I feel stupid and naïve for having this belief that there must be good guys somewhere who can do something. But it breaks my heart that it's not true, that the people who should have been protecting African Americans were literally in charge of the groups that were harming them.

And to what end? Hoover claims it reduced violence among Klan members, but that's just not true. Klan members who couldn't be violent in the UKA, because the FBI was influencing it to be more peaceful, joined groups that were plenty violent—like the Dixie Knights or Asa Carter's crowd or J.B. Stoner's circle. I think we should consider the evidence that the FBI running the Klan without aiming to shut it down might actually have increased racist violence because it drove violent people into these fringe groups full of deeply radicalized assholes who could gin each other up to actually do the things they'd been talking about.

This left the FBI monitoring the racists most likely to be non-violent, not the violent splinter groups. Clearly, someone like Gary Rowe was supposed to be an answer to that problem. He was willing to be violent and present for violence and he was the FBI's guy. And while the FBI was running him, he claimed he killed someone; he may have killed Viola Liuzzo; and he beat up the Freedom Riders, among other things. Would those things have happened without Gary Rowe? Sure. Maybe. But it feels deeply disingenuous to argue that the FBI's infiltration efforts made things less violent when people were being murdered by violent extremists so that the FBI could stay close to violent extremists.

More troubling, and something I think a lot about in the wake of all the "lone wolf" racial terrorism happening as I write this book: is the rise of the one angry white dude who steps into a gathering place and opens fire occurring in part because of the presence of law enforcement in racist groups?

If the way racist terrorists kept the FBI from stopping them was to leave the infiltrated Klan, it seems likely that a response to the FBI figuring out how to infiltrate these smaller violent terror cells would be to not have terror cells at all—to plan acts alone and keep them secret until it's too late for anyone to stop you.

And I can almost see the logic of the FBI. Maybe they really did believe that taking over the Klan was the way to make it less violent. But it's tough to argue that it worked. If we want to circle back around to our superhero discussion, we're deep in the Batman problem. To what extent does the presence of Batman spur the rise of worse and worse villains? Except we have the added twist of learning that Batman was the Joker's boss all along.

I think our tendency is to try to view this as some great moral conundrum in which our heroes must compromise their good beliefs in small ways in order to advance their good beliefs in large ways, but it's not really.

You know who runs the Klan? Bad people. It's that simple.

I would have hoped that the FBI would have recognized that early on. But here we are.

CHAPTER 7

THE JEWISH COMMUNITY CENTER BOMBING

Guide to the Racists in this Chapter

Kenneth Adams Anniston Klan leader and member of the Dixie Knights

Robert Bromley Wallace Rider's tenant

Jack Brown Leader of the Dixie Knights

Emmett Carr Nashville Klan leader

Crimmons brothers Suspects in the Hattie Cotton bombing

Donald Davidson Poet and unrepentant racist

E.S. Dollar Nashville Klan leader

Ed Fields J.B. Stoner's partner and founder of the National States Rights Party

Frank Houchin Fire marshal informant and FBI informant, involved with the earlier truck bombings

John Kasper Racist activist

William Hugh Morris Alabama Klan leader and, as we're about to learn, law enforcement informant

Ezra Pound John Kasper's mentor

Wallace Rider Nashville man who bragged about the Hattie Cotton bombing

Gary Rowe FBI Klan infiltrator

Robert Shelton Alabama Klan leader

J.B. Stoner Racial terrorist

Rev. Fred Stroud Leader of the Bible Presbyterian Church

Allen Tate Another white supremacist poet and friend of Donald Davidson

James McKinley "Slim" Thompson Wallace Rider's Alabama friend

Okay, back to Nashville.

In the wake of the Hattie Cotton bombing, there were a lot of dramatics and political maneuvering, but long story short, Nashville kept John Kasper in jail as long as it could, then ran him out of town. At the end of September 1957, Kasper went to D.C. to commiserate with

Ezra Pound, and in October, he went to federal prison for his role in the Clinton riots.

In November, Kasper's buddies, Ed Fields and J.B. Stoner, held a meeting in Knoxville to begin organizing the group that would eventually become the National States Rights Party (NSRP).[127] The NSRP was both a political party—meaning they ran candidates for office—and a terrorist organization.

The Rise of the Dixie Knights

At roughly the same time as the start of the NSRP, Emmett Carr and E.S. Dollar were leaving the US Knights of the Ku Klux Klan and helping to form the Dixie Knights of the Ku Klux Klan. Much of the known history of the Dixie Knights is hilarious. They got embroiled in a trademark lawsuit over Klan rituals. They tried endorsing candidates only to find the candidates appalled by their support. Then, in typical Klan fashion, people started leaving because the "one true" Klan they founded wasn't being true to Klan principles, whatever those Klan principles were supposed to be.

I had substantial difficulties in nailing down any reliable information about the Dixie Knights, but what I found beyond the hilarious public failures was disturbing. As we've discussed, the group came into being when Klavern no. 317 in Chattanooga got kicked out of the Klan, and Emmett Carr took the Middle Tennessee Klans under his control (including Nashville) out of the UKA to join forces with 317. Birmingham Klan leader Robert Shelton may have been involved early on, but he and Chattanooga leader Jack Brown didn't get along, so it's hard to know. I have to suspect that Asa Carter was either involved or a strong influence on the Dixie Knights. We can say with certainty that J.B. Stoner knew many of the men who formed the Dixie Knights. Stoner also worked with the notorious Birmingham Klavern with their infamous bombing unit. Were Klansmen from Birmingham somehow tied into this group? If

Shelton was indeed involved, it seems like yes, maybe. If not, then maybe no? (Investigative reporter Harold Weisberg spent years trying to sort this out while investigating the King and Kennedy assassinations, and even he wasn't clear on who was affiliated with what, when.)[128]

The publicly available story of the Dixie Knights is that they started in 1958 and had petered out by the time of Brown's death in 1965. The US Congress's House Un-American Activities Committee (HUAC) didn't even bother to subpoena any of them during their Klan hearings, saying that they "had dwindled to a position of relative unimportance."[129] But, and this is a big *but*, the HUAC did note that the Dixie Knights had a Klavern in Anniston, Alabama, which means that the violence committed against the Freedom Riders in Anniston by local Klan members, including Kenneth Adams, was committed by the Dixie Knights.[130] Also involved in the Anniston attack on the Freedom Riders were Klansmen from all over Alabama, including controversial FBI informant Gary Rowe. That would seem to indicate that the Dixie Knights were very important, or at least that understanding how the Dixie Knights operated was important, to understanding Southern segregationist violence. I couldn't find anyone who has studied them. No one nationally who understood their regional efforts. No one in Chattanooga who understood what they had been up to in that city. No one seems aware of the full scope of their activities.

I asked the National Archives for their file on the Dixie Knights, assuming I was looking for a small file on a fringe group. It's 30,000 pages long. I wrote back assuming that they had misunderstood which group I was talking about. They had not. The file on the Dixie Knights just from the end of 1957 is 500 pages. The file continues into the 1970s. So much for petering out.

And here's another thing that suggests there's much more for scholars to investigate. It's clear from available FBI files and Birmingham police files that other Klans were terrified of Jack Brown. Klan members warned each other not to cross him, that he was unstable and violent, that he had killed people. I couldn't find any murders Jack Brown was suspected of, but I also didn't get into his FBI file. The scope of his terrorism, what he was doing that had other Klans so afraid of him, is not yet known.

We have some hints, though. Alleged members of the Dixie Knights, much like members of the NSRP, had a habit of being present when bad, racist shit went down in the South. Jack Brown allegedly had a plot to kill President John F. Kennedy. Two Dixie Knights were suspected in the bombing death of Ringgold, Georgia housewife, Mattie Green.[131] Shelton's group may have been involved in at least two murders. And Weisberg found evidence this crowd was trying to pay someone to kill Rev. Martin Luther King Jr.[132]

The Start of the Confederate Underground

At this same time, the Confederate Underground must have come into existence. As we're about to discuss, they started bombing Jewish community centers and places of worship in late 1957. The Confederate Underground was a network of bombers headed up by J.B. Stoner, who had come out of the Chattanooga Klan scene. This is a known fact. And it was a fact known by some people almost as soon as the Confederate Underground started bombing Jewish targets.

There is no mystery about who, ultimately, is responsible for the bombing of our Jewish Community Center. And there hasn't been for sixty years. It was one of a series of anti-Semitic bombings perpetrated by J.B. Stoner's terrorist network, the Confederate Underground, in 1957 and 1958.

Except that no one in Nashville seems to have known this. It doesn't appear that anyone from the FBI or the Anti-Defamation League, which by the end of 1958 had a very thorough report about the network that pulled off these bombings, informed anyone in the Jewish community here. If they did, no one remembers it.

We don't know what the police were doing, but the little evidence we have of their thinking seems to indicate that they either didn't know about the Confederate Underground, or they didn't take it seriously.

So, though this bombing is still officially unsolved, it has, historically, been the least unsolved of the three bombings. But this information hasn't ever made it into public knowledge in Nashville. And that's a mystery I have no good explanation for.

If the answer to who bombed the JCC was "the same folks who were bombing all those other Jewish buildings throughout the South," and that answer was known in 1958, why don't we know it now? And if the Nashville police had known, or taken seriously, the fact that J.B. Stoner was behind the bombing of the JCC, shouldn't that have led them to look at whether Stoner could have been involved in the Hattie Cotton bombing? Shouldn't they have discovered he was in town in August of '57?

While it's true that an integrating elementary school and a Jewish Community Center seem like very different targets, the Confederate Underground went to great lengths to make sure the two would be connected in the public consciousness. They failed.

We know NSRP members took part in some of the anti-Semitic bombings by the Confederate Underground, so we know that those two groups had overlap. But how much overlap was there between the Confederate Underground and the Dixie Knights?

I suspect a lot.

The simplest answer may be that the Confederate Underground was just a name used by J.B. Stoner and whichever Dixie Knights and/or NSRP members he could rope into bombing people. If the Confederate Underground and the Dixie Knights had considerable overlap, then when the Confederate Underground bombed our JCC, a prime suspect should have been the person who went to the media two months before to announce that he was helping to form the Dixie Knights—Emmett Carr.

But it doesn't appear that Carr ever was a suspect.

A thing I've wondered about, too, is what role J.B. Stoner may have played in encouraging his Klan buddies to accept Kasper's ideas. We know Carr didn't like Kasper, but Carr and Stoner ran in the same circles, and Stoner liked Kasper a lot. It looks to me like Stoner was the "translator" of Kasper's ideas. Kasper said some dumbass thing or made some dumbass plan that wouldn't work because the Klan didn't trust Kasper; Stoner would make it okay for the Klan to do what Kasper said. He would make a plan that would work.

This brings us to the Jewish Community Center bombing.

How Anti-Semitism Got Tied to Anti-Black Racism

While there had been a rise in anti-Jewish terrorism in the late '50s, officials were slow to link it to integration until the Confederate Underground started taking credit for bombings. In part, this was because Southern segregationists weren't uniformly anti-Jewish. A North Carolina Klan, for instance, was opposed to John Kasper coming to the state because of his attitude toward Jewish people. This seems strange now in an era when racism and antisemitism go hand-in-hand, but back then, the men who were of an age to be leaders in the Klan were, by and large, World War II veterans who saw themselves as patriots fighting to preserve a distinctly American way of life. They were wary of anything that smelled too much like Nazism, the thing they had fought and watched their friends die to defeat.

So, an important rhetorical strategy of men like Stoner and Kasper was to link Jews to communism in the minds of racist whites. If Jews were communist, then opposing them wasn't taking the side of the Nazis against America, it was taking the side of America against the Reds. Their theory was that Black people were not smart or ambitious enough to want equality for themselves, that they were, normally, happy in their lot. It was the communist Jews who were putting ideas in Black people's heads, telling them they were unhappy, and planning and directing Black protests behind the scenes. Black aspirations for equality were just a symptom of a Jewish communist plot to ruin America.

J.B. Stoner had a parable he would tell his Klan buddies to help them understand why he was such a virulent anti-Semite and to try to convince them to join his cause. Here's how Birmingham Klan leader William Hugh Morris recounted said story:

> [Stoner] also told me yesterday that he had much rather that his Confederate underground had much rather bomb Jewish targets than negro targets. He compared it this way and these are his exact words. He said 'Suppose you were walking down the street and passed a house where there were a bunch of vicious dogs and the fellow in the house kept sicking [sic] those dogs on you, and you kept knocking those dogs over, and the man who kept sicking [sic] the dogs on you didn't stop them, then if you got the man who sicked the dogs on you, you could stop them.' He had reference to the Jews sicking the negroes on us. He said that acts of violence against the Jews would stop integration faster than on the negroes. He said that the acts of violence perpetrated against the Jews by bombing their synagogues and threatening their Rabbis and threatening their Federal judges has been solely responsible for slowing down integration.[133]

Once the Jews became the secret bogeymen behind the Black civil rights movement, they became fair game in the minds of the people opposing integration.

The Explosion

The local papers reported that the Nashville Jewish Community Center had been hosting integrated community meetings, though there hadn't been one for weeks. According to Gilbert Fox, who was the vice-president of the JCC at the time of the bombing, there had been an integrated activity, though. The JCC youth basketball team had recently hosted a Black youth community basketball team.

Fox and other Jewish leaders suspected that electricians who had been in the building that week had seen the children playing together, and that either the electricians were the bombers, or they had alerted the bombers to the situation.

Some witnesses remembered seeing a man sitting in a truck parked nearby as they left the JCC on the evening of March 16, 1958.

At 8:07 P.M. that night, the building, which then sat at 3500 West End Avenue, was bombed. Its front entrance was damaged, and windows on neighboring houses were blown out. No one was injured.

Damage to the JCC was mostly cosmetic. Unlike the Hattie Cotton bomb, which was detonated by electric charge, this bomb had a lit fuse. The FBI recorded that the explosive was placed near the door in such a way that indicated the bomber could have used the building's shrubbery for cover while coming and going. The FBI said that the Nashville Police Department and the Tennessee Bureau of Criminal Identification (TBCI) found two pieces of Orange Wax Clover Safety Fuse about five feet long and "taped together with light-colored masking tape, which was approximately three quarters of an inch in width."[134]

Rabbi William Silverman of The Temple out in Belle Meade received a call before he had even heard news of the explosion. His wife answered the phone and according to the *Tennessean* and the FBI, the caller said, "I am a member of the Confederate Union. We have just dynamited the Jewish Community Center. Next will be The Temple, and next will be any other nigger-loving place or nigger-loving person in Nashville. And we're going to shoot down Judge Miller in cold blood." Judge Miller, you recall, was the judge overseeing Nashville's school integration.

A few minutes later, a man called the *Tennessean* and said, "This is the Confederate Underground. We just blew up the center of the integrationists in Nashville. Now we are going after Judge Miller." An hour later, an anonymous caller reached the United Press and said, "This is the Confederate Underground. We have just blown up the integration center. Our next target is Judge Miller. We are going to shoot him down in the street. The dirty son of a bitch."

The FBI went out of its way to note that the caller "had the voice of an educated man, low-pitched, and no particular accent." We can gather from the FBI's report that there was something the TBCI recognized in this bombing, whether it was the description of the anonymous caller's voice or the way the bomb was put together—what exactly, we don't know. But the TBCI told the FBI that "REDACTED was the only suspect in this bombing and that a piece of masking tape, similar to that found on the fuse, was located in a garage operated by REDACTED. This was also sent to the FBI Laboratory, but no identification could be made between this and the tape found at the scene of the explosion."[135]

Based on the fire marshal's report, we know REDACTED was Wallace Rider, the garage owner who insinuated to Frank Houchin that he had been involved with the Hattie Cotton bombing.

The Message

On March 28, Rabbi Silverman addressed his congregation with a message entitled "We Will Not Yield." As you can imagine, the Jewish community in Nashville was shaken. My understanding, after talking with people who were alive then, is that Nashville Jews had very mixed feelings about how to, or even whether to, take a public stance on integration, for fear of being targeted. There was, apparently, shock and confusion about the bombing because Jewish people in Nashville hadn't been particularly vocal in support of integration. If they were targeted in order to dissuade them from publicly supporting integration, it wasn't clear to a lot of folks how they could do less.

Of course, most Jewish people in Nashville were completely un-aware that J.B. Stoner and other white supremacists were targeting Jews because of their conspiratorial belief that Jews controlled Black people and getting rid of the Jews would cause Black people to settle back down into their rightful, subservient place in society. They were used to much more straightforward antisemitism.

But Rabbi Silverman—who, remember, had been singled out by the JCC bomber—stood before his congregation and urged them to use this act of terrorism to galvanize them toward social justice. The sermons we are most familiar with from the civil rights era, like King's "I Have a Dream" speech, were for a large audience that King knew included the general public. Silverman's sermon wasn't published until 2008 and it is heavily focused on what he thought his congregation and the larger Jewish community in Nashville needed to hear.

Even with that focus and context, it's a deeply stirring message. At the end, Silverman says,

> WE WILL NOT YIELD TO EVIL. We will not capitulate to fear. We will not surrender to violence. We will not submit to intimidation but, as Reform Jews, we will continue to speak for truth; we shall continue to dedicate ourselves to social justice and to the brotherhood of ALL men, knowing and believing that all men are created in the divine image, and this includes Negroes as well as Caucasians. And even as we stand at the threshold of Passover, our Festival of Freedom, the Season of liberation, with resolution and reverence, our hearts touched, warmed and ignited by the Eternal Flame of an eternal faith, we shall continue to consecrate ourselves to human rights, and civil liberties—we shall, with God's help, continue to dedicate ourselves to the cause of freedom and justice for all the children of man.[136]

The Suspects

Donald Davidson shared his theory of the bombing with fellow poet and white supremacist Allen Tate in a letter.

> As to the "anti-Semitic outburst" in Nashville, that's the usual propaganda stuff put out by the press services. It is serious only because the incident will be exploited to cast discredit on the South and especially on all "segregationists", including such people as me. ... As to who planted the dynamite, nobody knows, and the police have no clues.[137]

In April, the police were questioning Elmer Robinson, a local Klansman, who was arrested in Carthage, a town about an hour east of Nashville. The *Tennessean* reported that he had "four timer clocks with electrical contacts and about 50 feet of electrical wire." Robinson claimed he was going to store the clocks "in his garage, although police said he later admitted he did not have a garage."[138]

Robinson fell through.

Nashville police shared a list of suspects with the Birmingham, Alabama, police as part of the region-wide initiative to stop these bombings: Robert Lewis Bromley, Wallace Lester Rider, James McKinley Thompson (who we know was called Slim), John Houston Prater, and Joseph Edward Prater. Rider and Thompson were fingered by Frank Houchin as two of the three Hattie Cotton bombers, so it's not surprising to see them pop up on this list. Bromley had been Rider's tenant, so it makes sense he might be tied in. But the Prater brothers? I don't know why they were on the list. They have similar backgrounds to the others—they'd been busted for robbing gas stations and liquor stores a few times. But I never came across their names at any other point. They're not on Kasper's witness list. They're not mentioned in any Klan meetings. I didn't find anything that connected them with the rest of the men on the list.

I can't exonerate them, but I also can't explain why they were suspects. Which leaves us with Robert Bromley.

Bromley and his wife were on Kasper's witness list when Kasper went to trial for his Nashville activities late in 1958, so he was at least tangentially tied to the crowd we'd expect to see the bomber come out of.[139] But Bromley is buried in Calvary Cemetery. He's Catholic.

Now, clearly, there were Catholic segregationists in Nashville.[140] The police beat some of them in the Hattie Cotton investigation. And Catholics can also be anti-Semitic. So, it's not like the fact that Bromley was Catholic would, ordinarily, prevent him from hating Jewish people. And we know Kasper and Stoner welcomed Catholics into their ranks and that Carr had been doing some Klan outreach work to that community.

But I'm still stuck on this. Nashville literally had a white supremacist church in Rev. Fred Stroud's renegade ex-Presbyterian congregation. The vast majority of racists who'd come to town to scream about segregation were Protestant. Some of these Protestants were clearly on a path to Christian Identity beliefs, and Christian Identity, by the 1960s, believed that Jews and Blacks were descended from Eve and the serpent—literally children of the Devil who needed to be annihilated in a holy war.[141] That was a theological teaching. You might find some Catholics who believe that Black people are the children of Ham (one of Noah's less-cool sons). You might find Catholics who believe that Jews had their shot at being God's favorites, but they screwed it up, and now He loves Christians best. But "Jews and Blacks are descended from Satan" is a theological leap most Catholics at this time wouldn't have made, especially because the unspoken goal of the annihilation of the serpent's descendants was so that proper white Christians could rule. And every Catholic in the South in the 1950s knew in their bones that white Protestants aiming for white Christian rule had no intention of including white Catholics in their paradise. The big Klan revival of the 1920s viewed Catholicism as incompatible with democracy and had happened in the adult memory of these folks' parents.

I'm going to admit that this may just be a place my imagination can't reach. I've been listening to Rachel Maddow's podcast, *Ultra*, which covers the America First movement and discusses the popularity of Father Coughlin and his anti-Semitic message. And I get, listening to that podcast, how he was carving out a space for Catholics in a very anti-Catholic society by appealing to a shared antisemitism. I get it. And, like I said, I have plenty of evidence that some Nashville Catholics were so opposed to integration that they joined the Klan.

But, man, how did it not occur to the Crimmons brothers or Bromley that they were doing the dirty work for men who, when it came right down to it, belonged to an organization that would happily turn on them?

The Other Anti-Semitic Bombings of the Confederate Underground

Later that year, the Anti-Defamation League (ADL) put out a pamphlet on the rise of anti-Semitic hate in the South: "Between June 1, 1954 and October 12, 1958, there have been 83 bombings in the South, of which the seven [anti-Jewish] bombings and attempted bombings were only one part."[142]

Here are those anti-Jewish bombings: November 11, 1957, an attempted bombing at the Temple Beth El in Charlotte, North Carolina; February 9, 1958, an attempted bombing at the Temple Emanuel in Gastonia, North Carolina; the Beth-El temple in Miami was bombed the same day as Nashville's JCC; April 27, a Black high school and a Jewish synagogue in Jacksonville, Florida, were bombed; the next day, April 28, the Temple Beth-El in Birmingham had a bombing attempt; and then October 12, the Temple in Atlanta. The Confederate Underground claimed responsibility by phone in many of these bombings. In the case of the Jacksonville bombing, the caller said, "This is the Confederate Underground. We've just blown up the Jacksonville Jewish Center of Integration." The same wording as the caller in our bombing.

The ADL report goes on:

> With regard to the bombings of Jewish institutions as such, several patterns seem to emerge. In all cases, an apparent attempt was made to avoid causing injury to human life, to time the explosions in such a way that they would only cause physical damage to property—with the evident intention of intimidating the Jewish communities.
>
> Almost identical shopping bags were used to conceal the dynamite in Gastonia and Birmingham. It also appears that in all cases with the possible exception of Birmingham, the dynamite employed was of a common variety readily purchasable or easily stolen.
>
> In Nashville, Miami, Jacksonville and Atlanta, telephone calls were placed to prominent individuals by anonymous persons identifying themselves as members of the "Confederate Underground." In each case the caller indicated a familiarity with what had transpired before it became a matter of public knowledge. Finally, it is generally believed by police and other experts that one group of individuals is responsible for all of the bombings against Jewish institutions.[143]

According to FBI files, an informant was also claiming that Stoner was trying to plan something against a Jewish target in Chattanooga. According to Birmingham police files, the St. Louis, Missouri, police were looking at Stoner for a threat against a "Jewish Center Home." Someone (the St. Louis police believed it was Stoner) called and said, "'The same thing can happen here as in Nashville, Tennessee,' and it was also remarked that it was the Confederate Union or Underground that was calling."[144]

You'd think that a criminal conspiracy that cut across state lines would be right up the FBI's alley, but no, the *Tennessean* reported that the FBI was still convinced that "it lacks authority to enter the cases."[145]

But Why Target These Places?

Kasper had visited many, if not all of these cities, before the bombings, and I suspect that's not a coincidence. I think Stoner really wanted Kasper to be in the National States Rights Party; this was the terrorist equivalent of flowers and an invitation. But there's another possibility we need to consider. It's possible Stoner was trying to impress Kasper because Stoner wanted Kasper, period.

We need to tread carefully here. Obviously, people were gay in the 1950s, and obviously, gay people can also be terrible racists. But it's also obvious that the FBI used "homosexual" and "deviant" as synonyms and saw part of their mission as ridding the country of deviants. And it's clear that the FBI often accused people of being homosexual or engaging in homosexual activity in order to prove that they deserved FBI scrutiny. The FBI also knew that calling someone a homosexual at this time was a great way to ruin his life.

So, for instance, when the FBI suggested that John Kasper had slept with a Black man in New York City, it's hard to know what to make of that. I didn't find any other evidence he slept with men as well as women, but I can't rule it out. But the FBI in this case wasn't interested in whether it was a fact. They wanted to suggest that Kasper had not only crossed a racial taboo, but a sexual one as well. They wanted to ruin Kasper's ability to lead racists. They nearly did.

The FBI's proof, such as it was, that J.B. Stoner was gay is a little more solid. By the end of 1959, the FBI had a really good informant very close to Stoner and Fields. This informant told them:

        Stoner was still going fiercely on the

> F.B.I. studded with "Kikes and queers" and
> "pervert agents committing all kinds of
> sexual abominations." This had now been
> going on three hours and I had never been
> submitted to a more refined brand of torture
> than listening to Stoner's outpourings. But
> in all this there remains some questionable
> point. "Methinks he does protest too much,"
> as Shakespeare would put it. Besides the
> fact that they were living together, Fields
> and Stoner were sharing the same bed, and
> there may be more than meets the eye in
> this situation.[146]

The irony is that everyone was right. Hoover and Tolson were more than friends. Stoner and Fields slept in the same bed whenever Fields's wife was out of town (the FBI heard this from multiple informants over the years).[147] Everyone's protesting too much and pointing out the real deviants far from themselves.

Stoner never married. As we've seen, there was no shortage of radical racist women. If Stoner had wanted a female companion, I think he could have found one.

So, let's entertain the idea that the FBI is right about Stoner and not just looking to slander him. Fields was a tall, handsome, smart man with what appears—though it's hard to tell with black-and-white photos—sandy brown hair. If this was Stoner's type, then Kasper fits it—tall, passably good looking, smart, and with brown hair.

How does a violent racist flirt with another violent racist? Maybe by bombing the cities the first violent racist visited and called for violence in?

CHAPTER 8

J.B. STONER DECIDES BOMBING EMPTY BUILDINGS ISN'T ENOUGH

After careful perusal and thought the following is a summary of the synopses which have already been detailed, relative to the conference held at the Roosevelt Hotel, 9 A. M., May 3, 1958, and we trust that the salient points listed herein will be helpful for analysis purposes.

1.   There is evidenced by the facts herein that in most of the bombings more than one fuse was used, and that one or both of the fuses in each of the instances failed to ignite the dynamite charge.

2.   With respect to the defect in the fuse resulting in the bomb failing to ignite, there is no apparent application to tamper with the fuse, but there must be a patent defect in the application, or the fuse itself. Facts appear to be clear that all bombs were placed at a strategically planned time, day or night, so as to not result in personal injury. It is also believed that total destruction of the property was not planned because, in most instances, had the bomb been placed in a more desirable position, looking toward greater destruction of the building, this purpose could have been achieved.

3.   In reference to the Miami, Birmingham and Jacksonville bombings, it is apparent that the bombs in these three cases were not thrown, but were placed in the position where they were exploded.

4.   It was established that the bombs were transported to the scene in some type of container, namely: The Birmingham, Alabama attempted bombing, that the dynamite was found in a blue canvas bag and the materials found at the scene of the explosions in Jacksonville, as reported by the report of the examinations made by the FBI Laboratory, reflected that materials of this type -- that is, a canvas hand bag, was present, and also, a ladies train bag was found containing the dynamite in the Gastonia attempted bombing.

5.   As in the Jacksonville bombings, a witness stated that she saw a light colored car with a tag, bearing white background, with black letters, the first two numerals which she believed to be A-9, at the scene, just before the bomb went off, and it is possible a car with numerals similar to this might be a Morie County, Tennessee tag, as was seen in the area of Nashville and near the vicinity of the explosion at the time of the bombing.

Immediately after the explosions in Jacksonville, Miami and Nashville, telephone calls were received from a party identifying himself as a member of the Confederate Underground (the details of which are related in previous sections of this report).

It was stated by ███████████ National Fact-finding Director of the Anti-Defamation League of B'nai B'rith, who was

21

Guide to the Racists in this Chapter

Dick Ashe Florida Klan Leader who was working with or for the FBI

Richard and Robert Bowling Brothers who worked with J.B. Stoner

Raymond Britt Montgomery Klansman and bomber who moved to Jacksonville

Asa Carter Alabama Klansman and enemy of Bull Connor

Robert "Dynamite Bob" Chambliss Birmingham bomber

Eugene "Bull" Connor Birmingham commissioner of public safety

Admiral John Crommelin Racist activist and retired Navy man

Eldon Edwards Imperial Wizard of the US Klans

John Kasper Racist who vexed Nashville

Floyd Fleming John Kasper's acquaintance and friend of Nazi George Lincoln Rockwell

Robert Pittman Gentry Florida Klansman who grew up in Murfreesboro

Barton H. Griffin, Jacky Don Harden, Willie Eugene Wilson, and Donald Eugene Spegal Florida Klansmen who, along with Robert Pittman Gentry, committed acts of terrorism in Jacksonville

Fred Hockett Violent racist and FBI informant

Sonny Livingston Montgomery Klansman and bomber

William Hugh Morris Birmingham Klan leader and informant

George Lincoln Rockwell Founder of the American Nazi Party

Gary Rowe Alabama Klansman who was working for the FBI

M.B. Sherrill Florida Klansman, member of the Pro-Southerners, and acquaintance of Emmett Carr

Vance Maxey Stevenson Nashville Klansman

J.B. Stoner Terrorist

Robert and Carrie Wray Friends of John Kasper he sometimes stayed with

Southern officials were upset about the Confederate Underground's bombing campaign. They wanted the FBI's help, and the FBI was still farting around claiming that they didn't have jurisdiction. We were lucky to have the TBCI, which could coordinate investigations in Tennessee that contained multiple municipalities, but many states didn't have an analogous department. Florida, for instance, didn't. So even if police in Jacksonville and Miami knew their bombings had been done by the same group, it was very difficult for them to coordinate their investigations and share information. There just wasn't the infrastructure for it.

Scale that up to a region-wide series of attacks and the problems compound. Someone who had a national perspective, who could track people's movement and trace long-distance phone calls, needed to be coordinating the investigation, but the FBI wouldn't. This kind of myopia at the FBI was still a problem ten years later. See Stuart Wexler and Larry Hancock's *Killing King*, where they found that one of the reasons the FBI never suspected Stoner's involvement in the plot to kill Rev. Martin Luther King Jr. is that Stoner was in Mississippi when the assassination occurred. As if Mississippi isn't directly south of Memphis? As if phones didn't exist?

Unless, of course, the myopia was deliberate, because the FBI didn't want Southern law enforcement to get too close to their informants.

The Southern Conference on Bombing

Anyway, this forced states to say, in essence, "forget the FBI, we'll do it ourselves." In May 1958, Southern governors held the Southern Conference on Bombing, where they shared information with each other about known dangerous racists in their states. I know they shared lists of names of people, because the list of dangerous people in Alabama from that conference is in the Birmingham city archives. The most complete paperwork from the conference I was able to find, in the State Archives of Florida, doesn't include any of those lists. Which is a shame.

But the file from the State Archives of Florida does reveal some interesting stuff. For one, the Jacksonville police had looked closely at

a person from Montgomery, Alabama, in the Jacksonville bombings—
"REDACTED was tried and acquitted in the case of a bombing in
Montgomery, Alabama last year. His modus operandi in those cases
was the same as the ones committed in Jacksonville."[148] Two men
had confessed to, been tried for, and been acquitted of bombing four
Black churches in January 1957—Bell Street Baptist, Hutchison Street
Baptist, First Street Baptist, and Mount Olive—and the homes of
Rev. Ralph Abernathy and Rev. Robert Graetz, who had been active
supporters of the Montgomery bus boycott. Those two bombers were
Klansmen Raymond Britt and Sonny Livingston. Britt had also been
involved in the lynching of Willie Edwards that same month. Judging
by the shortness of the black mark redaction over the name in the
Florida archive, the Jacksonville suspect was Britt. The Jacksonville
City Directory shows a Raymond Britt living in the city in 1958. If
Jacksonville police were right to suspect Britt—and with his history
of violence, it seems like they were—then we know Britt was in the
Confederate Underground, because the Jacksonville bombings were one
of the sets of bombings where the Confederate Underground called to
take responsibility, which means Britt had ties to Stoner.

There's another interesting, but confusing, bit in the report that reads,
"a ladies train bag was found containing the dynamite in the Gastonia
attempted bombing. As in the Jacksonville bombings, a witness stated
that she saw a light colored car with a tag, bearing white background,
with black letters, the first two numerals which she believed to be A-9,
at the scene, just before the bomb went off, and it is possible a car with
numerals similar to this might be a Morie [sic] County,[149] Tennessee tag,
as was seen in the area of Nashville and near the vicinity of the explosion
at the time of the bombing."[150]

This seems to indicate three sightings of a light car with Maury County
plates. "As with the Jacksonville bombing" makes it seem like that car was
spotted in Jacksonville. The car was also spotted in Nashville during the
JCC bombing, most likely, since there's no discussion of Hattie Cotton

in the file. Wherever this witness was, she also saw such a car. I'm guessing, from context, that she was in Gastonia, North Carolina. Nashville and Miami were also looking for an unidentified man who took a flight from Miami after the bombing there and arrived in Nashville prior to the JCC bombing.

My guess is that J.B. Stoner was in that car and on that flight. We know that J.B. Stoner was discussed at this meeting, and we know that he emerged as the suspected mastermind. He's not specifically named in the documents available, but we have an overwhelming amount of circumstantial evidence that suggests he was specifically named at the conference, starting with the fact that the FBI and various local law enforcements all took up the assumption that Stoner was the bomber thereafter, or at least the head of this bombing network.

In the first half of 1958, Stoner was still employed by State Farm and had a bit of money. According to the FBI file on the Atlanta bombing, "when STONER first came to Dublin, he did not have a car of his own and he drove a 1955 Ford, four-door, cream colored, bearing a Florida license which belonged to State Farm and had been used by a company nurse in Jacksonville, Fla.[151] STONER used this car until August 1957, when he obtained a 1957 Chevrolet, yellow body and cream top, which the company purchased for him."[152] As for the plates, Stoner often talked about switching them out. It wouldn't be a problem for one of his Middle Tennessee acquaintances to get him plates from Maury County to use when he was doing non–State Farm things.

Oh, but here's where it gets ridiculous.

The Time Bull Connor Decided to Catch J.B. Stoner

Bull Connor, yes, Bull "turn the firehoses on peaceful protesters" Connor was one of Alabama's delegates to the conference on bombings. He was also on Alabama's list of known dangerous racists in their state. He was furious and embarrassed (even though it was true!) and the conference organizers scrambled to apologize and appease him.

Still, Connor was motivated to do something dramatic to show that he wasn't a violent racial terrorist. When he got home to Birmingham, he was determined to catch a high-profile racial terrorist. Except he needed someone who wasn't one of his friends.

Conveniently, Bull Connor wasn't friends with the man Southern law enforcement had just spent days warning one another about—J.B. Stoner. I've never heard why Connor was hostile to Stoner, but it may be as simple as Stoner being buddy-buddy with Asa Carter, who had run against Bull Connor for office. So, Connor set out to catch Stoner being a racist terrorist. But for that to happen, he needed Stoner to have a racist terrorist plot in Birmingham. Connor had Klan leader William Hugh Morris vouch for two undercover police officers who were posing as businessmen, assuring Stoner they were prominent townsfolk. They then hired Stoner to bomb local civil rights leader Rev. Fred Shuttlesworth's church. For another $1,500, Stoner offered to throw in the assassination of Rev. Martin Luther King Jr.[153]

Judging by the FBI file, it doesn't appear that Connor's men agreed to pay Stoner to kill King, but let's note that we now know—and the FBI knew at the time—that by 1958, Stoner was entertaining plans to kill King, meaning King was on Stoner's radar, and Stoner was already looking for excuses to go after him.

Through his intermediaries, Bull Connor paid J.B. Stoner a small amount of money to indicate that they were serious about the plot to blow up Shuttlesworth's church. The plan was that Stoner would come to town to do the bombing in July, then Connor would arrest him, thus proving that Connor could do something no other Southern authority could—get Stoner for a bombing everyone knew he was involved in—and thus prove that Connor wasn't one of the bad guys.

Unfortunately for Connor, Stoner was well-connected, and he wasn't an idiot. He likely knew the plan. Stoner came into town on or right before June 29, 1958, and his crew placed a bomb at the church.

Fortunately, a church employee found the bomb and moved it into the street, where it exploded without injuring anyone. While this was going on, someone on the bomb crew tried to call Bull Connor to taunt him about the bombing. When he could only get through to the switchboard operator at the police department, he told her the Confederate Underground had just bombed a "Communist center of integration".[154] [155] Then Stoner left town.

Which meant that Bull Connor had paid a known racist bomber to bomb the church of a prominent Birmingham civil rights leader. Which, again, did not assuage anyone's fear that Connor was a violent racial terrorist.

At this point, Connor—who is really failing to learn from recent history here—went to the FBI for help. The same FBI that has heretofore utterly refused to help Southern authorities, of which Connor is one, with interstate racial terrorism, hence the reason for the conference Connor attended and was embarrassed at, which then led him to this cockamamie scheme in the first place.

Guess what happened next.

That's right. They refused to help Connor. Congratulations—we all have more ability to predict people's present behavior based on their past behavior than Bull Connor had.

Of all the evil Stoner was involved in, this is the thing he eventually went to prison for. Thirty years later. Just for three years. But he did go to prison. Ultimately, this was because it was a sting operation. Prosecutors had Connor's plan and could show a trail that led to Stoner doing this bombing. It's tempting to believe that Connor straight-up hired Stoner to bomb the church, because we know the kind of monstrous things Connor's on the verge of doing. But I do think it's clear he did intend to catch Stoner in the act.

Klan Leader William Hugh Morris, Police Informant

There's a little tidbit in the FBI's NSRP file that adds an interesting Nashville wrinkle to this Birmingham story:

> STONER contacted the source, stating he wanted to organize an air-tight group with the purpose of perpetrating violence against the Jews. STONER "intimated strongly" to this source that he was responsible for the bombings of a school and synagogue in Nashville, Tennessee, and a synagogue in Birmingham. STONER spoke knowingly of other acts of violence. STONER, having been contacted by the source under the pretext of representing a group which wanted to arrange for some act of violence against Negroes, indicated that he would set a price for such work. STONER thereafter met with this source and members of the Birmingham PD, who impersonated members of the source's "group". STONER represented that he could, through "his boys", arrange for bombings or killings, and implied that he had arranged bombings in connection with anti-Semitic and anti-Negro activity in the past. Following the attempted bombing of a Negro church in Birmingham, Alabama, in June 1958, STONER again contacted the source and members of the Birmingham PD (still under pretext) representing that he had arranged for the bombing and attempted to collect a sum of money for the "service".

On December 8, 1958, Commissioner EUGENE
CONNOR, Department of Public Safety,
Birmingham, Alabama furnished SAC CLARENCE
KELLY a copy of a statement dated 12/8/58
by REDACTED to Commissioner CONNOR and
Birmingham Police Officers (Bureau refer to
Birmingham airtel to Bureau 12/9/58 in the
REDACTED ET ALL matter). In the statement
dated 12/8/58 REDACTED included the following:

Source had "gathered bit by bit," from
STONER, that STONER had "planned and put
into execution" bombings of the Hattie
Cotton School, Nashville, Tennessee, a
synagogue in Atlanta, the Clinton, Tennessee
High School[,] at Jacksonville, and Miami
bombings and The Temple Beth-El, Birmingham.
STONER said, according to the source, that
he bore the expenses and bought the dynamite
for all the bombings. STONER deplored, the
source said, that so many people who believe
in segregation and the White race, will sit
around and do nothing. The source expressed
the opinion that STONER is insane.[156]

Okay, so let's make sure we all understand what this is saying. Stoner
came to this source sometime before June 1958 and told the source he
wanted to put together a terror cell to target Jews in Birmingham. Then,
in June, Stoner tried to get paid for bombing the "Negro church." All
the while, he was telling this source about all the places he had bombed
and how he supported the bombings. So, why didn't the FBI nail Stoner
to the wall?

```
In view of the possible doubt as to the
reliability of REDACTED and the fact that
past intensive investigation by the Bureau
or local authorities regarding the various
bombings mentioned by REDACTED has failed
to corroborate REDACTED's information re
STONER'S involvement in such bombings, the
information originating with REDACTED has not
been included in the body of this report.[157]
```

If there's one thing we know, though, it's that these investigations were not as intensive as they could have been with the FBI's help. The fact that Nashville couldn't piece together Stoner's involvement in the JCC bombing, for instance, isn't an indication that he wasn't involved; it's an indication that Nashville needed the FBI to help them put together clues from other anti-Semitic bombings throughout the South.

Though the copy of the FBI file I have has this source's identity redacted here, based on later references in other FBI files and Birmingham police files, this source was Klan leader William Hugh Morris,[158] the very Klan leader who had facilitated the meetings between Stoner and the undercover police.

Morris gave the Birmingham police, and then the FBI, a lot of information about Stoner and about our bombings, so the question of whether he's reliable is important. Can we trust the FBI's take on him? Frankly, I'm not sure.

Morris told the Birmingham police,

> [Stoner] has talked to me about that on numerous occa-
> sions in a general way and has intimated very strongly to
> me that he was responsible for the bombing of the school
> in Nashville, Tennessee, the placing of the bomb at the
> synagogue here in Birmingham, also the bombing of the

synagogue in Miami, Florida, and of calling by telephone the Rabbi down in Miami and representing himself as a member of the Confederate Underground and it
was either to the Rabbi in Miami or to the Federal judge
in Nashville that he said he would shoot them down in
cold blood. I don't remember which of them that was.[159]

Morris seemed to know that Stoner had been in both Miami and
Nashville, even though those bombings took place on the same day
(Miami in the very early morning, Nashville at night). That's not a detail
anyone else but the people at the Southern Conference on Bombing
seemed to have known,[160] which suggests Morris heard it directly from
Stoner. I could not find any source saying definitely that anyone in
Miami got a phone call from the Confederate Underground, so I had
been assuming that Morris just mixed Miami up with Jacksonville; but
I have since learned that Miami likely did get a call. This would mean
that Morris knew something that didn't make the papers and wasn't
widely known.

I went down to Birmingham and read through the Birmingham
Police Department Surveillance Files. Morris gave Bull Connor a lot
of information that isn't in the FBI file I saw. Morris told Connor that
Stoner was driving a blue-and-white Chevy early in 1958, the same color
car witnesses saw driving away from the Hattie Cotton bombing in late
1957. The early '50s Hudsons and Chevys did not look that different,
especially from the back. And, more incredibly, not only did Morris tell
Connor that Stoner had told him that Stoner had supplied the dynamite
for the Hattie Cotton bombing, but Morris also claimed that Stoner and
John Kasper met with Morris and asked for help bombing a school in
the fall of 1957.

Worse than that, after Stoner and his crew bombed Rev.
Shuttlesworth's church, when Stoner showed back up in Birmingham
looking for the money to pay his crew, he had a younger man with him.

Morris got out of paying Stoner by telling him the non-existent financial backers of the plot had come to believe that Stoner wasn't actually behind the bombings he claimed to be behind—that Jews had bombed the Birmingham synagogue themselves and that perhaps someone in Rev. Shuttlesworth's congregation had tried to blow up their church. The man traveling with Stoner supposedly told Morris he was the one who placed the phone call in which the Confederate Underground took credit for Shuttlesworth's church bombing and heavily insinuated that he (and maybe someone else) had done the bombing for Stoner. Morris identified that young man as a "Richard Bowling" from Atlanta.

Morris was telling Connor this in June 1958.

After the Hebrew Benevolent Congregation Temple bombing on October 12, 1958, in Atlanta, one of the men arrested was Richard Bowling of Atlanta, along with his brother, Robert. This bombing was also attended by a call from the Confederate Underground. J.B. Stoner, supposedly, supplied the dynamite and then, as was his way, left town so he had an alibi.

As a side note that may be relevant to Nashville, the Birmingham police took a statement from the operator who had talked to the man who identified himself as being from the Confederate Underground, the man Morris claimed was Richard Bowling. She said he was well-spoken and easy to understand.[161] It immediately put me in mind of how witnesses described the voice of the Confederate Underground caller in the Nashville JCC bombing. Let me be clear, I don't think this proves anything. But I do think it's enough to put Richard Bowling on our list of possible bombers of the Nashville JCC.

So, here's where we are with William Hugh Morris, Klan leader and police informant: Some of his information is not quite right. It's true that Bull Connor had every reason to want to make Stoner out to be the worst of the worst and Morris into Connor's brilliant inside man instead of a doofus in over his head. It's mighty convenient that Morris just happened to link Stoner to most of the unsolved bombings of the era.

But Morris also seemed to have really, really good information—like the name of one of J.B. Stoner's bombers—that no one else had.

Kasper had invited a ton of KKK leaders to Nashville in August 1957. Why couldn't Morris have been there? Kasper himself wrote that Stoner had been. Is it so hard to imagine that Stoner and Kasper might have met up with Morris, who had once been the regional head of our Klan and still had ties to those men?

I don't think we should do like the FBI and dismiss everything Morris has to say, but I do think we should be cautious about accepting anything he says without something other than his word to give some credence to it.

Still, what appears to have happened is that the FBI had okay—not great, but okay—information about the extent to which Stoner was involved in the Nashville bombings, which they kept from local law enforcement and even many FBI agents who could have used it, because someone else, namely Bull Connor, had stumbled across this lead.

I'm going to give the FBI a little benefit of the doubt here, at least to the extent that this was Bull Connor's source, not theirs. Bull Connor, as we've seen, was not making wise decisions, and it seems reasonable that the FBI should be suspicious of his source. Also, they knew Connor was looking to nail Stoner for something, anything, so it does seem super convenient that Connor has a source that links Stoner to *everything*.

But this is also what the evidence points to—that Stoner was in fact involved, to a greater or lesser extent, in most racist violence in the South in this era.

Another Nashville School Year, Another August of John Kasper Being an Asshole

This brings us back to Nashville in late summer, 1958. At the beginning of August, Kasper was released from federal prison in Atlanta and made his way back to Nashville. According to our stair-step integration plan, first grade and now second grade would be desegregated. White people were still pissed about integration. The Nashville Klan had switched allegiances from the United Klans to the Dixie Knights, a more violent faction. Many of Kasper's followers had joined the National States Rights Party while he was in prison. In other words, integration was spreading, racist whites were radicalizing, and the city's main suspect for being the mastermind behind the bombings was back in town.

It should have been a recipe for disaster, and Kasper tried to make it so. He did all the things he did the year before—big public spectacles of asshole-ishness, warnings of impending doom, an alleged terrorist plot—but nothing came off. Which suggests that there was some necessary component for racial violence in Nashville that Kasper didn't have at the time or didn't know he needed. He knew how to advocate for violence, but it seems like he didn't know how to ensure it would happen. He could shout "dynamite" repeatedly, but without that mystery factor, no one was going to be Kasper's terrorist.

I have many theories as to what this factor was, but I think the most likely one is that the people involved in the JCC bombing, and thus maybe the Hattie Cotton bombing, were laying low while Southern states were making noises about actually trying to catch them. Another possibility is that they knew the October 5 Clinton High School bombing was in the works and that's where their attention was. Another distinct possibility is that they were all busy planning the bombing of the Atlanta Hebrew Benevolent Congregation Temple, which took place on October 12. You don't want to risk getting caught doing piddly crimes in Nashville when the grand finale of your region-wide anti-Semitic bombing campaign is so near. Racist bombers may just have been too busy getting ready for October's events to come fart around in Nashville in September.

Still, Kasper's activities in 1958 are alarming.

On August 22, 1958, the FBI in Alabama received a tip that "John Kasper was planning to assassinate a colored city councilman in Nashville, Tennessee, by the name of Frank Luby [sic]; that Kasper had selected him [the tipster] for the job and REDACTED [the tipster] was to go to Nashville when Kasper directed him to do so; and that Kasper was to furnish the rifle with which to commit the murder."[162]

The tipster gave the FBI other information—that Kasper and Admiral John Crommelin "had formed a third political party on which ticket Crommelin would run for President" and that some of Kasper's followers were plotting to assassinate Bishop Sheen of New York. An agent from the Mobile office went to interview the tipster and found him "not trustworthy and possibly psychopathic."

In fact, Crommelin would announce his run for president on the National States Rights Party[163] ticket a couple of weeks later at the NSRP convention.[164] Now, we know that Kasper and Crommelin hadn't really formed the party. But the informant's information about Crommelin's political ambitions was accurate. Yet there was a note in the margins of the Mobile Office's letter: "No dissemination."

In other words, the FBI knew Kasper was back in Nashville and had good reason to believe he was possibly literally gunning for Looby, and they appear to have decided to keep that a secret.

On August 23, someone called now–school superintendent W.H. Oliver and warned him to stay away from a meeting being held the next day about desegregating Nashville's second grade. Both Oliver and the FBI were convinced Kasper was the caller. On the 24th, Oliver attended that meeting at Clark Memorial Methodist Church. Kasper, Carrie Wray and her daughter, and some of Kasper's men also attended the meeting. During the meeting a bomb threat was called in. Kasper and his group tried to leave while the church was evacuated and searched, but other attendees persuaded them to stay.

First, let's take a moment to admire the brilliance of that crowd at Clark Memorial that day. Remember, at the time most everyone was convinced John Kasper had bombed Hattie Cotton. There he comes, this nationally known terrorist, to sit in on their meeting about school integration. That must have been incredibly unsettling. Then there's a bomb threat, while you have a suspected bomber in your midst. Then that suspected bomber and his friends start to leave the event. I don't know who had the idea to gather a crowd and make it clear that Kasper would be rejoining the group in the church once the police gave the all-clear, but it was so smart. If Kasper's followers wanted to bomb the church, fine, but they were going to bomb Kasper with it.

Second, and I'm not some investigative genius here, but if you have a known terrorist in a building with one half of the couple he used to live with, and there's a bomb threat against that building, isn't the first person you go ask about the bomb threat the other half of that couple? I mean, Robert and Carrie Wray both appeared to be big Kasper supporters and yet only one of them has shown up to this little intimidation effort. Isn't it likely that's because the other one had a role in the event he couldn't execute from inside the church?

The Wrays may have lucked out here because Kasper's reputation for sticking his dick where it didn't belong was already very well known. When the police saw Carrie Wray with Kasper, I think it likely didn't dawn on them that they should wonder what her husband was doing while she was with Kasper. If anything, they probably thought Robert Wray should wonder what, or who, his wife was doing.

Over the weekend of August 30 and 31, Kasper was one of the keynote speakers at the National States Rights Party convention in Louisville. The FBI recorded that he talked about the bombings:

```
Just look what happened while I was in prison
even; those folks that have heard the truth
in Clinton, Tennessee, and other places have
a reaction even then, a synagogue was bombed
in Miami, and Nashville, attempts were made
in Gastonia, North Carolina, and Nigger
schools were bombed and dynamited. All this
was done only after a little communication
```

```
work had been accomplished.

[ . . . ]

We as leaders couldn't be blamed because
we are non-violent, but we tell the truth,
and when the people find out the truth, such
reaction is normal.¹⁶⁵
```

It's hard to know how true this is. On the one hand, it's kind of surprising that Kasper wouldn't want to take more direct credit for the bombings. On the other hand, he didn't want to go back to prison and, though he couldn't have possibly known how many FBI informants were in the room, he certainly would have guessed it was a number greater than zero. Probably best to distance himself.

The Clinton High School Bombing, October 5, 1958

With all his talk of dynamite, it's not surprising that Kasper still gets the blame, or the credit, for the bombing of the Clinton High School on October 5th, 1958. He had been active in Clinton, he had incited a riot, and he'd just gotten out of prison on charges related thereto.

But this time, the FBI had a close eye on Kasper and usually knew right where he was. Kasper was in Nashville when the Clinton High School was bombed. Yes, he could have planned the bombing and directed it from afar, except, remember, the segregationists in Clinton had come to loathe him. Who would he have made this plan with?

We're going to have to devolve into straight-up gossip here, but the unsubstantiated gossip I have heard is that the identity of the Clinton bomber or bombers is known in elderly racist circles in Clinton, that there were two brothers and the bomber was one or the other of them, and that they were tied to the NSRP.

The fact that this gossip exists and that I can hear it, sitting nearly 200 miles away from Clinton, never having visited Clinton, and doing very little heavy research into the Clinton situation, is one of the stranger things about this. Not that the Clinton gossip exists, but that the Nashville gossip doesn't.

I assumed when I started this research that our situation would be similar to the 16th Street Baptist Church bombing down in Birmingham, where a lot of people knew who did it but it just couldn't be legally proven at the time. I figured we never received justice because the right group of people to prosecute the case and serve on the juries didn't exist in the late '50s and early '60s in Nashville.

But I have tried to find the right gossip network that could at least informally say who bombed us. If that gossip network exists, and surely it must, it must be very small and very insular.

The Clinton bombing is important to our story not just because it's an important part of the "John Kasper was obviously a racist nightmare, but was he a bomber?" debate, but because Z. Alexander Looby was the lawyer on the Clinton desegregation case.

As far as I can tell, no one has explicitly made this connection. Among some people, it goes without saying that, of course, Looby was involved in all this. Who else was there to be? If African Americans in Tennessee needed a lawyer to take on a civil rights case, they were likely going to turn to Looby. But I think law enforcement, if they were looking for connections between the bombings at all, looked at who was bombed and who the suspected bombers were. No one seems to have stepped back to see if these cases had anyone else in common.

This is also what pisses me off about the way Nashville has erased the JCC bombing from our collective memory. If you don't know it happened and you don't know why the bombers said they did it, then you don't see the pattern developing with Looby at the center.

We don't have to continue to make that mistake. Let's look at the racist violence against Looby's causes.

In 1956, we have the Clinton Riot. Looby was the lawyer for the folks who wanted to desegregate the Clinton school system. In 1957, Hattie Cotton blows up. Looby was the lawyer for the family who wanted to desegregate Nashville schools. In 1958, the JCC blows up and the Confederate Underground threatens the life of Judge Miller. Judge Miller was presiding over the Nashville school desegregation case brought by Looby. Then back to Clinton for that bombing. In 1960, Looby's house was bombed.

Five acts of racist terrorism in five years and Looby is connected to all five.

I don't think it's unreasonable to believe that a secondary purpose of the first four incidents was to scare Looby into backing off. When he would not, the fifth incident was supposed to guarantee he couldn't be involved in any more desegregation efforts.

The Looby bombing wasn't just one in a string of bombings. It was the culmination of a five-year effort to scare folks, especially Looby, away from school integration.

Anyway, we'll get to Looby's bombing in the next chapter. For now, let's get back to Clinton High School.

In October 1958, Clinton High was bombed. Kasper was blamed. But finally, the FBI had eyes on Kasper almost all the time, so we know a lot of what he was up to and bombing Clinton wasn't among those things.

Who did bomb Clinton? By November 1958, the FBI had a suspect:

```
Recently, however, there has been some in-
dication of a general interstate pattern to
these bombings. For example, one of the 5 men
indicted on October 17, 1958, (Richard Bowl-
ing) for the bombing of the Jewish temple in
Atlanta, received from one of his fellow con-
spirators two checks [handwriting] amounting
to [typed] worth nearly $200. One of these
```

checks was dated October 4, 1958, the day
before the Clinton, Tennessee, High School
bombing; the other, October 9, 1958, three
days before the Atlanta temple bombing.[166]

Richard Bowling, who, as in the gossip I heard, had a brother and was in the NSRP. Who, along with Stoner, bombed Rev. Shuttlesworth's church. That's three bombings in 1958 this guy was linked to in three different states. He was Stoner's crony. Everyone knew that. Kasper was the face of the movement, but it was Stoner who had his hands in so many of the bombings.[167] Well, Stoner and Asa Carter. I just finished Rachel Martin's book, *A Most Tolerant Little Town: The Explosive Beginning of School Desegregation*, which is about the Clinton bombing. It's brilliant and you should read it. Possibly, you would have benefitted from reading it before you read this book. She makes two points that could be relevant—there was a lot of dynamite floating around Clinton, the police had confiscated at least two large caches of it; and "Asa Carter's branch of the Klan had established an office in downtown Clinton just one block from the school."[168]

So, another possibility is that Bowling was not paid to bomb these two buildings, but was, instead, repaid for buying dynamite from whoever was stealing it in Clinton. Same network, just a slightly different structure.

John Kasper's Scary Nashville Friends

Okay, back to Kasper.

In November, a couple of friends from D.C. came down to Nashville to visit Kasper. He showed them around town and introduced them to his racist buddies here. Kasper didn't know it, but his D.C. friends went home and told the FBI all about their trip.

Here's what the couple told the FBI about meeting a particular group of Kasper's friends:

KASPER called on Thursday night and said
that he would pick up the REDACTED [the D.C.
couple] at 8:30 in front of the hotel and
that he would be in a red and white Nash
station wagon. He arrived, with REDACTED and
her daughter, who goes to Antioch school, in
the eighth grade. Everyone was introduced,
and drove to the REDACTED who now live at
REDACTED. KASPER said that they had been
moved from the Jay Street address for almost
three weeks.

REDACTED were introduced, and told about the
REDACTED working for Seaboard WCC. REDACTED
started talking, and said that just a few
people had passed out thousands of handbills
around REDACTED. He likes to talk, and
the subject of weapons came up. He showed
everyone his weapons, and he had a small
arsenal. He brought out first a .25 cal.
automatic pistol, chrome, and either Spanish
or Italian. He said that he got it for his
wife to carry in her purse. He then brought
out either a M1 or an M2 Army carbine, and
said that he had close to 300 rounds of ammo
for it. He said that a friend of his and
REDACTED had suggested that the gun be taken
to a Negro park around Nashville, and that
a group of Negro outers be told to take off
down the road, and then worked over with
the gun. He then showed a 1903 Enfield rifle,
and said that he had close to 500 rounds of

ammo for this gun. He paid $25.00 for it, he
said. He said that he also had a .45 cal.
government automatic pistol, and ammo for
it. The carbine and the pistol were picked
up in the Pacific in 1942, and were supposed
to have been lost in action. He said that
none of the guns are registered, and that
several people know that he has them. He said
that he could make aluminum knuckles at the
plant he works at, and wished that REDACTED
could carry a pair. KASPER said that the
police could really get him then. REDACTED
said that he knew where he could get a half
case of dynamite at any time, without the
owners knowledge, "at that there was always
plenty of dynamite around." He seems to know
a good deal about dynamite, and talked about
several different types of fuse. REDACTED
carries an 18 inch British bayonet in his
car, sharpened on both edges, and said that
one swing would take a man's head off.[169]

There's one more ominous bit the D.C. couple recounted that seems
to be about this same man, "Kasper stated that REDACTED was not
hot-headed and if he did anything violent would not broadcast it before
or after and would do anything he did alone, with no help from anyone."

The Wrays lived on Jay Street. Robert Wray was listed in the city
directory in 1957 as living on Jay Street and working at AVCO. In 1960,
he still worked at AVCO, but now lived on Lutie Street. Working at
Avco would have given Wray access to aluminum to make aluminum
knuckles. Wray was born in 1920, so he certainly could have been in the
Pacific to pick up a gun during World War II.

Judging from the FBI file, the information this D.C. couple gave the FBI was very similar to what the FBI had been hearing from other sources. In a memo dated 4/29/58, the SAC wrote, "It is noted that information was furnished by REDACTED to the effect that ROBERT WRAY, in approaching him regarding possible membership in the Dixie Klans, Knights of the Ku Klux Klan, stated that he had picked up a carbine and one or two other rifles with ammunition in service in Europe and that he had smuggled these out of an Army camp when he returned to the United States." The FBI interviewed Wray's boss at Avco. They looked into his credit. They interviewed his grocer. And they called on someone, "REDACTED PSI, former Exalted Cyclops, Klavern 13, US Klans, Knights of the Ku Klux Klan, Inc." who "advised that he is acquainted with WRAY by reputation only and has seen him on one occasion. He advised that he has no information that WRAY has any Army guns."[170] The FBI determined that the situation had been somewhat inflated. Wray didn't have the arsenal that rumors attributed to him. He hadn't served in the Army, but in the Navy. And, even without adjusting for the sexism of the time, what comes through in the files is that, while Robert was a true believer, Carrie was the one who was actually carting Kasper around and doing organizing work for the Tennessee White Citizens Council and becoming an elector for the NSRP. Carrie, supposedly, has no FBI file.

Return to the Florida Klans

But we do get two bits of important information here. One is that Wray was sniffing around about possibly joining the Dixie Knights and that the FBI already, by April 1958, had a Dixie Knights source. This is a different person than the REDACTED who was the Exalted Cyclops of Klavern No. 13. That's the second important thing: the FBI had an informant who was the Exalted Cyclops of Klavern No. 13.

Can we know who that was, even with the redaction? Maybe. But it requires returning to Florida.

We're going to get more in-depth into this when we discuss Robert Pittman Gentry, but in June 1964, five men would go on trial in Jacksonville, Florida, for bombing the home of Donal Godfrey, a first grader integrating his neighborhood school. Those men were Barton H. Griffin, Jacky Don Harden, Willie Eugene Wilson, Donald Eugene Spegal, and Middle Tennessean Robert Pittman Gentry. The UPI reported that "the FBI said Griffin was the Exalted Cyclops or President of Klavern 13, Harden was Exalted Cyclops of Klavern 8, Wilson was former Old Titan or Goodwill Ambassador for the Florida Klan organization, Spegal was Klokard or Lecturer for Klavern 13, and Gentry was Kligrapp or Secretary of Klavern 8 and Grand Klexter or Outer Guard of the State Klan group."[171]

We have to go out on a bit of a limb here. As we've discussed, Klans were constantly breaking apart and reorganizing. We only have even odds that if Klavern No. 13 was in Florida in 1964 it was in Florida in 1958. But what if it was? Any interesting Exalted Cyclopses in Florida in 1958?

In June 1958, a Florida legislative committee was looking into the Klan. They cited Suwannee County sheriff Hugh Lewis with contempt for refusing to tell them about a 1955 attack on a Black farmer, Richard Cooks. Eldon Edwards, the Imperial Wizard of the US Klans, Knights of the Ku Klux Klan, was also forced to testify. He told the committee that Dick Ashe, of Lakeland, Florida, had told him folks were trying to start a rival Klan (as we've already discussed). Edwards also said that Ashe was the Exalted Cyclops in the Lakeland area.

As a side note, M.B. Sherrill was also called to testify.[172] He refused on state and federal constitutional grounds, since he didn't have his lawyer. But what's interesting is the question the committee attorney asked him. According to the *Tampa Tribune*, "One question Hawes asked was: Did Sherrill have any connection with the bombing of a Jewish Synagogue in Nashville, Tenn. Sherrill has been linked to Ku Klux Klan activities at Nashville and with anti-Jewish organizations. A letter purportedly written by him was introduced into evidence. The letter said the Klan was prepared to show Nashville residents how to make bombs and control fires and gasoline. Sherrill blurted out that he didn't write the letter."[173]

The next day, we get this bombshell:

> A self-proclaimed FBI undercover agent today laid the 1951 bomb slaying of a NAACP leader and his wife at Mims at the door of the Orlando Klavern of the Ku Klux Klan. Richard L. Ashe, 31, Winter Haven public relations man, testified before a Legislative investigating committee he had learned also that Klansmen at Jacksonville, Orlando, Lakeland, and Tallahassee have large stores of firearms and ammunition ready to oppose school integration with violence. He said the Orlando Klansmen have stockpiled dynamite in a warehouse.[174]

There's a lot here we suspected but didn't know—folks had already made the connection between Florida and Nashville. The umbrella organization of the Klan headed up by Eldon Edwards was active in connecting and overseeing various Klans under it. There were explosives and weaponry that were set aside for segregationist violence and moved to communities where it was needed. There were terrorist workshops available to local Klans. (It'd be interesting to know if this was Stoner or if this is just where he got the idea. I suspect this was Stoner.)

And then there's something we learn I'm not sure anyone has realized. Here's the prototype for Gary Rowe. Like Rowe, Dick Ashe wasn't in the KKK before he started working with the FBI. Like Rowe, the FBI recruited and placed Ashe into the Klan and then used him as a funnel for information. The FBI publicly claimed—like they did with Rowe—that Ashe wasn't an FBI agent, per se, but just someone who worked with the FBI. Ashe told the committee that he got a salary and his expenses covered and that he was run by Special Agent Rae Jett.

Now let's relook at that bit from Robert Wray's FBI file: "REDACTED PSI, former Exalted Cyclops, Klavern 13, US Klans, Knights of the Ku Klux Klan, Inc." PSI is Personnel Security Interview, the interview you have to go through to work for the FBI. People who just gave the FBI information didn't have to go through that process. If REDACTED had a PSI, then REDACTED was genuinely working for the FBI. He wasn't just an informant. And, if REDACTED is Ashe, then this file confirms that he went through an interview process with the FBI.

If I had to guess, I think the semantic game the FBI is playing here is that in order to be an FBI agent, you have to go through training. In today's terms, it means you go to Quantico. Clearly, neither Ashe nor Rowe did that. They were just guys hired by the FBI to infiltrate Klans and report back. They weren't going to have jobs with the FBI when this task was done. But how much does that matter to us out here in the real world? These men may not have been FBI agents, but they were sure acting as agents of the FBI. And, in this case, the FBI's guy was running the Lakeland Klan—not just informing on people in it but running it at the behest of the FBI. To spell this out: the FBI ran the Lakeland Klan for a time.

I'm harping on this so much both because it tells us that Gary Rowe wasn't a one-off mistake, but a longstanding FBI strategy, and now one we know they were employing in some fashion in Klans throughout the South.

But we're not quite done with Florida racists yet. Who was this D.C. couple who visited John Kasper in Nashville and gave the FBI all this information on Robert and Carrie Wray? They appear to have known John Kasper through the Seaboard White Citizens Council in D.C., which he was one of the leaders of. The man could be Floyd Fleming, who would go on to be good buddies with George Lincoln Rockwell, founder of the American Nazi Party. Kasper and Fleming would split over this because Kasper thought Nazis were losers and he wanted a winning kind of American racist fascism and nothing to do with George Lincoln Rockwell.

If so, it's a huge deal that the FBI had an informant in Rockwell's inner circle from the start.

But I don't think it was Fleming.

How Fred Hockett Stayed out of Trouble

In another place in Kasper's file, they fail to redact who came to visit Kasper. Oops. The special agent in charge of the Washington, D.C., field office wrote to Hoover on November 6, 1958, to provide Hoover with a little more information about Fred Hockett, who Agent Norwood had said was staying in the Boxwood Motel in Nashville with John Kasper and a blonde who could have been Hockett's wife: "It should be noted that FRED HOCKETT participated in burning fiery crosses Washington, D.C. 1956, and was arrested Miami, Fla., either 1956 or 1957 for attempting to burn cross on lawn of Negro. HOCKETT was characterized as dangerous by WFO sources in 1956. Information was also received that HOCKETT at times is armed."[175]

Hockett was a member of Kasper's Seaboard White Citizens Council who had moved to Florida and had been arrested not just for burning a cross on a lawn (the lawn of local musician Frank Legree, who had purchased a home in a formerly all-white neighborhood) but also for plotting to kill five NAACP leaders and dynamite Black homes in Miami.

It seems likely that we're seeing here why Hockett didn't get in more trouble for that. He found he had some friends in the FBI he could approach in order to stay in the clear.

But this also shows the dysfunction of the FBI. The D.C. field office clearly had no idea Hockett was an informer. They're operating as if he could be a danger to FBI agents. Meanwhile, other parts of the FBI are treating him like a valuable asset giving them a ton of information on Kasper and his associates. The right hand didn't know what the left hand was doing. No wonder they couldn't catch people.

How Stoner Set Up and Ran His Bombing Squads

In December 1958, William Hugh Morris told the FBI (or told the Birmingham police who told the FBI) that he and Stoner had been driving to Louisville and Stoner made a big deal of stopping in Nashville to get a map. Morris alleged that Stoner had confessed to him again about several bombings in the South on this trip. Stoner also apparently gave Morris details on how he set up his bomb squads:

> I know that there is a group in Chattanooga.
> Now, those groups, I don't believe any of
> them would consist of over five men, probably
> three. He has talked about a group in At-
> lanta and one in Florida. He says it is not
> necessary for over three men to go on any of
> them unless they wanted to ride "shotgun".

> . . .

> Now, STONER, so he says, needs a car. He
> did tell me this. You see he would pick out
> a target—this is the way it operates—and
> he would go get his man on the weekend. The
> company[176] furnished him a car and to keep
> from showing so much mileage on these trips,
> he would disconnect the speedometer. He
> didn't try to cheat the company—he paid for
> his own gasoline and everything except for
> the wear and tear on the car. He would go
> and see the target for himself. He has a map
> of all of the southern states and all of the
> major cities, showing the major highways and

roads. He would get his man who was going to do it and they would look it over together and then he would furnish him the dynamite, gasoline and oil for his car and if that man's car needed a tire or anything, he would furnish that, and then he would also furnish the whiskey after it was over to celebrate the victory. He didn't tell me exactly how much it would cost, but I just imagine that it would cost $100.00 a job. He said he had spent about $1,500.00 of his own money to get this stuff done and nobody has been interested enough in it to help him out. I got the impression from talking to him that his man in Chattanooga is the best man he has got. He says some of these boys use just one fuse but this boy uses three. They have no timing device, they make the fuse long enough so they can get away. He said it wasn't necessary for a man on any job to be there over one minute. They light the fuse before they get there and set it out burning, and get back in the car and are gone. They ordinarily find a place where there is a concrete porch or something and they always like to be on the upper side because it has a tendency to go down, and the more travel there is, the more they like it because, if somebody saw them, they would be gone and the person wouldn't think about what kind of car they were in.[177]

There's a lot about what Morris is saying here that resonates with what we know happened in Nashville. The Hattie Cotton bombing crew was small, or so one of the alleged bombers claimed—just three men. Both Hattie Cotton and the JCC were bombed in covered entryways. We may have had a man from Chattanooga in Nashville for the Hattie Cotton bombing. And it seems ominous that Morris wanted authorities to know that Stoner wanted a map of Nashville.

But let's take a minute to step back and think about what Morris is describing here. At this time, Stoner lives in Atlanta, where he apparently knows some guys who, in mob parlance, can do the thing—one of whom was Richard Bowling. He also knows a guy or two in Chattanooga and a couple in Florida. I'm just guessing, based on the fact that it was a hot-bed of violent racist activity at the time, that this crew was probably in Jacksonville, which should give us cause to raise our eyebrows when we encounter Robert Gentry in Jacksonville later.

Chattanooga and Jacksonville are both a day's drive or less from Atlanta. This means Stoner has guys he can deploy who are less than a day's drive from most of the South. Looking at the bombings we're discussing (our three in Nashville and the ones that have come up tangentially): Clinton and Nashville are both easy drives from Chattanooga; Charlotte, NC, and nearby Gastonia are easy enough to get to from Atlanta, as is Birmingham; and someone in Jacksonville could get to Miami.

Let's not lose sight of the fact that the main reason these bombings were never solved is racism. But second to that was the assumption that these were mostly local incidents, that even if John Kasper or J.B. Stoner or someone else had come in and riled folks up, these bombings were planned and committed by locals.

When the facts didn't line up well with the roused-up locals theory—like how could a bunch of folks in a bunch of Southern towns all decide independently to bomb Jewish buildings in their towns and all independently call themselves by the same group's name and all come up with nearly identical language to use when they took credit?—then the impulse has just been to credit Stoner solely: he organized this and planned it and came to town to direct the locals on how to do it.

But what we're seeing is that there was a layer of middle management in some of these bombings. Stoner could come up with a bombing plan, deploy a regional bomber to your community, and that regional bomber could help you set up a crew (or be on your crew) and leave town so that the local investigations were always missing one crucial piece of the puzzle when it came to solving the crimes and prosecuting them.

Stoner didn't need to be there. Just his regional bomber.

It's pretty easy to see the benefits of this setup. Locals willing to do acts of terrorism don't have to spend time learning how to bomb things (which would open them way up to the possibility of getting caught). They can rely on the expertise of whoever Stoner connects them with. Stoner's expert doesn't have to run around any particular town getting better at bombing. He has the whole South to practice in.

And it seems very possible to me that the locals and the regional bomber wouldn't even know each other. The regional bomber could just be "Stoner's guy." The local guys are just the local guys. In this scenario, there'd be very little they could tell police, if they did get caught.

If the crew is three people, the local police are never going to see a likely group of three suspects, because at least one isn't from there. They might be deeply suspicious that, say, Joe, was on a three-person crew, but if they only ever see Joe with Brad, then can they really be certain Joe was involved? Joe doesn't have a third trusted friend.

And that third person isn't going to pop back up, because the third person doesn't live in town.

You can also see how this protects Stoner, too. He can funnel a lot of resources through his regional person without ever being the person who hands the bombers the dynamite or places the bomb himself.

Which brings us back to the Birmingham situation. Morris had to do a lot of work to get Stoner to agree to bomb Rev. Shuttlesworth's church, and even after Stoner agreed, he still changed the plan, and the bomb went off early. This suggests that Stoner didn't completely trust Morris.

Part of the reason Stoner must have been wary is obvious: Birmingham had bombers. Rev. Shuttlesworth's home had been bombed on Christmas Day, 1956. On April 10th, 1957, the home of the pastor of 1st Baptist Church Kingston, George Dickerson, was bombed. On April 28th, the Allen Temple AME Church in Bessemer, a suburb of Birmingham, was bombed during services. And, as mentioned, in 1958, also on April 28th, terrorists tried to bomb Temple Beth-El. This last one was Stoner, but there's no clear indication that the others were. Stoner must have wondered why Morris was coming to him and not to the locals who knew what they were doing.

But it's also likely that the reason Morris came to Stoner was because Stoner had a fourth node, a fourth city where he knew a guy who could do a thing, if a thing needed doing—Birmingham.[178] Stoner had deep Birmingham ties, and the city was important enough to him that the NSRP headquarters, along with Ed Fields, moved to Birmingham in 1960. Morris, being a Klan leader, would have been exactly the kind of person who would have approached Stoner about getting something done.

I don't think Stoner was some kind of boss man. He seems like a supervillain in part because he was functionally unstoppable, and he was audacious. But in reality, he was more of a facilitator. If someone in your town wanted something bad to happen there, but didn't know how to do it, Stoner could help. But I haven't found any clear examples of Stoner doing something without local cooperation. Stoner (or his guys) didn't come into town and do a thing without the local bad guys being okay with it and without locals helping him pull it off.

I want to show how Nashville's bombings fit into the larger patterns of segregationist violence in the South at that time, and the direct link is Stoner. But I don't want to give the impression that Stoner was the only one with brains, motivation, and plans, and that everyone who fell into his orbit was an unthinking minion.

Stoner was, for a great portion of the South, the guy who knew a guy who could do a thing. But someone had to want Stoner to have his guys do the thing.

This doesn't look to me like some kind of top-down organization where Stoner gives an order sitting in Atlanta and that activates the people in his network to go do it. It's more mutually beneficial and the power balance more equal.

On May 9, 1959, John Kasper held a rally for his candidates for mayor and vice mayor of Nashville, Bessie Williams and Henry Jerrell, on the steps of the county courthouse. Very few people showed up—mostly local media and college students who heckled Kasper. But one of Kasper's speakers was J.B. Stoner, who, judging by the FBI files, the FBI did not have as close a watch on as one might hope. They didn't know when he'd arrived in Nashville, how he'd gotten here, or where he was staying. He spoke out against school integration and Jews.

In March 1960, Stoner mailed Klan literature to Kasper in jail.

CHAPTER 9

THE BOMBING OF Z. ALEXANDER LOOBY'S HOME

Guide to the Racists in this Chapter

Emmett Carr Dead Nashville Klansman
Donald Davidson Nashville racist poet
John Kasper Incarcerated Racist
George Lincoln Rockwell American Nazi
J.B. Stoner Racial Terrorism Instigator
George Wallace Segregationist Governor of Alabama and Asa Carter's new boss
Carrie Wray Kasper's old friend and National States Rights Party member

As soon as I realized that the story of these bombings was more complicated than we knew, I contacted the FBI and did a bunch of Freedom of Information Act (FOIA) requests for files on the bombings and files on people I thought might be involved. The FBI informed me that most of the files that still exist had been transferred to the National Archives. I could request said files from them.

The response they sent to my FOIA request for files pertaining to the Z. Alexander Looby bombing was different. It read, in part, "Records which may have been responsive to your request were destroyed in September 1996."[179]

An unsolved assassination attempt on a sitting US politician and the FBI destroyed the files? To put it simply, what!?

I spent a year trying to find someone—either at the FBI or with knowledge of how the FBI operated back then—who could explain to me why the FBI would have done this. I had conspiracy theories—there was something in the file the FBI never wanted anyone to see—and crazy conspiracy theories—my god, the FBI itself must have tried to kill Looby—but I didn't have good answers. And without the FBI files, the TBCI files, or the police files, trying to piece together what had happened was going to be difficult and incredibly tentative.

Still, that was the work that had to be done.

Then, finally, I was having a casual conversation with Keel Hunt, who had been Senator Lamar Alexander's right-hand man back when Alexander was governor of Tennessee and had remained close with the senator. I asked Keel for his opinion on why the FBI would have destroyed the Looby bombing files. He insisted I immediately call Hal Hardin, a local lawyer and former US attorney. If anyone would have insight into why the FBI destroyed those files, it would be Hardin.

So, I called Hal Hardin and told him that the FBI told me it had destroyed the Looby files, and he incredulously told me he didn't believe it. I didn't know if he meant he didn't believe me or if he meant that he didn't believe the FBI.

Turns out it was the FBI story he doubted. He told me to call John Lewis's office right away. Yes, Georgia representative and civil rights icon, John Lewis. That John Lewis. So, I did. Shortly I got in touch with the person in his office who deals with civil rights issues. I went through my whole spiel again, and she told me, since I wasn't a constituent of Representative Lewis's, that they couldn't open up an inquiry with the FBI on my behalf. I explained that I was merely trying to gain some insight into the FBI's decision-making process, and she again apologized for not being able to help me and told me that I needed my representative to open an inquiry with the FBI.

Oh, okay. Message received.

I emailed the office of my representative, Jim Cooper, explained everything to them, and they said they were in. Long story short, after his staff exhausted all avenues of trying to understand why and how this happened outside of contacting the FBI, Cooper sent the most delightfully nerdy and badass letter to Christopher Wray, the head of the FBI, informing Wray about Looby's importance, expressing concern that these files had been destroyed, and demanding an explanation for why.

And lo and behold, Cooper's involvement got the FBI to admit that the Looby bombing file hadn't been destroyed after all. Turns out, it too was sitting at the National Archives.

Now I just needed to wait two years for the review process so I could get it. This was both great news and a bit of a bummer. So much for having the book out in time for the sixtieth anniversary of the Looby bombing.

But still, I would be on track to have the book out in 2021, maybe 2022. And then COVID hit. And here we are, the end of 2023, and I still don't have the Looby bombing file. All that work, all that help from the most powerful people I know, and who knows when I'll get it?

It's not all bad and frustrating. The National Archives not only has the Looby bombing file, but also has what's left of Looby's personal FBI file—the file the FBI kept on him. All twenty pages of it. The National Archives sent it to me.

Those twenty pages contain a little information on the Columbia Riots and a little information on Looby's supposed feud with NAACP member and perhaps communist, Lee Alexander Lorch. And that's it.

The guy who was the lone attorney devoted solely to civil rights in the state of Tennessee for years? The guy who made Tennessee the home of many of the first public schools in the South to desegregate? NAACP leader? Attorney for the students who led the sit-in protests at downtown lunch counters? Looby's FBI file had twenty pages in it the first day they opened it. I would put money on that.

My guess is that *this*—Looby's personal FBI file—is the file decimated by the FBI, not the bombing file, and whoever responded to my FOIA request was just sloppy in his or her search for the files. As for why Looby's personal file was mostly destroyed, who knows? My guess is because the optics of the FBI carrying out massive surveillance on a US politician and failing to stop a terrorist attack aimed at him are pretty bad. But also, it's possible that the surveillance of Looby could have violated attorney-client privilege in some way. We don't know.

The FBI did a lot of terrible things during the integration era, but at the moment I believe the destruction of the Looby file is just about getting rid of proof of the FBI's stupid and unethical behavior, not about covering up something infinitely more evil.

Doing without the Looby Bombing File

But since we can't get into the Looby bombing file, let's go over what can be known or surmised without it.

Our local Klan leader, Emmett Carr, had an unbreakable alibi for the bombing of Z. Alexander Looby's home on April 19, 1960. He'd been dead fifteen days.

John Kasper's alibi was pretty good, too. He was in the Nashville workhouse.

The general understanding of the bombing is that the sit-ins were going on; Looby was one of the lawyers for the protesters; Looby's house was bombed because of that; the protesters marched downtown and Diane Nash asked Mayor Ben West to desegregate downtown; he did; then Martin Luther King Jr. came to town to tell us how awesome and inspiring we were.

One of the reasons we think this is that the *Tennessean* reported that Looby thought the bombing was because of his legal work on behalf of the sit-in protesters who were getting arrested trying to desegregate downtown businesses. But the sit-in movement had been going on for weeks. There hadn't been any action or event that would seem to have galvanized racists into violent acts. At first glance, it just appears they picked a random day to bomb Looby.

Without the FBI files or police files, without any suspects, without any precipitating event that obviously inspired the bombers, how can we even begin to say why Looby was bombed, let alone who did it? Let's all shake our heads and give a collective shrug and move on with our lives.

The story as we know it has the excuse for the bombing's unsolved status built right in.

But once you start to dig into this bombing, even a little bit, a clearer—though not entirely clear—picture begins to emerge.

The Precipitating Events

Let's start with the bit where there doesn't seem to be any precipitating event, no build-up to this bombing. First of all, we now know that segregationists in Nashville had been targeting Looby by name since 1957 (or earlier, if we count the note with the cross burning near Belmont University's campus). We also know that the FBI had good reason to believe Kasper was trying to figure out how to assassinate Looby in 1958. And we know that Looby was at least tangentially tied to our two previous bombings.

Then there's this: on April 5, 1960, the *Tennessean* ran a story informing everyone in town, "The Rev. Kelley Miller Smith [sic], president of the Nashville Christian Leadership council, announced that the Rev. Mr. Martin Luther King Jr., president of the NCLC's parent group, the Southern Leadership conference, will speak at the next mass meeting here April 18, 'if we can find a place big enough.'"[180]

Martin Luther King Jr. didn't come to town in response to the Looby bombing. The Looby bombing was, it appears, planned to be a response to the meeting King was supposed to have on the 18th. The April 5 announcement must have pissed racists off, or at least some small group of racists, enough to plot to do something dramatic.

I think John Kasper knew something was in the works. Look at why the *Tennessean* reported he was dissolving the Seaboard White Citizens Council on April 17, 1960.

> The 30-year-old segregationist said the council he orga-
> nized in 1956 is being taken over by neo-Nazis and he
> wants no part of them.
>
> "I am nearly broken by jails, niggers and rock quarries
> and the cruel life that this is," Kasper recently wrote a
> former associate from the Davidson county work-house
> where he has been confined for about three months. "I

have a definite fear of being railroaded to jail again for something I don't believe in."[181]

Sure, yeah, maybe he's talking generally. Of course, it's a safe bet that neo-Nazis might do something in the future that he's going to get blamed for. But two days in the future, Looby's house is going to get blown up.

There's no further mention in the white papers of this King rally until April 19, when a *Tennessean* story announced, "A mass meeting to hear Dr. Martin Luther King Jr. will be held at Fisk university gymnasium tomorrow night, instead of at War Memorial auditorium, as originally scheduled."[182]

Which, oops, if your plan was to bomb the Looby house in response to the King rally, you've just bombed the Looby house only to grab a paper and discover the rally didn't happen the night before.

Then there's the story of the bombing itself, which also becomes more complicated when you look a little more closely at it.

The Bombing

Civil rights attorney, NAACP leader, and sitting city councilman Z. Alexander Looby's house was bombed at 5:30 A.M. on April 19, 1960. The blast damaged Looby's home at 2012 Meharry Boulevard, his neighbor's home on one side, and the apartment building on the other side. It also shattered 147 windows across the street at Meharry Medical School. Police Chief Douglas Hosse told the *Tennessean* that, "If that bomb had gone in the window, Looby's house would have been blown off the face of the earth."[183] Hosse told the *Tennessean* that he thought it was a bomb made up of ten or twenty sticks of dynamite "thrown from the street at a picture window in the front of Looby's house. The bomb apparently missed the window by about four feet, fell to the ground and exploded at the foundation as the bombers drove away."

I spent an afternoon at the NAACP listening to old men reminiscing about Looby (who, they relayed, was always a snappy dresser) and the old neighborhood. Cars, they said, usually lined Meharry Boulevard. So, we're supposed to believe that someone in a car on the street threw a five-to-ten-pound package out a car window, possibly over a parked car, up a slight ridge, and maybe 50 feet to Looby's house on the first try? Well, put out an all-points bulletin for a racist shot putter with some quarterback experience, because who else could have done it? We're talking about someone tossing the equivalent of a bowling ball at the house from a car.

In the other bombings, initial reports were also that the bombs were tossed from passing cars. Only later was that revised to the bombs having been carefully placed. I think we have to guess that the same is true here. I have a caveat, though. One afternoon, local journalist Brian Mansfield and I were out at the Looby house with a gallon of water, since a gallon of water weighs about the same as the amount of dynamite investigators thought was used. I was telling Brian that authorities reported that the bomb was thrown from the car, but I just couldn't see how anyone could throw something this heavy out a car window and get it to go very far.

Brian, holding the gallon jug, went out to the middle of the street and stared for a minute. Then he said, "But what if you were in the back of a truck? And you could just stand up and . . . " he swung his arms back and then forward and the water arced over the street and across the lawn and landed almost exactly where the Looby bomb had landed.

Because Looby's house didn't appear to be destroyed, white Nashville quickly assumed that the bombing was more cosmetic than deadly, just as the other two bombings had turned out to be. The kinds of follow-up stories that happened with the other two bombings didn't happen in Looby's case. We know very little about whether and how the police might have revised their thinking on the Looby bombing. But the house and his neighbor's house had to be condemned. We do know that. Both Hattie Cotton and the JCC could be fixed. Looby's house could not.

Maybe a truck was used (though we're about to get into why I don't think that's so), but I think the bomb was placed near the corner of the house deliberately, to try to ensure that if the Loobys weren't killed by the blast, they'd be killed by the house collapsing onto them. What the bombers likely didn't know was that the Loobys' cute brick house hadn't always been brick. A photo in the Looby collection at Fisk University shows that same house, but with light-colored wooden siding. If you look closely at the bombing photos, you can see that wooden siding under the brick.

I didn't find any information about why he bricked up the house or when, but I am tempted to assume it was to make the house harder to set on fire—a common danger civil rights leaders faced. But this also meant that the outside walls of his house were much thicker than the bombers would have expected.

Something else, though, about the placement of the bomb that may tell us something about the bombers. An alley ran behind Looby's house. It still runs down the middle of that block. Looby's driveway ran the whole length of his property, from the street to the alley. Directly behind Looby's house—right across that alley—was the office for the organizers of the sit-in protests. Another really juicy target. Across the street from Looby's house was the hospital, where people would have been coming and going at all times of night.

The bombers would have been much better served to use the alley to plant the bomb under Looby's bedroom. Their chances of being seen if they were on the street were fairly high (though not high enough, apparently) and their chances of being seen in the alley were very low. Plus, they would have literally been bombing the sit-in office's back yard. Why didn't they use the alley?

I'm guessing it's because they weren't familiar with the neighborhood. I don't think they knew there was an alley. This differs from the Hattie Cotton bombing, where the bombers knew how to get out of a rabbit warren of a neighborhood with no problem. Also, it suggests that, unlike the JCC bombing, they hadn't adequately staked out their target and considered how to use the landscape as cover.

I also think the timing of the bomb is a clue. The generally-sympathetic-to-the-civil-rights-protesters *Tennessean* published in the morning. The more conservative *Banner* was the afternoon paper. By the time the *Banner* came out, civil rights protesters had already gone downtown and confronted Mayor West. What would have obviously been the biggest story of the day in the morning—the Looby bombing—was old news by the time the *Banner* hit newsstands. Obviously, the bombers couldn't have known what would bump the bombing from the *Banner*, but it was a sure bet the *Banner* would found something else to highlight.

And the bombing happened late enough in the early morning that the *Tennessean* was already being delivered when it happened. That meant the *Tennessean*'s first story about the bombing was the next day. If you needed to give your bombers a window of opportunity to get out of town before anyone even knew to look for them, you couldn't have planned it more perfectly.

The Police Response

I also wonder about the police. They canvased the area repeatedly looking for someone who might have seen something, and the most they got out of it was that someone had seen a newer model car with two white guys in it. The police don't appear to have gone back to the Whites Creek guys who had initially been arrested for bombing Hattie Cotton to see what they were doing that morning. They don't seem to have checked in with any of the suspects in the JCC bombing. There's not even a report of them going to talk to Klan leaders to see what they might have to say.

The police sent officers to guard the homes of the following people: Mayor Ben West; Rev. Kelly Miller Smith; Councilman Robert Lillard; Dr. C.J. Walker (the chair of the citizens liaison committee for the Nashville Christian Leadership Council); and Fisk president Dr. Stephen Wright.

In retrospect, those seem like obvious people to guard. But why were they obvious on the day of the bombing? The past two bombings had been spurred in part by Judge William Miller's actions or a hatred of him. How did the police know they didn't need to protect him in this case?

I don't want to inadvertently downplay Rev. Kelly Miller Smith's importance to the civil rights movement when I ask this, but it's a question we need to consider: Why guard Smith's house?[184] Smith wasn't the only clergy supportive of and active in the civil rights movement. Just as an example, we talked about Clark Memorial Chapel hosting desegregation talks, which John Kasper attended, and getting a bomb threat in response. How did the police know they didn't need to guard that parsonage?

Plus, students from every historically Black college and university in town participated in the sit-ins. Why would the police guard Fisk's president and not TSU's?

The only way the police's strategy makes sense is if we look at it with Dr. King's presence in Nashville in mind. King and Smith were dear friends. When King came to town, he often stayed with Smith. I didn't find any confirmation that King was with Smith on this particular stay, but it's a reasonable assumption. The Nashville Christian Leadership Council was the local branch of King's Southern Christian Leadership Council. Dr. C.J. Walker and King worked closely together to coordinate strategies of resistance to segregation. Looby was one of the lawyers representing the sit-in protesters, who were under the guidance of the NCLC. And, of course, King spoke at Fisk.

In other words, the police behaved as if the attack on Looby was a threat against King.

But why did they believe that?

Mayor West Leads the Investigation

There was another very odd thing about the police investigation. Mayor

West participated in it. He canvased the area for clues and interviewed witnesses. The mayor of the whole damn city took time out of his regular mayoral duties to conduct a police investigation? What?!

One of the few remaining police files I was able to find is the transcript of the interview Mayor West conducted with the night watchman at Fisk, Lem Dawson, the day of the bombing. At the start of the interview, Mayor West announces "Present is the Chief of Police, D.E. Hoss, Chief of Detectives, Mr. Sidney Ritter, and Mr. Avon Williams, attorney and law partner of councilman, Z. Alexander Looby."[185]

Let's list what's weird about this: 1. The mayor is interviewing a witness in a police investigation. 2. On the day of the crime. 3. In front of the bosses of the people you'd expect to be doing the interview. 4. With a lawyer who is intimately invested in the investigation in the room with them.

This is the very same day the silent marchers came downtown to confront the mayor about segregation. Mayor West was right out in front of Looby's house looking for anything out of the ordinary. The chances that he and the marchers left North Nashville headed for the mayor's office at the same time are pretty high.

Lem Dawson, the Fisk night watchman, told West a lot of interesting things that may give us some clues as to who did this. First, the night of the bombing, he saw a two-tone Ford—cream top, dark bottom, maybe a 1958 or 1959 model—circling around campus. Dawson recounted, "Well, last night at 2:00 o'clock I met a car that I saw for three weeks prowling around there you know—two white men and one colored man in the back."[186] He saw them again at three o'clock and four o'clock. He got off work at five, "but I thought I better make another search and so I circled around and couldn't see nothing you know, where nobody had been around or nothing and so by that time I went down on 18th to make one more last circle down by the boiler room and I heard this explosion and by the time I got to Herman Street and 18th I heard the explosion and I turned around and looked at all my buildings to see if they had blowed and they hadn't and I didn't know where it was—then the police come through flying and I trailed them to Mr. Looby's house and that's where it was."

The interview then moves to when Dawson had seen this car before:

Q[uestioner]: Now, before last night—had you seen this car there in this neighborhood?

Dawson: I saw it a week ago.

Q: A week ago—now where did you see it that time?

Dawson: Around on Jackson.

Q: On Jackson.

Dawson: 17th & 18th.

Q: Now, you know, of course, Mr. Avon Williams lives on Marina?[187]

Dawson: I didn't know where he lived.

Q: And President Wright lives on Marina?

Dawson: That's right.

Q: About what block on Marina—where President Wright lives?

Dawson: He lives at 1803.

Q: Now—where and what time of the night did you see it a week ago?—tell us about that occasion.

Dawson: That was just all around the buildings and coming through up Jackson and back around to Herman and back up around Meharry Blvd.

Q: How many were in it at that time?

Dawson: That's 4.

Q: Four (4) were in it that time?

Dawson: Yeah—four (4) whites.

Q: Four (4) white you saw—all four of them were white?

Dawson: That's right.

Q: And—how many times that night did you see it?

Dawson: I saw them at 2:00 o'clock and I saw them again at 3:00 o'clock—I didn't see the car at 3:00 but I saw two men up behind the building.

Q: Now where did you see the men—behind what building?

Dawson: Behind Scribner Hall.

Q: Scribner Hall?

Dawson: In front of it—I looked from 18th and seen one man standing at the corner and I put my lights out and went up behind the building and then—

Q: Were you armed at that time?

Dawson: Yeah—I was armed.

Q: What did you have?

Dawson: I had a shotgun.

Q: A shotgun?

Dawson: And a pistol.

Q: Now then you came up to that building tell us what happened.

Dawson: I went to the corner of the building and peeped around [smear] this fellow was trying to get the door open and then I blasted right on him that time.[188]

There's a lot to unpack here. But let's start with geography, since most of us aren't intimately familiar with 1960 Nashville streets. I'm going to simplify some, but basically "Fisk" was the area south of Jefferson Street and north of Herman Street. Sixteenth Avenue marked its east boundary and 21st its west. The north-south streets were numbered. Seventeeth Avenue took you right into the heart of the academic buildings. Eighteenth Avenue ran between the academic part of campus and Meharry Medical School. Most of the cross roads don't make four-way intersections on 18th. So, to the west going south, you have Jefferson

Street, Meharry Boulevard, Alameda Street, Albion, Morena, Hermosa, and then Herman. To the east, you have Jefferson, Meharry (though it doesn't intersect with the Meharry to the west), Phillips, Jackson, and then Herman. Jackson is the nearest street on the east side of 18th to Morena on the west.

What Dawson is describing when he talks about how these cars were circling around campus, is that they were staying fairly close to 18th Avenue and seemed to be exploring the blocks just to the left or right of it. Like they kind of knew the location they were looking for, but not exactly.

Also, Scribner was a woman's dorm. When Dawson shot at the white men who were trying to get into Scribner in the middle of the night, he was shooting at white men trying to get into Black women's bedrooms. This explains why the police treated the bombing like it was about the sit-ins. They knew what was never made public—that these men who blew up Looby's house had been skulking around Fisk's campus all month, driving by Avon Williams's house and Looby's house and, perhaps, trying to get their hands on Fisk's most famous female student at the time—Diane Nash.

Just as a cool side note, when Dawson retired in 1962, he gave an interview to Robert Churchwell at the *Nashville Banner* where he explained why he worked until deep into his seventh decade of life at Fisk: "I was raised up in the woods . . . I didn't have no education and I tried to stay here so people could get one without fear."[189]

I also want to take a minute to talk about the Black guy in the back of the car the night of the bombing. I think the obvious assumption we can make is that the white guys couldn't nail down the location they were looking for, so they grabbed a Black guy to make him show them. I can't imagine that poor man having to live with that for the rest of his life. I hope he had a rest of his life, considering he was likely kidnapped by racists who were about to try to murder someone. Would they have had any compunction about killing a Black witness?

But this goes back to the point I made earlier: a Black person familiar enough with that area to point you to Looby's house would have known about the alley. If this man was smart enough to keep the bombers out of the alley, he saved the Loobys' lives.

A Confession

Then there's this: the police quickly got a confession. According to the *Nashville Banner*, two days after the bombing, Lucian Arzo Neely[190] was arrested after drunkenly telling a bunch of people at the Tennessee Theater that he had bombed the Looby house. He told the two police officers who arrested him that he had done it, and the next morning, after he'd sobered up, he told three detectives he'd done it. For reasons that are unclear, one of the detectives told the *Banner* "the statements he made Thursday night undoubtedly was alcohol speaking," even after his sober confession.[191] Neely was only charged with being drunk in a public place.

Neely looks like a very, very poor suspect, confession aside. He didn't seem to have any trouble before this incident, and he didn't seem to have any trouble after this incident. According to the *Banner* story, he was an interior designer. According to the city directories, he was a painter. Neither profession gives you a lot of access to or experience with dynamite.

But here's the thing that might make you wish the police had taken a little more time with him: Neely lived at 2113 Scott Avenue, two blocks away from where police found John Kasper the night of the Hattie Cotton bombing.

By the end of April, the NAACP and other Black organizations in town were calling for the Justice Department to step in and lead the investigation. Only ten days had gone by, and it seemed like Black Nashville was already convinced no one local was going to catch anyone. Little did they know that no one national was either.

Busy Looking the Other Way

In 1967, John Britton interviewed Looby for the Civil Rights Documentation Project. Before they talked about the bombing, they talked about the kinds of racists Looby had problems with. Looby told Britton about a deputy sheriff who tried to make him move from the lawyers' section in a court room and a district attorney who tried to fight him. Britton then asked, "Did you ever have any problems with the citizens in these communities, like maybe the Klan or anything like that?" Looby said, "No." Britton said, "It was just the officers—"

Looby explained that he wasn't out in the crowds that ran into the Klan. The racists he had trouble with were the racists he met. Due to his profession, the racists he met regularly were police officers and city officials and other lawyers.

A few minutes later, Britton asked him, "Did anybody call you or tell you in any kind of way why your house was bombed? Do you have any indication why it was bombed?"

Looby answered, "Never. It was during the time of the demonstrations. Now, the city council put up a reward of $10,000, of course, nobody's ever claimed it. I knew nobody was going to claim it, at least I didn't think anybody would, but I'm afraid that some people do actually know. Somebody knows. I think the police could have found out, but they didn't. They were very busy looking the other way."[192]

Who Gets Credit? Who Gets Blame?

The rumor started flying around town, or at least around the white parts of town, that Black people had bombed Looby. This (shamefully) became white conventional wisdom on the bombing. And worse, supposedly the bombing happened not because anyone in the Black community disagreed with Looby, but to try to drum up sympathy for the sit-in movement.

This means that the seemingly viable suspects in each of these bombings were not the middle-class white Protestant racists who actually had
the means, motives, and opportunities to do these bombings. It was
some "other people": dirt-poor racist rural folks, some of them Catholics
who could never be wholly accepted into the Klan, Jews, and Black people. In every case, we see someone arguing that "they" are doing this stuff
to make "us" look bad: Emmett Carr said as much about John Kasper;
Donald Davidson made that argument about how the JCC bombing
was covered; and the chair of the United Church Women's committee
on Christian social relations, which was trying to raise money for the
Loobys, had to take to the *Tennessean* on May 21, 1960, to "scotch a
'widespread rumor that the bombing was planned by the Negro community and executed by one of their number.'"[193]

Debbie Elliot, on NPR's *Weekend Edition*, in trying to understand
the popularity of the "false flag" conspiracy theory, tried to get to the
bottom of why whites were so quick to blame anyone but segregationists
for the bombings of the '50s and '60s.

> "That's the most inhumane thing you could think of,"
> [Birmingham resident Jeff] Drew said. "Who would
> bomb their own house?"
>
> But that rumor was widely circulated in white circles
> says Diane McWhorter, who wrote a Pulitzer Prize-win-
> ning history of the Birmingham Civil Rights movement
> called *Carry Me Home*.
>
> "The understood motive was that blacks were bomb-
> ing their own churches and buildings in order to raise
> money and get publicity for the movement," she said.
>
> She says it was repeated publicly by politicians,
> including Alabama's segregationist governor, George
> Wallace. Other common theories were that the bombings
> were ordered by Martin Luther King Jr., or were part of a

communist plot, or were orchestrated by the FBI.

"It was repeated so often—I mean I grew up hearing this from my own father—that, you know, I think they started believing it," she said. "And part of the reason they were able to believe it was that, until the 16th Street Church bombing in September of 1963 when four young girls were murdered, there had been no real fatalities."[194]

I think this is most of the truth. I do think that many white people were desperate to believe that they were good people and the beliefs they had were good beliefs and that it simply wasn't possible that good people with good beliefs could be doing these terrible things. Let's call that 50 percent of what was going on with that.

Then I think another 40 percent was about making it utterly clear to the victims that they weren't ever going to see justice. A way the police and the justice system upheld white supremacy was by keeping justice inaccessible to non-whites. Appreciate, as Jeff Drew is getting at in the interview, how cruel that is. Not only are you the victim of this terrorist violence, if you involve the police to aid you, you have to know it means they're going to jack up the life of some Black dude who you know had nothing to do with it. You have to calculate into your calls for help if you're willing to sacrifice an innocent Black man to the sham investigation that will follow. And if you don't call the police, then, really, you must not mind getting bombed. It's sickening.

But there's also another factor that I think is important, but I'm not sure if I'm a good enough explainer to get at it. Bombers wanted credit for their bombings without consequence. It's why the Confederate Underground called and took responsibility for the JCC bombing. It's why J.B. Stoner ran all over the place bragging about the bombings he'd participated in. It's why Emmett Carr went to the *Tennessean* to brag about joining up with the Dixie Knights. They wanted to believe that they were beyond the law and that all of white society was on their side—that they could say they did these things, and no one would touch them for it. It's not hard to imagine the power trip that would be and why bombers would desire it.

But the flip side of this is that it means either the police were hugely corrupt and letting these guys get away with these bombings, or they were idiots who couldn't solve bombings the bombers were bragging about committing. Don't get me wrong, both of those things were probably true. But the point is that no matter how racist the system is or how widespread the support for that racist system is, those bombers were making fools of the police, and it's clear that the police often resented it.

The rumor that the Jews in Birmingham had blown up their own synagogue started *among the police and their informants* as a way of denying Stoner and his group the credit for it. This was ostensibly to keep from paying Stoner for blowing up Shuttlesworth's church, but reading through the Birmingham police files, it's also clear that taking credit for the bombing away from Stoner was deliberately supposed to belittle him and humble him back into doing what the police wanted him to do.

I don't know how much wanting to deny credit to the assholes you, for whatever reason, weren't going to arrest played into things here in Nashville, but I think it must have been part of why Black people got blamed for the bombings.

Nazis

If we're talking about who gets credit and who gets blame for these bombings, here's one last strange thing. On April 20, the day after the bombing, John Kasper, sitting in the Nashville workhouse, demanded to talk to the FBI. The FBI waited five days to meet with him, and when he launched into a rant about how he wasn't involved with Nazis, they don't seem to have questioned him about why he was so anxious right then for them to know that.

This is weird for a lot of reasons. Someone just tried to assassinate a sitting US politician. Regardless of how the FBI and the police might have felt about his civil rights activities, they had to know that other politicians, many of whose politics lined up more with law enforcement's, wanted to feel assured that would-be assassins are caught. The police were almost instantly behaving like they knew the scope and focus of the plot and that they knew they weren't going to catch who did it. Then the FBI gets a call from the guy who they knew may have already had an assassination plot against Looby and they lollygag around for five days before going to see him? Perhaps because they knew he wasn't going to have any information they didn't already have? And then, who were these Nazis Kasper was trying to distance himself from? If there were Nazis in Middle Tennessee in 1960, they weren't some new unknown crowd of strangers. They were the same people we've been talking about all along, who didn't like whatever group they'd previously been associated with, so they reconstituted themselves as Nazis.

Or, and this is important, possibly they didn't consider themselves Nazis, exactly—but Kasper did.

George Lincoln Rockwell started openly calling himself a Nazi and his movement the American Nazi Party at the end of 1959. But Rockwell, especially at that time, kept himself in the D.C. area and farther north. With one exception, when he briefly worked for the NSRP.

I'm less clear on whether Stoner considered himself a Nazi, but he hated Jewish people, thought they were intentionally upending the social order and ruining the world, and he wanted them all dead or deported. Plus, he'd been pen pals with a Nazi in his youth and hung out with people who were straight-up American Nazis in the late '50s.

Also, I think we have to consider who would have been able to get information to Kasper about any kind of plot. His mail was monitored. There had been a couple of instances when women smuggled letters to him, but there's nothing in the FBI file to suggest that the smuggled letters were from a different crowd than the people regularly sending him letters—the same old assholes who always hung around Kasper.

Carrie Wray was an elector for the NSRP in 1960. Many of Kasper's followers had, indeed, followed him to the NSRP and stayed active in the NSRP when he went to prison. If there was some kind of "Nazi" plot against Looby that Kasper was aware of, the likeliest place to look for the Nazis whose plans Kasper might come to know was in local Klan groups and the remnants of Fred Stroud's church—with the people who had further radicalized and joined the NSRP.

The NSRP gave the impression throughout the early '60s that Kasper was still a vital and important leader of their group. But going through Kasper's FBI file, it seems like he was burning out quickly on racist advocacy. Not that he was softening in his racist stances, but he was really tired of going to jail[195] over and over when very few other racists were. And he was growing very bitter over other racists not making more of an effort to appreciate what he was doing for them. Could he have been attempting to turn on the NSRP?

Let's assume everyone is right: The attack on Looby was aimed at both Looby and King. Nazis (possibly the NSRP) were involved. Looby never had problems with the Klan. His problems were with lawyers and judges and cops. Who does that point to?

Answer: lawyer, would-be King assassin, NSRP leader, organizer of the other bombings here in Nashville, acquaintance of Emmett Carr, and man who was deeply appreciative of his relationship with John Kasper (and thus might try to kill a man Kasper seemed to want dead)—J.B. Stoner.

I know by this point, I'm like Giorgio Tsoukalos on *Ancient Aliens*. He's always saying, "I'm not saying it was aliens, but it was aliens," and here I am, not saying it was J.B. Stoner, but it was J.B. Stoner.

Is there a simpler explanation?

Like I said, in order not to get mired down in bizarre conspiratorial thinking—a risk when you're trying to figure out a conspiracy—I'm trying hard to make sure I keep asking myself for the simplest explanation.

Is it more likely that we had three completely unrelated bombings in a four-year period? That there were three different, unrelated groups of racial terrorists willing to bomb us, but who each stopped after one? Or is it more likely that there was some through line, some person who wasn't in jail and wasn't dead, who would escalate, who was common to all three bombings?

Kasper had written down in his private notes that Stoner was here in August 1957. Considering that Carr was on the verge of chucking his and his Klan's affiliation and joining them up with the Dixie Knights, it seems very likely that Carr knew Stoner. There's no doubt Stoner was behind the JCC bombing, and his shared links to Carr again suggest that Stoner's accomplices probably came from Carr's circle. Everyone—the FBI, the ADL, the Southern Conference on Bombing—knew that Stoner was behind the anti-Semitic attacks in 1957 and 1958. They knew that by May '58.

The facts we know in the Looby bombing are few, but what we have also fits Stoner's methods and mindset.

Was Stoner the bomber? We absolutely cannot say.

But here's an interesting question no one seems to have ever asked: Are there any known racist bombers with ties to Stoner who also had ties to Middle Tennessee during these bombings?

The answer to that question is yes—two.

CHAPTER 10

NASHVILLE'S KNOWN RACIST BOMBERS— ROBERT GENTRY AND GLADYS GIRGENTI

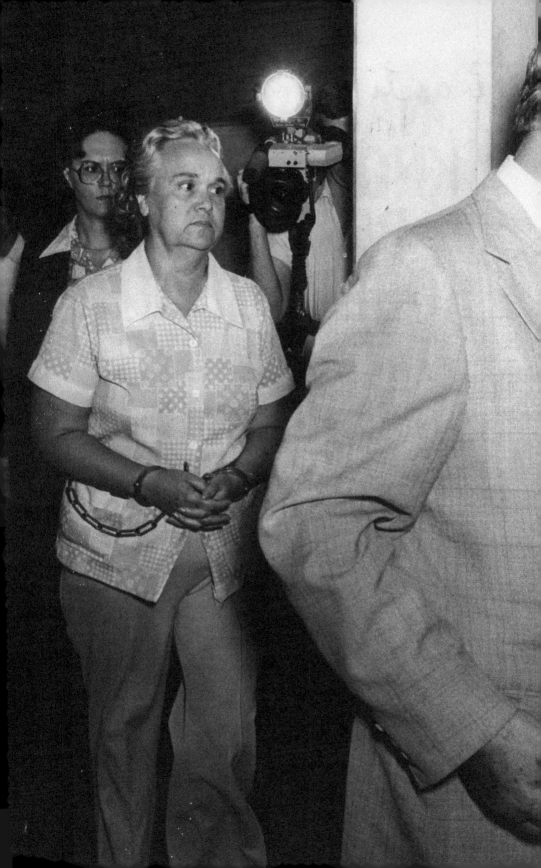

Guide to the Racists in this Chapter

Kenneth Adams Anniston Klan leader

Richard and Robert Bowling Stoner's brother bombing buddies

Charles Boyer Nazi

Johnnie Burnette Member of Bessemer Klavern 20

Emmett Carr Deceased Nashville Klan Leader

David Duke Yes, that David Duke

William Foutch Nazi

David B. Garrett Klansman in the Invisible Empire

Stanley King Grand Titan for Tennessee Invisible Empire

Lynn McCloud Klansman that Girgenti sent to kill Stanley King

James E. Nellums Klansman in the Invisible Empire

Bobby Joe Norton Klansman in the Invisible Empire

Hubert Page Grand Titan of Eastview 13

William Rosecrans Compatriot of Robert Pittman Gentry

Gary Rowe FBI infiltrator of the Klan in Alabama

Robert Shelton Head of the United Klans of America

M.B. Sherrill Pro-Southerner, Klansman, and acquaintance of Emmett Carr

Frederick Smith Alabama Klan treasurer

J.B. Stoner Yes, him again

Ronald Tidwell Birmingham Bomber and member of Eastview 13

Bob Lee Vance KKK leader who was cooperating with the ATF

Bill Wilkinson Head of the Invisible Empire of the KKK and FBI informant

I've been operating under the assumption that this violence has to have a pattern, has to fit a pattern, and, if only we could figure out the pattern, we could use that pattern to recognize the culprits. These bombers did not wake up one day, commit one act of terrorism, then return to their ordinary lives. Whoever did this—I felt certain—it would *make sense* that they were responsible.

So, I started my search for Nashville's unknown racist bombers with Nashville's known racist bombers. Was there anyone in Nashville at the time who we know committed acts like this, if not in Nashville, then maybe somewhere else?

We had two: Gladys Girgenti and Robert Gentry.

Robert Gentry

Let's start with Robert Pittman Gentry.[196] Born in 1938, Gentry's story is that he lived up here peacefully until he went into the Army sometime in the late '50s. He was discharged in 1961, at which point he moved to Florida, became a Klan member (though he didn't exactly say he hadn't been a Klan member here in Tennessee; he pled the Fifth when asked), and then got accused of all kinds of unseemly things that he insisted he did not do. Like bombing the home of Donal Godfrey, the first grader integrating Lackawanna Elementary School in Jacksonville on February 16, 1964.

The lawyer who got him off on those charges?

Yep. J.B. Stoner.

Gentry had also admitted to the House Un-American Activities Committee that he was in Birmingham on September 15, 1963, during the 16th Street Baptist Church bombing, but he never would say why.

His lawyer when he appeared before the HUAC?

Right again. J.B. Stoner.

Right after Godfrey's house was bombed, Gentry came back to his family's home just north of Murfreesboro. Nashville police took him into custody at the behest of the Jacksonville police. According to Nancy Bradford at the *Tennessean*, while Nashville police had him, they questioned him about whether he was involved in the Hattie Cotton bombing or the JCC bombing. Branford did not mention the Looby bombing as being a topic of discussion, most likely because Gentry was in the Army at the time.[197]

In 1966, Gentry told interviewers from the House Un-American Activities Committee that he had joined "the Klan shortly before June 25, 1961. At the time he joined, the Florida Klan was affiliated with the newly formed United Klans, which split from the United Klans and became independent."[198] It's not clear if Gentry meant that he was in a Klan in Florida that was briefly associated with the United Klans or if he was in the "Florida Klan," meaning the Association of Florida Klans. There are two reasons this might be important. One, if Gentry was in the "Florida Klan," then he's a dude from Middle Tennessee tied to one of M.B. Sherrill's groups and it might behoove us to wonder if he might have known another dude from Middle Tennessee, Emmett Carr, who was in another one of Sherrill's groups, and, if so, what the extent of their relationship was, especially before Gentry moved to Florida and became a known racist terrorist. The other is that Stoner was Gentry's lawyer, which, if Gentry was indeed in the "Florida Klan," shows more links between Stoner and Carr's circle.

I had initially dismissed Gentry as a suspect in our bombings because he was so young—19 at the time of the Hattie Cotton bombing, 22 at the time of the Looby bombing. That was before I learned that Emmett Carr was trying to organize white teenagers to terrorize students at Father Ryan. Gentry was young during our bombings, but not younger than other people participating in and being recruited for racial violence in Nashville.

I wanted to know how early Gentry had been on the FBI's radar and I wanted to know if they ever suspected him in any of our bombings. I did a FOIA request. They told me his file had been destroyed on May 6, 2005, four years before he died.[199]

Let that sink in. A bomber who tried to kill two people in Florida,[200] who was admittedly in Birmingham before one of its most infamous bombings, and who was in Nashville for two of our bombings, and the FBI suddenly decided—years after his activities, but before he died— that they didn't need a file on him anymore. A known racist terrorist with strong ties to other racist terrorists.

That's weird.

Here's a thing that may or may not be relevant. Most living people's identities are redacted from FBI files available to the public. Sometimes, like in the case of the Wrays, the FBI will leave enough identifying information that you can make a good guess who's being referred to, but sometimes not. Also, with rare exception, you can't get someone's FBI file unless they're dead. Once a person dies, though, their identities normally don't have to remain redacted, and if your FOIA request reasoning is sound, you can get the FBI files of dead people. The simplest explanation for the destruction of Gentry's file is that there was some piece of information or some identity that the FBI never wanted known. So, instead of letting that file become available after Gentry's death, they just got rid of it (unless they're lying, like they lied with the Looby bombing file).

That's . . . not cool, to put it mildly, and it really hampers our ability to understand Gentry's role in racial terrorism in the South in general and whether and how he was involved in Nashville. It's also problematic for us as we try to understand what happened in Nashville because, as full of shit as Gentry apparently was, the House Un-American Activities Committee investigators learned a lot of interesting things about him and his buddies.

The HUAC investigator wrote that Gentry told him that J.B. Stoner was "capable of planning acts of violence; expert in demolitions; although alleged to have no affiliations with the Klan, in fact belongs to a Jacksonville (Fla.) Klavern and carries a Klan passport, which affords him access to and entry into any Klavern of the Klan; Subject's trial lawyer."[201]

HUAC investigator Philip Manuel also managed to track down FBI informant Gary Rowe in a hotel in Los Angeles. Manuel recounted a lot of disturbing stuff Rowe told him, but here are the paragraphs full of names familiar to readers of this book:

Rowe identified two former Klansmen and former state officers of the Alabama Realm as two violent individuals whom Rowe is positive were participants in the Birmingham bombings. These individuals are Ronald Tidwell and Hubert Page. Rowe stated further that at the time of the bombings J.B. Stoner and his associates were very close to Robert Shelton and during his life, Matthew Murphy was very close to J.B. Stoner. Murphy and Stoner along with members of the UKA in Alabama, namely Tidwell, Page, Johnnie Burnette and possibly Frederick Smith, along with members of the NSRP especially Robert Bolling, were described by Rowe as the guilty parties in the Birmingham Church bombings. Rowe claims he has no direct knowledge in this regard but claims that those inside the Klan know those persons to be the guilty parties.

With further regard to Murphy, Rowe claimed that the late Klan attorney always maintained good contact with Stoner and the NSRP, and Rowe believes that Murphy was a constant cause of violence in the entire South. Rowe had no direct knowledge of where the Klan obtains their dynamite, but he knows that Kenneth Adams had an excellent contact at the Anniston Ordnance Depot where it was rumored that the Klan was obtaining explosives. Further at the time of the Birmingham bombings there was, according to Rowe, excellent relations between Ken Adams, Matt Murphy, Robert Shelton, J.B. Stoner and certain members of the Dixie Klan in Tennessee. When questioned by this Investigator, Rowe stated that he had also heard the name Robert Gentry in connection with the Birmingham bombings, and he seemed to recall that Gentry was on a state Klokan Committee. (This statement of Rowe's seemingly lends credence to a prior statement of Gentry made to this

Investigator and Investigator McConnon with respect to
his involvement with acts of violence.)[202]

Okay, let's pick through the information Rowe provided. Ronald
Tidwell was, indeed, known to be a bomber in Birmingham. He was
said to be behind the bombing of the home of Birmingham civil rights
attorney Arthur Shores's house in 1963. He was a member of the infamous Eastview 13 Klavern. Hubert Page was the Grand Titan of
Eastview 13. Johnnie Burnette was a member of the Bessemer Klavern
20, and he allegedly once pulled a gun on FBI agents who were tailing
him. Frederick Smith was an Alabama Klan treasurer. Robert Bolling is
obviously Robert Bowling, but I suspect, based on what we know, that
Rowe got the two brothers confused and he's referring to Richard, who
did seem to have bombed a church in Birmingham. We've already met
Kenneth Adams. These are all, indeed, violent dudes.

The thing is that Rowe's not exactly trustworthy. We don't know if
he's conveniently leaving his own name off the list here (I suspect he is),
but he does seem to know things that other people hadn't put together
yet—namely that the flow of dynamite into Alabama had something
to do with the Dixie Klan in Tennessee and Kenneth Adams. He also
knows a Bowling brother involved in church bombings in Birmingham.
That wasn't common knowledge. So, when he throws Gentry into the
mix here, I think we have to consider that he's telling the truth.

Based on how Investigator Manuel is careful to use "bombings" and
not "bombing," I think we need to be careful, too, and not jump to
the conclusion that, of course, Gentry must have been involved in the
16th Street Baptist Church bombing. There were plenty of bombings he
could have been involved in. But which ones?

Investigators had been able to coax a lot out of Gentry.

Subject also admitted to this Investigator, under the previous stated stipulations, that he was the trigger man in the

Tamiami case. He stated that he had deliberately missed the intended victim, as he had never killed a man in his lifetime. Subject, under further questioning, stated he was able to accomplish this deliberate miss at high speed, because he is an expert marksman, since a child has had guns for hunting, and holds a National Rifle Association instructor's certificate. His excuse to the Klan for missing, he said, was that the victims' car was station wagon and he had fired at the second set of windows in passing the vehicle, thus the middle windows, behind the driver, rather than the front windows. He states that the Klan believed this story.

Another admission subject made to this Investigator (under same stipulations) was that he <u>has</u> committed some of the Klan bombings of which he is not suspected and possibly one of which he is. Also, he claims to have knowledge of those persons who have committed bombing of which he is suspected, but of which he is innocent. He declined to name these people and the locations and dates of the bombings.[203]

The "Tamiami case" was when Gentry and William Rosecrans (who was on the Godfrey bombing crew with Gentry) opened fire on Tamiami Freightways employee Eugene Striggler, a Black man. Other than the Godfrey bombing, I haven't found any indication of any other bombings where he was named as a suspect. Granted, the FBI destroyed his file, but still, if he was a serious suspect in other bombings, you'd think his name would have come up in other files. Much as I'm not sure what conclusions we should draw about Gentry, the HUAC investigators also seemed confused by him. The investigator said Gentry was "bent toward dramatics," but he still recommended someone look further into his stories.

We don't know if anyone did.

Gladys Baker Carney Girgenti

We have a much better understanding of Gladys Girgenti's place in the racist paradigm. It's highly unlikely that Girgenti was involved in these early Nashville bombings. By the late '50s she was living outside of Detroit and had small children at home, and no woman was ever seen in the vicinity of our bombings. But the reason I want to discuss Girgenti is that she is a known racist bomber with ties to J.B. Stoner who lives in Nashville and grew up here. If there is anyone in a position to know who bombed us, or to at least have heard plausible gossip, it's her.

Gladys Girgenti was born Gladys Baker in 1930 up in Bordeaux. Yes, near where possible Klan member and definite FBI informant Thomas Norvell lived, and near where the Whites Creek suspected bombers lived. She married for the first time at fifteen to a thirty-seven-year-old man, Charles Carney, a neighbor.

After that marriage broke up, she married Nick Girgenti, a small-time criminal from Michigan. By the mid-50s, she had moved north. Most people seem to have forgotten that she started life here.

When she moved back to Nashville in 1971, her few appearances in the local media before she went full Klan Granny told the sad tale of a Detroit widow who had moved here after her house was firebombed in a race riot, the stress of which killed her husband.

These stories were about her kids being involved in some school program or another, so it's probably not surprising that no one fact-checked Girgenti's claims, but there were no race riots in Detroit or the surrounding area in 1971. No one's house had been firebombed.

There was, however, a firebombing: the Klan had firebombed the Pontiac school buses. In reading through the coverage of the Pontiac school busing situation, we find story after story of white women standing in front of buses, hurling rocks and hateful words at the vehicles. Yet, when the bombers were arrested, they were all men.

There is an element of sexism that runs through the events of this book that I have been assuming you probably already picked up on. But if part of my purpose is to try to understand why we don't know who did these things to us, then I think I need to state it explicitly. Women were a fundamental and crucial part of the segregationist movement in Nashville (and throughout the country). They headed up the protests at schools. They sheltered and cared for John Kasper when everyone else had had it with him. They called in death threats and bomb threats. And yet, even though they're standing there in plain sight doing terrible things, history has often overlooked them.

You'd like to think that when the *Tennessean* ran into Gladys Girgenti decked out in her full Klan regalia, when she and other Klan leaders went to the state capitol and posed with the bust of Nathan Bedford Forrest in October 1980, they'd have been like "Who is this woman and what has she been up to?" Instead, they treated her as a joke.

After she moved back to Nashville, Girgenti spent the '70s becoming more open about her Klan affiliation. She sent robed Klansmen to her son's school to lecture him when he got in trouble, for instance. By the end of the '70s, she wanted to be a Klan leader. After all, according to her, she was a third-generation Klan member who had been in the Klan for thirty years.[204] But sadly for Girgenti, there wasn't a Feminism for Evil movement to help her realize her full potential, and like so many women before her, both good and bad, she got shunted off to lead the children's group.

But wait! When was the last time we had a confusing and public meltdown of the Klan in this story? Back when Emmett Carr took his Klan and joined up with the Dixie Knights, who may have been part of the Confederate Underground, I think? Or maybe when the Dixie Knights got embroiled in their stupid copyright case?

Well, here's another one.

Girgenti had been in the Knights of the Ku Klux Klan, David Duke's group in the 1970s. But for some reason no one seems to know, she had joined up with Bill Wilkinson's Invisible Empire of the KKK by the end of the decade.[205] The Knights of the Ku Klux Klan and the Invisible Empire of the KKK were bitter enemies. The Grand Titan for Tennessee in the Invisible Empire was a guy named Stanley King, who made Girgenti the state director of the Klan Youth Corps. King told the media that he fired Girgenti on April 17, 1981. He said he fired her because she'd "taken some Klansmen and weapons and went to Murfreesboro to intervene in a fight between some blacks and whites, and I found out about it."[206] He also believed that right before he fired her, Girgenti sent her friend and fellow Klansman, Lynn McCloud, to try to kill him. Which seems like a pretty good reason all on its own to fire someone, but what do I know?

McCloud never denied assaulting King, but claimed he did it because King assaulted Mrs. McCloud. They took their bickering to the media. Meanwhile, in the spring of 1981, Girgenti was starting a new clandestine terrorist organization—the Confederate Vigilantes.

King ran to the media repeatedly to tattle on Girgenti. He told reporters that Girgenti and her husband were active members of the United Klans of America[207] until its leader, Robert Shelton[208] went to prison. King said Girgenti was a member of the National States Rights Party[209] and that she "maintains a five-drawer filing cabinet in her home, filled with letters, documents, charters and other papers[210] collected during a 20-year[211] career in these and other groups."[212] King also told the *Tennessean* that Girgenti had been involved in the Pontiac bombing.[213]

So, here's Girgenti, in the Confederate Vigilantes, which sounds very close to J.B. Stoner's Confederate Underground. She's allegedly a member of the NSRP, Stoner's political group. And she's old buddies with Robert Shelton, another one of Stoner's pals.

What was it Stoner's Confederate Underground promised us back in 1958? "We have just dynamited the Jewish Community Center. Next will be The Temple."

In 1981, Gladys Girgenti tried to bomb The Temple in Belle Meade, a ritzy suburb just west of Nashville.

That spring, Girgenti put together a terror cell—herself, KKK leader

Bob Lee Vance (who it turns out was cooperating with the Bureau of Alcohol, Tobacco, and Firearms), Nazi party member William Foutch, Nazi party member and steel guitarist Charles Boyer, Bobby Joe Norton of the Invisible Empire, James E. Nellums of the Invisible Empire, and David B. Garrett of the Invisible Empire.[214] As you'd expect from someone tied to Stoner, she had a whole huge plan to basically go to war with Nashville's Jewish community. She was going to bomb The Temple, the WSM tower, which she believed was owned by Jews, and various Jewish-owned pawn shops around town.

The reason Gladys failed is that when Vance went home to "make the bomb," he actually got a dud from the ATF. Girgenti went to prison.

I think it's unlikely that Gladys would have ratted on fellow bombers by the time she was on trial for the attempted Temple bombing. But back when she was pissed enough at Stanley King to supposedly try to kill him? Back when she was being publicly kicked out of the Klan? She might have spilled the beans on all she knew about local bombings and bombers. That was a real missed opportunity.

Another missed opportunity was not getting a search warrant and confiscating the Klan files she'd compiled. But this didn't happen, I think, because no one had put together that Gladys wasn't *from* Detroit. At least judging by the media coverage, no one realized she grew up in Nashville, that the Klan history she would have known well was our Klan history. Which is frustrating, since she, herself, told the *Tennessean* that her son was a fourth-generation Klan member, thus putting one or both of her parents in the Klan in Nashville, where they lived, and same with at least one of her grandparents. Who knows how far back her information on the Klan in Davidson County might have gone?

J.B. Stoner was finally convicted of bombing Rev. Fred Shuttlesworth's Bethel Baptist Church in Birmingham in 1980. In "things it would have been nice to know"—Did Girgenti decide to finish in '81 what Stoner had started in '58, targeting our Jewish community in retaliation for or in honor of Stoner, who looked like he was finally going to prison? How well did she know Stoner? Did Stoner give her the idea to bomb The Temple? Did she know who the earlier bombers were? If she didn't, who did she think could have done it?

Gladys Girgenti likely had the answer to all these questions, served up to us on a silver platter of bad decisions on her part. For whatever reason, Nashville didn't take the opportunity to ask.

So, I went to talk to her. To ask her myself. And I really liked her.

The Visit

I don't know what to make of that, but it seems like an important component of trying to understand why these bombings weren't solved. I've never been to a Klan rally. I don't, as far as I know, know any people who deliberately set out to hurt or scare others. And I'd never talked to a convicted terrorist before.

She was funny and charming. She had big round eyes that made her either seem perpetually surprised or perpetually delighted. She lived in a multi-story assisted care facility over in Madison, about fifteen minutes from my house. The place was spotlessly clean, but old. The hallway to her apartment was poorly lit and there were pipes overhead. It smelled like people used to smoke there a lot but hadn't in a long time.

Her apartment was small and cheery. She had a large window she sat beside, and sunlight flooded the place. She had an amazing, crocheted afghan draped over her loveseat. She had a cat, who seemed about a third longer than a cat normally should be.

Her son told me the cat would bite, but once he got some head pats and sniffed my bag, he settled in on the cat tree and paid us no mind. Once her son seemed to ascertain that I was harmless, he went upstairs to his apartment.

And there I was, alone with one of two known racist bombers to come out of Nashville.

She was very matter of fact about things. She launched right into telling me about Klan rallies and who she knew and how she had met them—J.B. Stoner, who she met through Ed Fields; Robert Shelton; David Duke. Folks I had only read about in books or, in Duke's case, seen on TV. They were her friends and she spoke about them with the fondness you have for friends.

She didn't use any racial slurs or launch into any lectures about the evils of the Jewish people. And, honestly, I didn't ask her about her beliefs. I wanted to focus on getting my questions answered.

But it's easy to see how, as a white bystander, you could seduce yourself into believing that a white supremacist like Girgenti isn't "that bad." Yes, she was talking about the Klan and talking about people who did really terrible stuff, but she was talking about it in the matter-of-fact way you might talk about your Sunday school class or the Rotary Club. The signals that tell you that this is dangerous aren't present or they're muted.

So, as I was sitting there, listening to this funny, charming woman tell these stories that were sometimes hilarious, sometimes sad, I could feel something happening to me, mentally. I came into that apartment knowing some really terrible things about Girgenti and having heard credible rumors of worse. And I had been warned not to underestimate her, that she was very smart. In other words, I was as prepared as I could be.

And I still felt this overwhelming urge to just go along with what she was saying. Not just for the sake of the interview—that much I could understand and not fret over—but for the sake of our rapport, for the psychological reward of having this woman I found funny and charming finding me funny and charming.

That scared and scares me.

Listening to her stories, it's very easy to see that the FBI took the wrong approach to her, over and over. It seems like they thought the button to push with her was her family. After talking to her, I agree that her family is very important to her. But threatening them never caused Girgenti to break and admit to crimes. It just strengthened her resolve to not cooperate.

Not that I got much farther. She wasn't in town for my bombings. She didn't want to tell me anything she, herself, didn't know as a fact. So, no gossip on who it might have been. But I definitely got the impression that there was gossip she had heard. I just didn't have the skills as an interviewer to overcome her reluctance to gossip with me.

But this was my first time interviewing a person with known ties to a terrorist network. Presumably the FBI does that all the time.

I had told a handful of people where I was going and that they should call the police if I didn't get back in touch with them by dinner. I was done long before dinner. I did my best to make sure I wasn't followed home. I felt stupid for worrying about it.

I couldn't sleep though. I found excuses not to go to my room, and then when I realized I was just sitting on the couch staring at nothing, I forced myself to go to bed. And then I lay there, in the dark, in the quiet, afraid I would hear someone in the house with me. I had this thought that I should not have met her, that I should not have let her know what I look like or given her my phone number. That, obviously, anyone with dangerous friends could still be dangerous.

But the thing that kept me up was that I wasn't having these thoughts until almost eight hours after I'd interviewed her.

The thing I'm struggling to put into words is how far down the path I was before my gut instinct to be afraid kicked in. I had already done the interview. I was already home. I had already assured everyone I had jokingly asked to avenge me if I was murdered that I was fine.

But while I was with her, I wanted her to like me. And I had years of research about her and her awful friends in my head.

There's something psychological going on here that seems important, if we want to truly understand how we're in this situation. Something about how your brain will push you to find connections and common ground with people, to find ways and reasons for you to like each other and see each other as being on the same side, even temporarily.

I keep thinking about that lyric from They Might be Giants, "Can't shake the Devil's hand and say you're only kidding." You become like the people you like. You can't have a racist friend and not be, at some level, okay with her racism.

And yet, if that person is charming and funny, smart and insightful, isn't it so very tempting to overlook her flaws?

No, no. Different than tempting. I would not have been tempted to overlook Gladys Girgenti's flaws.

This is something deeper and more fundamental to how white supremacy works, I think. Something so deeply ingrained in me, so deeply trained, let me like her and suppressed the warning signals I should have been getting—and obviously was getting, if my terror that night was any indication.

I came as prepared as I could be. I was raised to try very hard to not be a racist asshole by people who have tried very hard their whole lives to not be racist assholes, and I still had that psychological reaction to her. And I didn't even recognize that's what was happening until way later.

That's deeply troubling to me. But it also feels to me crucial for understanding why these bombings were never solved. I think there's a very good chance that the white people in a position to investigate these bombings had the same bad training or psychological shortcoming or whatever this is as me. I think a crucial component of why these bombings were never solved is that the people who could have solved them were not seeing them for the huge red flags that they were. And I have to allow that one of the reasons I haven't completely solved them is that I also am not picking up on obvious cues and am, instead, reacting in ways that work to thwart my own goals.

Like I said, she didn't know anything for certain about my bombings and she didn't want to gossip, but the interview did give me some important background. I asked her why so many Klan members were FBI informants, and she told me it was for the money. Being an FBI informant, it seemed to me, was, in Girgenti's world, like working as a stripper to get through college. It wasn't the kind of thing you wanted to brag about in polite company, but the money was good, and people understood why you would do it.

Until this moment, my understanding of FBI informants came from the movies. I assumed it was really dangerous, and if you were discovered, chances were you would be killed. But what Girgenti was telling me seemed very different—that being an FBI informant was more often just a character flaw, and a flaw most of your peers would overlook.

This is my speculation, based on my conversation with Girgenti, but I think, with the widespread understanding of just how much the money from the FBI might mean and how easily the FBI could jack you up if you didn't cooperate, the sin was not in being an informant. The sin was in being a useful informant.

If you could talk to the FBI and tell them things they either already knew or could easily find out, then, okay, it's distasteful but everyone gets it. But if you talk to the FBI and tell them things they couldn't otherwise know, or if you agreed to testify against your fellow racists, that was when you were putting your butt in peril.

And one of the reasons I think this is the dynamic at play is that I talked to Girgenti for a long time and got what I thought was a bunch of new information about her. But later, after I'd had time to go through my notes and revisit old newspaper articles, I realized she told me very little I hadn't either already read or couldn't have inferred from what I'd read. If that's how informants were supposed to handle the FBI, then being that kind of FBI informant wouldn't matter much at all.

She and I found common ground in our mutual frustration with the FBI, though her frustration was that they kept raiding her house and once sent her to prison. Mine was just that they weren't very forthcoming.

Still, it was easy to see how Girgenti and Stoner could be friends, not just because of their shared hatred of Black people and Jewish people, but because of their audacity in the face of the FBI. I told Girgenti how Stoner had figured out he was being tailed by the FBI and reported their own license plate numbers back to them.

She, in turn, told me about a time when the FBI put a car on her house while David Duke was staying with her and how, before bed, she brought out coffee to the agents in the car and asked them if they wanted her to wake them up in the morning so they wouldn't miss the opportunity to follow her or if they had their own alarm.

"I tell you what," she said to me, "I have more respect for the Klan or the lowest drug dealer than I have for the FBI. Get that on the record." I assured her I would. "They are the lowest people, and, like I say, if you want justice, look in the dictionary," insinuating that the dictionary was the only place justice could be found.[215]

She was still pissed at Stanley King for saying she was dangerous during her trial in 1983. She asked me if I was afraid of her. I didn't want to say yes, but I didn't want to lie to her, so I told her I was. I couldn't tell if she was flattered or not.

As I was leaving, she assured me that I didn't have to be afraid of her. "I'm not going to bomb you."

I have to admit, hearing out loud that the possibility had been on the table didn't leave me feeling particularly safe. But I did laugh, not just out of discomfort, but because the delivery was perfect. I kid about the Evil Feminism bit, but we're probably really lucky as a city and a country that Gladys was never given the opportunity to live up to her full potential.

The Ethics of It

As I'm writing this book, media critics are discussing the ethics of interviewing white supremacists—not just whether you should do it, but how you do it so as not to normalize or elevate their beliefs. A point the critics keep raising—and rightly so—is that the neutral ways of interviewing subjects give a kind of credence to the beliefs of the white supremacists. If one side of the "debate" thinks that Black people are human beings and the other side of the "debate" insists that they are apes, even holding the debate makes it seem like these are two reasonable positions in dialogue with each other. A thing good people can disagree on.

If one side believes that Jewish people are a Semitic people whose beliefs and practices coalesced in the Middle East a few millennia ago, the reasonable other side of the debate should be about how many millennia ago or if we should say "a Semitic people" or "Semitic peoples" or if that term is even relevant—not about whether Jewish people are actually the descendants of Eve and the serpent in the Garden and thus controlling the city through the WSM tower.

I'm not trying to let myself off the hook or put myself on the hook for interviewing Girgenti and liking her. I don't think I'm doing anything wrong by giving you a sense of how funny she was.

But I want to be clear that this is a trap. The white supremacist's ability to be charming and willing to talk is supposed to make other white people find them helpful and cooperative. Nice, even. To make them seem like reasonable people with whom I just have a difference of opinion. It's supposed to lure other white people into a sense of normalcy so they can use the other white people to disseminate their stupid, evil ideas.

I suspect one of the reasons Girgenti still loathes the FBI is that the FBI didn't seem to be willing to treat her like they might just disagree on a few things, but didn't they have a lot of common ground?

In a way, this level of white supremacy is like a cult. We seem to understand the dangers of putting religious cult leaders on TV and letting them ramble on mostly unchallenged about their beliefs. We don't yet seem to have developed the same sense about white supremacists.

Anyway, long diatribe short: white supremacists can be likable, especially if you're also white. But if we decide that our liking someone means they must have some core goodness we could appeal to if only we treated them with respect, we're not that much different from the crowds of people in Nashville who went out to hear John Kasper and didn't realize he was escalating, because they believed he was only talking about hurting Black people, not white people too.

CHAPTER 11

INFORMED SPECULATION

Guide to the Racists in this Chapter

Robert Bromley Rider's tenant
Frank Houchin Informant for the state fire marshal and the FBI
Charles Reed Kasper's friend and FBI informant
Wallace Rider Garage owner who bragged about Hattie Cotton bombing
Lloyd Shadrick Nashville Klansman and Charles Reed's neighbor
Slim Thompson Rider's Alabama friend

I feel pretty confident that we know what happened with the Hattie Cotton bombing and the JCC bombing. We've spent a lot of time looking at J.B. Stoner and what brought him to Nashville. I think he came to town at the behest of Kasper, perhaps with some buddies from the Chattanooga Klan, in August 1957. Possibly, he even brought the explosives.

Kasper then took the explosives and, with the help of Charles Reed, hid them in the abandoned house on Delta Avenue. This would have been just a few blocks away from Wallace Rider's garage at 17th and McDaniel. If Frank Houchin's account is right, then Wallace Rider, Slim Thompson, and some unnamed guy then went and bombed Hattie Cotton. I'm biased, but I believe that unnamed man was likely J.B. Stoner.

We now know that the only real suspects police had for the JCC bombing that make any sense were Rider again, and his tenant, Robert Bromley. We also know that Stoner flew into town that day, so it seems likely that he was involved in this bombing as well.

We know that a man from Alabama contacted the FBI about John Kasper trying to hire him to kill Looby, and we know that the FBI disregarded it. However, we also know that Slim Thompson lived in Alabama and was regularly in Nashville and the Klan talked about him almost like he was some kind of Klan hitman. Was he this man from Alabama who contacted the FBI?

If there's one thing I would like to impress upon you, it's just how silent all the FBI files I reviewed are when it comes to April 1960. With the exception of them noting that they got a call from Kasper but farted around instead of talking to him, it's hard to piece together anything they might have been doing in April, when someone tried to assassinate a sitting US politician.

More so, everyone already knew that the Nashville police department seemed to have lost interest in solving the case days after the bombing—but now we also know that it was initially so important to Mayor West that he helped conduct the investigation himself.

We have a puzzle with quite a few missing pieces. But we've discussed other times when evidence suggests the FBI shut down investigations to protect informants. It seems plausible that the Looby bombing investigation was also shut down to protect an informant.

But let's speculate why the Hattie Cotton bombing, at the least, wasn't ever prosecuted. There is a witness, Frank Houchin, who heard directly from Wallace Rider that Rider bombed the school. That bit of information wasn't even worth an arrest of Rider, to see what might shake loose under interrogation? Strange.

But imagine that you're Rider's attorney and Houchin is the State's star witness. Houchin is a known criminal who was somehow wrapped up in the Jesse Wilson truck scales bombing mess. If Wilson really was guilty of trying to kill a bunch of people here and in Chattanooga, why was his sentence so short? Or did the short sentence reflect some doubt by the judge of Wilson's guilt? Remember, part of Wilson's defense was that Houchin and his friend were framing and blackmailing him. If I'm Rider's attorney, the very first thing I'd get Houchin to admit on the stand was that, of him and Rider, he was the one associated with a known bomber and that, though Rider had been in and out of trouble over the years, never for things as serious as Houchin had been. Plus, way back in his younger days, Houchin had been in on a scheme with a corrupt cop. Houchin had the contacts and the experience to frame someone.

Did Nashville fail to convict anyone for the Hattie Cotton bombing because their main witness was too compromised? And same for the

JCC bombing? Plus, we now know that Houchin was an informant for both the fire marshal and the FBI. This adds some interesting shading to the Looby bombing. If the circumstances surrounding the abrupt end to the Looby investigations at a local, state, and federal level suggest that an informant committed the bombing and needed to be protected, there is only one informant I've come across who knew bombers in Nashville and who both state and federal officials might have wanted to keep safe, even if they suspected he was involved—Frank Houchin.

Still, let's be clear, these are a lot of dots very close together that look like they'd make a Frank-Houchin-and-friends-looking pattern if connected—but they are not connected. The biggest missed connection is that we simply don't know why every investigation into the Looby bombing seems to have fizzled out by the end of April 1960. My theory is that it was because the bomber was someone authorities did not want revealed. My opinion is that the most likely reason is that this person was an informant. But we don't know that for sure.

I heard a story about Gary Rowe, the Birmingham Klan infiltrator for the FBI. I don't know how true it is, but it goes like this. Supposedly, Gary Rowe was set to testify in one of the 16th Street Baptist Church bombing cases and when the defense lawyer heard this, he started laughing. The prosecutors demanded an explanation, but the defense lawyer kept laughing and said, "No, no, go ahead and call him." Then, allegedly, the prosecution called the FBI and asked why a defense lawyer in this case would be laughing about Rowe testifying and whatever happened during that phone call resulted in Rowe never being called.

I bring this up, not because it's factual, but for its folkloric value. What the story tells us is that people believed that the FBI had people so deeply embedded in these situations that it may have hampered investigations and derailed prosecutions, because no one knew just how involved the FBI's informants were in the crimes and no one wanted to risk the informants testifying under oath to that involvement.

We could have in Frank Houchins a Gary Rowe problem. Did he

know all this stuff because he was a witness or did he know it because he was a participant? And what would it have done to the city, and possibly the nation, for us to learn in 1960 that an FBI informant was involved in some way in an assassination attempt on a sitting U.S. politician? You think JFK conspiracy theories are wild now? Imagine if conspiracy theorists had the precedent of Houchins and Looby to fuel them?

I also feel very good about my theory that J.B. Stoner was intimately involved with at least the first two bombings, which makes it very likely that he was involved with the third. But all we have connecting Stoner to the bombings are men with a proven track record of shading the truth—Bull Connor, John Kasper, and Stoner himself. I'm all in on the "Stoner was behind it" theory, but you could have reasonable doubts.

Here's the thing, though. The FBI had a file on Looby that it started long before the bombing. The FBI also had informants in Nashville and (in April 1960, when the bombing occurred) good reason to believe that John Kasper was ready to start telling what he knew. They also knew that Kasper had tried to hire a hit man to kill Looby the year before. So, they knew there was a target on Looby's back. And then they lied about having the Looby bombing file.

All this leads me to the conclusion that either the FBI knew racists had a plot against Looby and they let it happen, or, for all their agents and informants, they didn't have good enough connections in Nashville and failed at their job, which means they let it happen, but with a slightly different inflection.

The only reason the FBI would be, to quote Looby, so "busy looking the other way" is if it was going to cause them problems to look squarely at the crime.

We may never know exactly what happened with these bombings and I hope that outrages you. Our history has been deliberately hidden from us by people who don't even bother to justify it.

But I also hope you will go by 2012 Meharry Boulevard if you get the chance and see the house that Looby built after his home was

Photo by Betsy Phillips

destroyed. The whole house is brick, with small windows. The front wall juts outward like the bow of a ship so that, if another bomb is thrown at the house, it will be harder to knock it down. Inside is a bomb shelter.

Z. Alexander Looby did so much to provide Black Tennesseans some shelter under the law and yet, when he most needed it, he found none. This house—this bunker—is a testament to the way law enforcement failed him and how he picked up and went on anyway.

239

A CITY CAN'T HEAL IF IT CAN'T SAY WHAT HAPPENED

I CAME TO
NASHVILLE
NOT TO BRING INSPIRATION,
BUT TO GAIN INSPIRATION FROM
THE GREAT MOVEMENT
THAT HAS TAKEN PLACE
IN THIS COMMUNITY

MARTIN LUTHER KING, JR.

In September 2017, I spoke before the Unsolved Civil Rights Crimes Special Committee of the Tennessee State Legislature about these bombings. Members of Elbert Williams's family—the NAACP officer lynched in Brownsville, Tennessee, in the 1940s—were also there to speak, as were family members of other NAACP workers who had been terrorized into leaving their homes.

Over the course of the morning, we heard stories about people beaten, killed, bombed, and threatened; families whisked away in the middle of the night; farms and businesses confiscated by white mobs. And yet, when each person testifying was asked what he or she was hoping would come out of this, what they all wanted was for the truth to be told, for what happened to their families to be fully investigated and acknowledged. They didn't ask for things stolen to be returned or for aid in suing towns where it could be proved that law enforcement was involved in these criminal acts.[216] They just wanted the truth to be told.

But it's stuck with me in the years since then that the people who made the effort to come all this way from Michigan or New York or wherever their families had fled to were asking for one thing: the truth.

It's such a simple thing. Just say what happened and stop bullshitting about it.

A number of people have heard about this project and asked me, in an accusatory tone, "What do you expect to come from this? Do you really think anyone is still alive or that there's enough evidence to put them in jail?"

At the time I'm writing this, J.B. Stoner's dear friend, Ed Fields, is still alive and living in Marietta, Georgia. Every time you hear of some law enforcement agency reopening a civil rights case from this era and then closing it again because there's supposedly no one who knows anything left to talk to, keep that in mind. People are still alive. Specifically, Ed Fields, who was in the middle of all of this evil and in a position to know who did what to whom, is still alive. Fields may not be in any shape to talk to people now, but ten years ago? Twenty?

But also, no, even if some people involved in these bombings are still alive, I don't expect them to go to jail. As Gladys Girgenti said, if you want justice, look in the dictionary. That's the only place you're going to find it in most cases.

But we can tell the truth. Maybe not the whole truth, because we don't know it. But we can be as honest as we can about what happened here. And we can let the truth become the story we tell about that time as a city.

Even though we can't say with certainty who bombed us, looking closer at the bombings of Hattie Cotton School, the Jewish Community Center, and Z. Alexander Looby's house shows us a much different story of Nashville's integration era than the one we've been told.

We've set ourselves up as the peaceful Southern city who did integration right. Unspoken in that is "unlike Birmingham." But we're not so unlike Birmingham, it turns out. We were actually, it seems, closely linked to Birmingham, not only through the bravery of the civil rights activists who organized and trained here and went to Birmingham in the 1960s, but also through the activities of the racists who organized here and took what they'd learned here and spread it throughout the South.

Nashville was the precursor to so much American tragedy in the 1960s.

The Shadow Nashville Cast on the 1960s

Some ways we shaped that terrible decade are, at this distance, unknowable. Did J.B. Stoner put together the terror cell that bombed Hattie Cotton and that's why it looks so much like the cells we know he put together later on? Or did he come here, see that cell, and take a lesson from it?

Also, I think we have to guess, even though we don't know, that Stoner was paying very close attention to how the Tennessee Federation for Constitutional Government swooped in, first in Clinton and then in

Nashville, to make sure that arrested Klansmen had the monetary support of rich racists and also a high profile public advocate. After Nashville, Stoner often made himself that high profile advocate. Throughout the 1960s, rich racists put a bounty on Martin Luther King Jr.'s head and funneled that money to working class racists willing to make attempts on King's life. Even now, in the last couple of years, the League of the South has provided financial and logistical support to more actively violent racists.[217] That financial model of terrorist funding, at least this iteration of it, was first worked out here in Nashville.

Also, this better understanding of the Looby timeline and the actions of the police in the wake of the bombing tell us that the Looby bombing deserves to be understood not only as the culmination of a series of escalating attacks on school integrationists, but also as an early attack on people working with Dr. King, not so different from what was happening in Birmingham and other Southern cities at the time. Plus, we can better understand—or perhaps understand for the first time—that the bombing of the JCC wasn't some anomaly but was part of a coordinated attack on Jewish institutions throughout the South. We can also now see how Gladys Girgenti's later attempted bombing of The Temple in Belle Meade fits into this history.

And then there's the plot against Looby that the FBI was informed of, where they decided the informant they had was nuts, so they didn't bother to tell Looby or anyone else in Nashville, that someone might be gunning for him.

This is so similar to what the FBI did to King, where they just failed to warn him about plots against him that they knew were at least semi-plausible. It's likely that we're seeing an early example of the FBI's approach to "protecting" civil rights leaders.

A Little More on Chattanooga

The targets of racist bombings in Chattanooga were very similar to our targets. On July 24, 1957, Black Chattanooga civil rights attorney R.H. Craig's house was bombed. According to the United Press story, "the porch and front door were splintered and a window shattered by the blast."[218] Z. Alexander Looby was, of course, a Black Nashville civil rights attorney. On January 19, 1958, Chattanooga's Howard High School was bombed. We had the bombing of Hattie Cotton School the fall before. On January 27, 1958, Chattanooga's recently integrated YWCA was bombed. Later that same year, we had a religiously affiliated community center bombed, the JCC. Also, like in Nashville, no bombings were carried out in 1959, but they resumed in 1960.

If I'm right about the Looby bombing being related to the presence of Rev. Martin Luther King Jr. in Nashville, then this suggests another possible tie between Nashville and Chattanooga—people willing to do violence to King. In 1960, the number of known people either trying to kill King or expressing a willingness to kill King was very small: whoever bombed his home in Montgomery during the bus boycott in 1955, and Izola Curry in 1958.

We have to think racist leaders were hoping that someone would succeed in killing King. But people making actual plans? We know that J.B. Stoner expressed a willingness to murder King to a Birmingham police department informant in 1958. Stoner claimed that informant offered to pay him; the informant claimed Stoner offered a monetary amount he'd be willing to do it for.

We also know that ardent segregationist and Klavern no. 317 leader Jack Brown was gunning for King in those early years. Since so little research has been done on his groups—Klavern no. 317 and the Dixie Knights—it's hard to know how early Brown started to focus on King. But we know he was focused.

And it turns out that Donald Davidson and Jack Kershaw[219] were not the only "respectable" racists who funneled money and support to Klan members willing to do violence. Lamar Waldron, Stuart Wexler, and Larry Hancock found evidence showing that "Southeastern businessmen raised the money to kill King, then transferred it to lawyer, James Venable,[220] who then turned to the most reliably violent and determined racist group in the country, Sam Bowers's White Knights, to finish the deed in 1967 and 1968."[221]

A lot of what we know about the plots of rich racists to kill King comes from Atlanta businessman and massive racist Joseph Milteer, who told Klansman and FBI informant Willie Somersett all about it. Milteer also told Somersett about Brown's focus on King in 1963. It came up while they were discussing whether Brown would kill President Kennedy:

Somersett: You think he[222] knows he is a marked man?

Milteer: Sure he does.

Somersett: They are really going to try to kill him?

Milteer: Oh, yeah, it is in the working. Brown himself, Brown is just as likely to get him as anybody. He hasn't said so, but he tried to get Martin Luther King Jr.

Somersett: He did.

Milteer: Oh yes, he followed him for miles and miles, and couldn't get close enough to him.

Somersett: You know exactly where it is in Atlanta don't you?

Milteer: Martin Luther King Jr., yeah.

Somersett: Oh Brown tried to get him huh?

Milteer: Yeah.

Somersett: Well, he will damn sure do it, I will tell you that. Well, that is why, look, you see, well, that is why we have to be so careful, you know that Brown is operating strong.

Milteer: He ain't going for play you know.

Somersett: That is right.

Milteer: He is going for broke.

Somersett: I never asked Brown about his business or anything, you know just what he told me, told us, you know. But after the conversation, and the way he talked to us, there is no question in my mind about who knocked the church off in Birmingham,[223] you can believe that, that is the way I figured it. [224]

Part of what's so frustrating about this is that it suggests that Brown, much like Stoner, played a crucial role in some of the segregationist violence in the 1950s and 1960s. Just like the FBI was quick to dismiss Stoner's possible role in the King assassination because he wasn't in Memphis at the time, the FBI also dismissed Brown's potential role in the 16th Street Baptist Church bombing because he wasn't in Birmingham that day. But as I found repeatedly, that's how Stoner operated—plan and provide the necessary equipment and then stay away from the area when the event was going down. Is it so hard to imagine Brown would act similarly?

On April 19, 1963, Florida Assistant State Attorney Seymour Gelber and Miami detective Lochart Gracey sat down with an unidentified

Florida Klansman, likely Somersett. The Dixie Knights came up. The interviewee told them that Joseph Milteer was at a meeting of many different Klans and Milteer was representing the Dixie Knights on behalf of Jack Brown and his brother, Harry. Gelber and Gracey asked the interviewee if the Dixie Knights differed from other Klans. He replied, "They don't, as far as I know, except they spread and are more powerful and violent. The Dixie Klan is considered the most violent Klu [sic] Klux Klan in America because they have committed all kinds of bombings and killings in the State of Tennessee."[225] [226]

The informant also goes on about how Brown and other people in a core group of racists wanted to start assassinating people—like US politician type people—which meant, since he was there on behalf of the Browns, that Milteer was already talking about assassinations.

There are earlier suggestions in FBI files that Jack Brown was talking about the necessity of assassinating US politicians at a Klan gathering in April 1960—coincidentally, the same month someone tried to kill a Nashville politician.

An informant told the FBI about a terror cell—a "den"—inside Klavern 1, the old Klavern no. 317, "consisting of ten members and two alternates, including Jack William Brown, Imperial Wizard (National President) of DK, KKKK,[227] Inc., Jack Leon Brown, Exalted Cyclops of Klavern 1, Chattanooga, Tennessee (the local chapter president), and others, all listed as members of Klavern 1, DK, KKKK, Inc., Chattanooga, Tennessee, during July, August, and September 1960, were responsible for five bombings of residences of Hamilton County, Tennessee during July and August, 1960."[228] So there were however many members of Klavern 1, and then there was this small group that did the evil that the other members were kept in the dark about.

Going back to Milteer and Somersett's conversation, there's another bit that seems like it could be relevant.

Somersett: I was talking to a boy yesterday, and he was

in Athens, Georgia, and he told me, that they had two colored people working in that drug store, and that them, uh, they went into the basement, and tapped them small pipes, I guess that they are copper together, and let that thing accumulated, and blowed that drug store up. He told me that yesterday, do you think that is right?

Milteer: It could have happened that way.

Somersett: Well, that is what he told me, and he is in town right now.

Milteer: Does he know who did it? Do they think these Negroes did it?

Somersett: Oh, no, they killed the Negroes, because they had two Negroes working in the place, that is what he told me. He is in town now, he is from Chattanooga. He knows Brown, he knows all of them, his uncle is in the Klan there. He is a young boy, he has been in the Marines, and he really knows his business. He went there, he went down and looked, and he told me that is what happened. So he has been involved in quite a little but [sic] of stuff, according to his story about Nashville, Chattanooga, and Georgia. I have no reason not to believe him, because he told me too much about Brown's operation.[229]

I wish the conversation here was as straightforward as it seems. Apparently, Stoner had that person in Chattanooga he liked to use for bombings. I haven't been able to confidently identify that person, but we know he was in the military and did demolitions. This conversation between Somersett and Milteer happened on November 9, 1963, in Jacksonville, Florida, while J.B. Stoner was speaking at a Klan rally nearby. If Somersett met a kid from Chattanooga who was in the military and who "has been involved in quite a bit of stuff" including stuff in Nashville and Chattanooga, it seems quite likely that this unnamed kid was Stoner's favorite bomber.

But get this! In May 1962, J.B. Stoner had sent Fred Hockett a letter, writing, "As you well know, Somersett is an undercover agent for the FBI."[230] That's a full year before Milteer sat down and yakked with Somersett. And if you read the full transcript of the Milteer-Somersett discussion with this in mind, I think you could argue that Milteer is playing Somersett. Even in what I've excerpted here, look at how much Somersett says and how little Milteer says. All Milteer gives up is that Brown wanted to kill King. Somersett's the one talking about Stoner's marine and who bombed what and whether someone will assassinate JFK.

Which raises the likely possibility that Somersett isn't having a straightforward conversation with Milteer but is trying to get Milteer on tape saying something that law enforcement could use against him.

At one point, Somersett says, "They have got a damn, this boy was telling me yesterday about, they have got an explosive that you get out of the army, it is suppose to be like putty or something, you stick it up, and use a small fuse, you just stick it like that, he told me, and I think that is what happened in the church in Birmingham, they stuck this stuff, somebody stuck it under the steps with a short fuse, and went on home. This boy is pretty smart, demolition is that what you call it?"[231] That boy is supposedly Stoner's Chattanooga bomber again. And Somersett is clearly talking about the explosive C4, or something like it. Except the 16th Street Baptist Church was bombed with dynamite.[232]

I tried to figure out what drug store explosion Milteer was talking about. There was none in Athens, Georgia. However, Atherton's Drug Store in Marietta, Georgia, had exploded as a result of a gas leak ten days before Somersett and Milteer had this discussion. Six people were killed. This appears to have genuinely been a run-of-the-mill accidental tragedy, but at the time Somersett and Milteer were talking, that wasn't clear.

I've been mulling over all of the facts that I know Somersett got slightly wrong—the location of the drug store tragedy, the kind of explosives used at the 16th Street Baptist Church—and I have this nagging suspicion. I think Somersett was trying to get Milteer to correct him, because that would get him on tape knowing information related to these events.

Imagine how Somersett might have been hoping this would go:

> SOMERSETT: That boy told me they used some kind of putty explosive in Birmingham.
>
> MILTEER: No, that was just regular old dynamite.
>
> POLICE: Somersett, you are a brilliant hero who has gotten Milteer to tell you a fact only someone involved in the bombing could have known! Here's a parade.

Or

> SOMERSETT: That boy told me he and Stoner blew up the drug store in Athens, Georgia.
>
> MILTEER: No, not Athens. The one in Marietta, Atherton's. He and Stoner were in on it.
>
> POLICE: Ooo, great work, Somersett. Here are your keys to the city.

Frustratingly for me, if I'm right about Somersett's rhetorical strategy here, I have to assume he is slightly, perhaps deliberately, wrong about other things in the conversation. I spent a great deal of time trying to figure out who Stoner's Chattanooga man was. I've been assuming he's a real person. I continue to assume he's probably a real person, but I also haven't been able to find anyone in Chattanooga who matches and who was seen with Stoner. This may change as more of Stoner's FBI file becomes available, but for now what I do have available to me suggests no one in the FBI ever laid eyes on this Chattanooga person. They had also heard he existed, but it's possible they heard he existed *from Somersett.*

Either scenario is equally likely. I have a couple of suspects I think could have been Stoner's Chattanooga man—men in Chattanooga who had ties to the Dixie Knights, military experience, and either knowledge of explosives or knowledge of chemistry. But I can't place them with Stoner or at any of the bombings I've linked to Stoner. And I have the Bowling brothers, young guys from Atlanta who hung out with Stoner all the time and who blew stuff up for him. But they weren't from Chattanooga and, as far as I've been able to find, they didn't have military backgrounds.

Somersett may have heard Stoner say something like, "This is so-and-so from back home," and assumed that meant Chattanooga, when it actually meant Atlanta, where Stoner was living at the time. He may have expected Milteer to say something like, "I know who you mean, that's so-and-so, from such-and-such." But that didn't happen. Milteer mostly went along with whatever Somersett was saying.

If Stoner had in fact tipped Milteer off to Somersett's informancy, it also suggests that—more than suggests that—Stoner had ways of learning who police and FBI informants were, which has interesting implications much broader than the scope of my story here. But if Stoner had someone or someones in law enforcement, perhaps in the FBI, sympathetic to his goals, it sure would explain how the FBI could accumulate thousands of pages of files on him without ever managing to catch him doing anything.

To sum up the little we know: folks in Chattanooga were up to really bad stuff that resembles the really bad stuff that went down in Nashville. The Nashville Klan was closely tied to the Chattanooga Klan, which had close ties to J.B. Stoner. We might not be able to say for sure what role the Chattanooga Klan played in our bombings, but it seems very likely that they're an important part of the puzzle, even if we don't quite know how it fits.

Atlanta Child Murders

I don't want to end this book without at least mentioning the Atlanta Child Murders. From 1979 to 1981, thirty or more Black children, mostly boys, were murdered in Atlanta. In 1981, Wayne Williams, a local music producer, was arrested for the murders.

In 1986, *Spin* magazine ran a story about an investigation they did into the murders. As publisher Bob Guccione explained in a 2015 introduction to the story,

> What had been a secret until we poked our noses into it, was that the Georgia Bureau of Investigation had been working on a parallel investigation and had extremely solid evidence tying members of the Ku Klux Klan to the murder of one small boy, and further evidence linking them to at least 14 of the other killings, but suppressed it, fearing a race war. When Williams, conveniently black, was caught on flimsy, circumstantial evidence, the GBI quietly, gratefully closed the book on their case, and, in the immortal words of Mark Twain, suddenly remembered another appointment.[233]

What the *Spin* writers, Bob Keating and Barry Michael Cooper, found was the Sanders family, members of which had been running around bragging about murdering Black boys. "According to these informants, 30-year-old Charles Sanders was incensed when 14-year-old Lubie Geter backed a go-cart into his car. Sanders swore: 'I'm gonna kill that black bastard. I'm gonna strangle him with my dick.' Several weeks later, Geter was found dead, strangled to death in a wooded area in the city. Shortly after, Sanders' brother Don was heard on a wiretap to tell another Klan brother that he was going out to look for 'another little boy.'"[234]

There's really too much to dig into here, at the tail end of a book about events a quarter of a century earlier. Atlanta is once again in the middle of retesting evidence and reexamining the crimes and we don't yet know where that will lead. But one detail stood out to me in the *Spin* article, a detail that had meaning and resonance to me because of this research and I trust the same will be true for you.

> A few days later, investigators, recognizing a shortage of information on the Klan, began to process more information on the various klaverns—among them the National States Rights Party/New Order of Ku Klux Klan, to which Charles Sanders and several members of his family belonged. One of five Klan groups active in the state of Georgia, the National States Rights Party was small but rapidly building, due mostly to its strong advocacy of violence. [235]

Here's what we know that Keating and Cooper didn't. The National States Rights Party wasn't a Klan. It was a pan-Klan movement. It wasn't small but growing. By 1980, it was practically dead. It was J.B. Stoner, Ed Fields, and some of their friends. If I had to guess, I'd bet they were down to two or three dozen true members. But what this means is that, if NSRP members were kidnapping and murdering Black children (if, indeed, they were) then Stoner and Fields knew about it. And, frankly, there's a lot about the Sanders clan that sounds familiar: here's yet another family—like the Cashes in Birmingham, the Adamses in Anniston, the Bowlings also from Atlanta, the Browns in Chattanooga, and we might even include the Rays[236]—of racist activists with ties to

Stoner and ties to terrorist activities. The race war talk was a hobbyhorse of Stoner and Fields's going back to the era of this book. Stoner's network was willing to target children—Donal Godfrey, for example—and murder them—Addie Mae Collins, Cynthia Wesley, Carole Robertson, and Carol Denise McNair. They went into Black neighborhoods. We know that because they went into a Black neighborhood to put a bomb at Z. Alexander Looby's house and into another Black neighborhood to put a bomb at Rev. Fred Shuttlesworth's church.

I didn't research the Atlanta Child Murders. From what I know, it does seem clear that Wayne Williams killed at least some of the people he's accused of killing. But the investigation into the Sanderses was not some implausible wild goose chase. They were good suspects, especially because of their ties to people who by that point were very well practiced at doing terrible things to African Americans and getting away with it. People who spent some of their early days here in Nashville getting that practice.

We Can't Heal if We Don't Know the Truth

We were not unique among Southern cities. We had exactly the wrong evil people here doing exactly the kinds of things they would go on to do more successfully in other places. They just weren't as good at it yet as they would go on to be. We were lucky. No one died. That's true. But people were terrorized, and they suffered. Leaving these cases unsolved didn't lessen that fear and pain.

Nashville has a story it tells itself about how we, unlike those other Southern cities, integrated peacefully and calmly after Diane Nash and her friends went for a walk and politely asked Mayor Ben West to make it happen. Even Dr. Martin Luther King Jr. complimented us by saying, "I came to Nashville not to bring inspiration, but to gain inspiration from the great movement that has taken place in this community."

We tend to gloss over the fact that King said those words not to all of

Nashville, but specifically to the civil rights activists in the Black community here. He was not complimenting the people who had blown up the home of great civil rights lawyer and sitting city councilman Z. Alexander Looby that morning, or the people who had spent hours on the phones since then calling in bomb threats to every college in town, or the people who had, in fact, delayed King's speaking engagement with a bomb threat.

It does say something good about the kind of city Nashville wants to be that we all want to imagine ourselves in the community King was addressing.

But in our hurry to reimagine ourselves as the kind of city where the sit-ins were barely necessary, we have left unsolved the crimes that prove we did need, desperately, to change—specifically the bombing of Hattie Cotton Elementary School on September 10, 1957, the bombing of the Jewish Community Center on March 16, 1958, and the bombing of Z. Alexander Looby's home on April 19, 1960.

You can't have forgiveness and reconciliation if you can't say what you need forgiveness for. Someone knows who did these bombings, and it's not too late to give the city the answers it needs to heal from the terror of those years.

I hope this book is a useful first step.

THE FILE FINALLY ARRIVES

November 2023

Of course, after the book has been turned in to the publisher, I get an email from the National Archive informing me that the Looby bombing file is ready for me to download. Of course.

I had been under the assumption that, if the FBI had to be cajoled by a US congressperson into revealing that the file even still existed, that it must contain some explosive (pardon the pun) revelations. I assumed I'd be pulling my book out of production and completely rewriting it. I had been fantasizing about the thrill of knowing this terrible secret and trying to keep it until the book came out. I expected some "Holy shit" moment equal to the headache getting the file had been.

There is no such moment. I wanted the truth. Instead, what I got was enough knowledge to know that the truth isn't in this file. More upsetting, it's only because I've been sitting with these bombings for so long that I know the file is … I don't want to say incomplete, because I have no way of knowing if this is all the materials that were ever in this file. This may be the complete FBI file. And anyone who had just received this file but hadn't been steeped in this stuff would find it complete. It looks like the FBI supported the Nashville police however the police asked them to. They helped chase down sources of evidence. They checked on the whereabouts of suspects like J.B. Stoner and Robert Wray. They seem to have shared everything with the police and the TBCI. The file reads like you are getting a complete document.

But things are missing. Whether they were ever in the file and now aren't or if the FBI–second only to the IRS for getting into the minute details of whatever has its attention–just wasn't interested in compiling these details, I'm not sure. Some things were clearly left out at the time. Take, for instance, the description of Looby that FBI headquarters was sharing with field agents:

```
As a background to this situation, it will be
```

> noted that sit-in demonstrations have been
> conducted in Nashville, Tennessee, by Negro
> students, from colleges in the Nashville area,
> which resulted in approximately 160 arrests
> in all. LOOBY, as a principal attorney for
> the NAACP, has been prominent in the de-
> fense of these students who were arrested.
> LOOBY has long been identified with NAACP in
> Nashville, and was largely responsible for
> successful court case integrating public
> schools in Nashville.[237]

See what's missing? Any mention of Looby being an elected official. And this is throughout the file. I can't be sure, but it seems that any typification of Looby as a councilman comes from the Nashville police, but memos generated by the FBI focus on his NAACP role. There are fewer than five mentions of him being an elected official at all. This is a file dealing with vandalism against an NAACP lawyer, not an assassination attempt on a sitting US politician.

A couple of other things stood out to me as being glaring omissions and there's no way to tell if these are things that were never in the file or if they were removed at some point. One is that we know from his FBI file that John Kasper was asking to speak to FBI agents right after the Looby bombing. We know from this file that the FBI didn't know where Robert Wray was the morning of the bombing: "All accounted for except Robert Wray, who got off work at twelve thirty am, nineteenth instant, and whose car believed missing from residence at five forty am, by neighbors. UACB, by eight pm, central standard time, Nashville, Tenn. PD being advised that Wray-s whereabouts cannot be accounted for. Bureau will note Nashville PD known to be aware of Wray-s close association with Frederick John Kasper and PD known to have interviewed him previously concerning racial matters."

To be clear, the FBI didn't know where Robert Wray was the morning of the bombing. They knew, and they knew NPD knew, that Wray and Kasper were friends. John Kasper asked to speak to the FBI and they took their sweet time getting to him. Well, okay, then. But they did go talk to him. Eventually. Why isn't there anything in this file about what Kasper told them? Maybe because, according to Kasper's file, they didn't talk about the Looby bombing at all, only Kasper's hatred of Nazis and the bad conditions at the Nashville workhouse.[238]

I also find it strange that there's no mention in the FBI file of Mayor West being the one heading up the investigation into the Looby bombing, especially with Avon Williams—Looby's law partner and fellow sit-in lawyer—being right there. The FBI was deeply worried about "the communist" influence on American society and there had been communists in the Nashville NAACP (white guys, though). If the mayor was breaching protocol to do police work with an NAACP lawyer at his elbow, wouldn't that have been right up the FBI's paranoid alley? And yet, there's no mention of it. Did they not know? If they didn't know, that suggests that the cooperative relationship between the FBI and NPD that appears in the file didn't exist in real life and that NPD, as in the other bombing cases, was not being fully open with the FBI. If they did know, why isn't it mentioned in the file?

Then there's the discussion of the information provided by Fisk nightwatchman, Lemuel Dawson. At first, it doesn't differ much from what he told Mayor West. But then we get to this:

```
In subsequent interviews with Dawson
by detectives of the Nashville Police
Department, he states that he had seen
this same automobile at the vicinity of
Fisk University on one or two occasions
since the bombing, but he did not report
it to the Nashville Police Department. As
```

> a result the Nashville Police Department
> specifically assigned two Negro detectives
> to keep a close contact with DAWSON and to
> attempt to locate instant automobile. These
> officers worked with DAWSON for some time and
> subsequently stated that they believed that
> he was lying about the whole incident, or if
> he believed it himself he was suffering from
> hallucinations.

What do we even make of this? Sure, maybe it's true, but this would require us to believe that Fisk kept an armed old hallucinating man as its night watchman for two more years after this (Dawson retired in 1962). Remember, this is 1960. Nashville had only had Black police officers for twelve years at that point.[239] Nashville got its first Black detective, Harold Woods, in January, 1960.[240] Judging by the FBI reports, it was Detective Harold Woods and Floyd Bailey who followed Dawson around three months later.[241] We had very few Black cops on a predominately white force that had already failed to solve two racist bombings before this. Tensions were also high because of the pressure of the sit-ins. I think we have to assume that Black police officers may have felt a little cautious of their white peers. We also have seen evidence that NPD, in general, was not completely forthcoming with the FBI in the past regarding bombings. And, in fairness, the FBI hid witnesses from them. NPD distrust of the FBI was warranted.

Did these Black detectives truly think that Dawson was lying or did they look around and realize this case, too, was not going to be solved any time soon and that putting Dawson's name out there as a credible witness was putting his life in danger if the bombers were looking to tie up loose ends to ensure it was never solved? Did they protect him by lying about his credibility?

I don't know.

I have also been thinking long and hard about what it might mean that Mayor West headed up the investigation into the Looby bombing, that the FBI didn't seem to know that, and that the Nashville police seem like they might have deliberately fed the FBI information discrediting a witness. Here's what's sticking in my craw. If Nashville knew it was being targeted by racist terrorists (they did), and if they were so aware of the FBI's refusal to help that they helped organize and participated in a multi-state conference on these bombings to share information because the FBI was being no help (they did), and if they had reason to suspect that the FBI had connections in Nashville's KKK scene (they did), might they have been concerned that the FBI was capable of feeding information to the KKK?

And if Nashville became suspicious that the FBI wasn't just unhelpful, but was actively working against Nashville investigators (and what other assumption could you draw after the Hattie Cotton debacle?), might Nashville have decided it couldn't trust the FBI? Might Nashville have gone rogue? And, if you were a city that had just decided that you actually weren't going to cooperate with the FBI in this case because you didn't trust them—maybe you even worried they were giving information to the Klan—might that explain why the mayor took over the investigation? To provide cover for his police force should it ever become clear they were not actually cooperating with the FBI? After all, he took charge. If the FBI was unhappy, West was to blame, not the police who would still need a working relationship with the FBI when this was over.

Obviously, I don't know. But damn, I wonder.

Also missing from the file is any information from the FBI's confidential informant, Memphis T-1, Frank Houchin. They had an informant who was in the Klan and who hung out with people who left the Klan because it wasn't violent enough and they didn't feel like talking to him about Looby? According to Kasper's FBI file, Memphis T-1 was still providing the FBI with good information during this time, just, apparently, not about Looby.

We know there's a whole network of people the FBI knows who would have been capable of harming Looby–some of whom, as far as we know, were unknown to Nashville police or the TBCI–and the FBI didn't include any information from any of them in the file. The file contains three pages of unrelated complaints about uncooperative communists but not one phone call to Frank Houchin.

Also, remember that the FBI knew about that guy in Alabama who told them Kasper wanted him to kill Looby? And how they dismissed him for being a lunatic? Okay, well, now someone has tried to kill Looby. You don't go back and talk to the Alabama lunatic?

I don't know what all might be missing from this file. But I know at least some of the things I'd have expected to be in there aren't there. And I don't know what these absences mean. Did the FBI really not talk to their informants in Nashville about this? And, if not, why not?

Here's the fundamental problem with this file, with this whole thing. If the FBI was running the Klan in Tennessee earlier than scholars know—and my opinion is that it's very likely this arrangement started in response to the Clinton riots in 1956 and not the mid-60s—and if the Klan blew up Looby's house, then the FBI is mixed up in the attempted murder of an elected official. There is simply no way that any information stating that clearly is going to be in any FBI file. They're not going to confess to being behind an assassination attempt on a sitting US politician.

So, when I look at this file and I see how it way, way downplays Looby's political role and that the Klan is mentioned only in passing, I can't help but wonder if this is to keep this incident from raising alarms that would ultimately implicate the FBI. And, I mean, if you wanted to make sure no evidence pointed to your guys, being the folks who analyze the evidence is a super convenient way to make that happen.

My gut tells me this is the most likely scenario. But the historian in me says it's a leap too far to say for sure. My whole goal for this project was to tell Nashville the truth about what happened during those terrible, turbulent times. Or at least the truth to the best of my ability. That truth is everything in this book AND that I still think there are important pieces of this puzzle we don't have. And I don't know if we don't have these pieces because, well, it's been almost sixty-five years and things get lost in that time or because someone dumped those pieces in the trash as soon as they realized what the puzzle would show.

The FBI did clear J.B. Stoner to their satisfaction. He had been in Louisville, Kentucky with Ed Fields the night of the bombing and no one had seen him leave. They didn't ask about Stoner's whereabouts the week before the bombing, even though, by 1960, they had enough experience with him to know that he was often in town right before a bombing but gone by the time the explosion happened.

I'll leave you with one last mystery from the file, one that on its surface doesn't seem like a mystery at all. But now you've read this book. So, you know some about J.B. Stoner. What do you make of this?

> On April 21, 1960, LS T-2[242] advised that on that date J.B. Stoner had remarked that the recent bombing of a Negro home in Nashville, Tennessee, had been done by the "Niggers" themselves in order to gain sympathy and to have a reason for the march by the "Niggers" on the City Hall at Nashville, Tennessee.[243]

Here's what strikes me. First, if Stoner didn't have anything to do with the bombing, why was it on his radar? As far as I can tell, the Louisville *Courier-Journal* ran one story mentioning the Looby bombing, that ran on an inside page, on April 20th. The big news in Kentucky was some scandal about the state leasing trucks from a company that maybe didn't exist for the Highway Department.

But second, we know this line of reasoning—Black people did this to themselves for sympathy—was used by the Birmingham police to deny Stoner credit for the bombing of Rev. Shuttlesworth's church. And we know that Stoner knew that. So, in saying this, is he thinking "Well, since 'Black people did it to themselves' equals 'Stoner did it' but without me getting in trouble for it, if I tell my friends who know my history that Black people did it, that's me bragging about doing it?" Or is he mad that he wasn't included in on this bombing and so he's using tactics used against him previously to deny the bomber the satisfaction of credit?

And should we make anything of the fact that this "explanation" for the bombing very quickly became conventional wisdom in white Nashville? Did the "explanation" come from Stoner to contacts in Nashville who spread it? Or was this a common enough white excuse for violence against Black people that it came from multiple places?

Is this a clue or isn't it? Is it just a villain saying villain shit or is this as close to a confession as we're likely to get?

Acknowledgments

First and foremost, this book would not have been finished if not for Steve Cavandish. I don't know what to say that would convey how grateful I am. He called me at a low point when I didn't see any way to finish the book, asked me what I needed, and then hung up on me. Twenty minutes later he called me back with a workable plan.

I'd like to thank Dr. Benjamin Houston for his support. Every time I've emailed him and given him an update on this project or asked his opinion on something, he's given me wise council, good advice, and enthusiastic encouragement.

I'd like to thank Congressman Jim Cooper, Lisa Quigley, and the rest of his staff. Without Congressman Cooper's intervention, the Looby bombing file would still be missing and people would still be told it had been destroyed.

I'm very grateful to all the folks at Third Man Records: Chet Weise, Jordan Williams, Amin Qutteineh, and Ben Swank, all of whom have been so enthusiastic about the project from the start. Sheree Renée Thomas, Siobhan Boroian, Anthea Gwynne, Caitlin Parker, and Sydney Bozeman and others I'm sure I'm forgetting.

I'd also like to single out Dr. Rachel Martin, whose advice to not get too hung up on John Kasper too early or I wouldn't see what was really going on kept me digging.

I'm very grateful to Daniel Jackson, who has worked on similar cases in Chattanooga. We shared files and bounced ideas off each other and I can't say enough how helpful it was to have someone else as deep in the weeds as I was to help me think things through.

I had been thinking that it goes without saying how much help I received from the Nashville Public Library, but this book is a testament to the fact that if you leave something obvious unsaid, eventually it becomes unknown. So, my deepest thanks to the Nashville Public Library and, specifically, Andrea Blackman, Chi Amaefula, and Beth Odle.

Beth's expertise in the *Banner* photos, especially, was so very helpful. I'd also like to specifically thank the people in the Nashville Room, who are jewels in the crown of the city: Linda Barnickel, Courtney Buggs, Kathleen Feduccia, Dixie Rose Johnson, Deborah May, Karen Piper, Tasneem Tewogbola, and especially Elliott Robinson. Sorry if I told you the same stories fifty million times, Elliott.

I'd also like to thank Tricia Gesner at the Associated Press who was so generous with her time and expertise. Over and over again, I'd email her something along the lines of "Hey, I see you all have a picture of this guy, but do you have one where he's facing the camera more straight on?" or "Here's so-and-so in a group shot. Do you have one of him alone?" and she would come back with exactly what I needed, often two or three options.

We are very lucky to have so many resources here in town and I would especially like to single out the Tennessee State Library and Archives.

Early versions of a lot of this material appeared at the *Nashville Scene*. I deeply appreciate their support over the years.

Special thanks to Tom Wood, who pointed me toward the FBI file that made everything in the book click into place.

I'm also deeply grateful to the staff of Vanderbilt University Press, who have been so supportive. Thanks, especially, to Zack Gresham for helping me read smoothly.

The list of people who've helped me on this project and to whom I owe a debt of gratitude is extensive: Kim Baldwin, Demetria Kaledemos, Hal Hardin, Keel Hunt, Daniel Harper, Henry Martin, Gladys Girgenti, Learotha Williams, Crystal DeGregory, Linda Wynn, Ludye Wallace, Eric Etheridge, Rip Patton, Sgt. Gary Smith, Stuart Wexler, David Garrow, Diane McWhorter, Carter Newton, Michele LeNoue-Newton, Samantha Yeargin, Amy Chau, Rich Blecker, Carolyn Cusick, Sara Harvey, Margaret Renkl, Elizabeth Duke, Gilbert Fox, Larry Brinton, Alex Little, Cari Wade Gervin, DeLisa Harris, Caroline Randall Williams, Ciona Rouse, Clive Webb, Michael Newton, Andrew Maraniss, Frederick Strobel, Debie

Cox, Larry Woods, Saralee Woods, Gail Terry, Caroline Eller, Brian Mansfield, Ken Whitehouse, Chicoya Gallman, Ansley Erickson, Daniel Horowitz, Wayne Dowdy, Jim Baggett, Gordon Belt, Jerry Mitchell, Gary May, Nina Melechen, Barry Mazor, Chase Stejskal, Bart Phillips, Holli Phillips, Ben Phillips, Courtney Phillips, and my parents, who worried.

Though he is not here to appreciate it, I want to acknowledge that I would not have been able to finish this book without also having the sculptor, William Edmondson, to research at the same time. To be able to stop and spend time looking at a man who loved his family and his community and who used his gifts to improve their lives was a sanctuary during this. Because Nashville is a small town, still, there is actually an Edmondson connection to this story. His supervisor at the WPA was Jack Kershaw.

Here's a funny story about William Edmondson and Jack Kershaw that is on the verge of being lost. It goes like this: William Edmondson, the greatest sculptor in Nashville in his day, carved a statue of a boxer. Supposedly, he was quite proud of the statue and brought it in to work to show known white supremacist, Jack Kershaw. Jack allegedly said, "That's pretty good. What's it called?"

Over the past year or so, I've seen art historians start to call this statue "Joe Lewis," and I assume that's because Edmondson carved hair on the statue. I also assume it's because they didn't know *who* Edmondson was talking to. Because the story as I've always heard it is that Edmondson told Kershaw the statue was called "Jack Johnson."

Joe Lewis was a great, legendary, even, boxer. He was a hero both to Black and white America. Jack Johnson was the same age as William Edmondson. White people hated him and tried to find any excuse to discount his talent. Yes, he was bald, but for Kershaw to point that out would have meant acknowledging that he paid even a little attention to Jack Johnson. I think Edmondson was making a little dig at Kershaw, using the name "Jack Johnson" to signify art about a Black man at the height of his talent who was better than his white peers, made by a Black artist at the height of his talent who was better than his white boss. You switch the name to "Joe Lewis" and you miss some of the pride and rage and knowing simmering just under the surface of Edmondson's comment to Kershaw.

Rest in Peace, Blackie Bromley. You deserved better.

I've been working on this project for a long time, so if I've left anyone off this list, please know it's more that my brain was scrambled by this, and things have slipped my mind and not that I don't appreciate your help.

I also had help from people who don't want to be named or associated with the project. I'm still very grateful to them.

Endnotes

1   Katherine E. Delmez, *We Shall Overcome: Press Photographs of Nashville during the Civil Rights Era* (Nashville: Vanderbilt University Press, 2018).

2   This sounds very dramatic, but it wasn't this project that almost killed me. I had a histoplasmosis infestation that formed granulomas in my chest that came bursting out of my neck, and it took six months for doctors to figure out that was what was happening.

3   There is so much information about Nashville in the Birmingham police files, handwritten notes about our suspects, pages out of our police reports, letters from other police departments about our bombings. I sat in the downtown Birmingham library, hand-cranking through their microfilm and taking pictures of useful pages as they appeared onscreen for a whole day and I'm sure I didn't find everything.

4   Crystal A. DeGregory, "Nashville's Clandestine Black Schools," *The New York Times*, February 17, 2015.

5   Bill Carey, "The Roger Williams Legacy," *The Tennessee Magazine*, July, 2012.

6   I found a number of different accounts of this incident—some saying it happened during the trial, not at the end, and some saying it was Weaver who was arrested, not Marshall. The facts of the matter have not been nailed down yet, clearly, but the version recounted here is the story you're most likely to hear. It's the version most people believe is true. I also believe it's the most likely, based on how racism worked. I don't believe the 1946 Columbia police would have arrested a white Tennessee lawyer and never taken him to the jail. But police harassed

Black people like that all the time.

7 These streets don't intersect, but I suspect the *Tennessean* means the cross was burned at that almost intersection where Grove runs into 12th Avenue South just north of where Acklen runs into it.

8 "Burning Cross Found Near Acklen, Grove," *Tennessean*, March 29, 1951.

9 Well, maybe it's fairer to say that Looby eventually supported these efforts. In the April 3, 1957, *Banner*, Looby said that while he respected the people who supported one government, he was worried that it would reverse gains Black people had made in the city. But by January 24, 1960, Looby was quoted in the *Tennessean* as saying, "A metropolitan government is the greatest need of the city of Nashville and Davidson county."

10 James Squires, *Secrets of the Hopewell Box: Stolen Elections, Southern Politics, and a City's Coming of Age* (New York: Crown Publishing Group, 1996).

11 Laura Riding was the only Fugitive who wasn't at Vanderbilt.

12 Paul V. Murphy, "Agrarians," *Tennessee Encyclopedia* (2017). http://tennesseeencyclopedia.net/entries/agrarians/

13 "Jack Kershaw Obituary," *Dickson Herald*, September 24, 2010.

14 I don't know who wrote Kershaw's obituary, but it sounds like he, himself, could have.

15 A towering stack of books and journal articles have been written

about how that wasn't really true or how they came to see the error of their ways, but mostly that's just scholars trying to justify to themselves why they like and respond so strongly to the art of these racists, as if racism and talent have to be mutually exclusive. The only Agrarian I feel confident in saying would have not oozed disdain and disgust for any Black person not in a position of servitude to him was Robert Penn Warren—and his contribution to the Agrarian manifesto, *I'll Take My Stand*, was chapter called "The Briar Patch," in which he defends segregation. So, sure, maybe folks improved in later years, but during the time we're talking about? Racist.

16   Paul V. Murphy, "Donald Davidson," in *Tennessee Encyclopedia* (Tennessee Historical Society, January 1, 2010). http://tennesseeencyclo pedia.net/entry.php?rec=357.

17   Fred Stroud had been the pastor at Nashville's Second Presbyterian Church on the corner of 9th Avenue North and Monroe Street. At the end of 1938, the Presbytery of Middle Tennessee removed him from the church. His views had become so radical that the overarching denomination no longer considered him a Presbyterian minister. The ideas that were so out of line with Presbyterian teaching were racist and sexist.

I've tried to find some solid history of exactly what these racist and sexist teachings were, but the renegade church Stroud would go on to form no longer exists and the Presbyterians didn't keep any records on Stroud once he was gone. Still, and this is no offence to the Presbyterians, who were (and still are) considered fairly liberal-ish, this was Nashville in 1938. What kinds of racist and sexist views must you have been expounding to have your denomination kick you out of the ministry?! It's mind-boggling. A great deal of racist and sexist attitudes were perfectly acceptable and seen as normal. I honestly can't imagine how bad Stroud must have been, but clearly his positions must have been wildly abhorrent for him to have been banishably outside the mainstream of the time.

18   I don't know if it means anything more significant than that AVCO was a large employer in Nashville, but John Kasper's buddy, Robert Wray, who we'll meet in a bit, and Robert Pittman Gentry, who we'll also discuss at length, both worked at AVCO.

19   "Tennessee Federation for Constitutional Government roster and newsletter," *University of Tennessee, Chattanooga, digital collections* (1955). https://digital-collections.library.utc.edu/digital/collection/p16877coll8/id/217.

20   Mark Royden Winchell, *Where No Flag Flies: Donald Davidson and the Southern Resistance* (University of Missouri Press, 2000).

21   For a brief but insightful view into the long-standing habit of powerful whites using the Klan to get their way, see NPR's *Codeswitch* podcast episode "The Story of Mine Mill" from December 5, 2018, about how US Steel created the vigilante group that would become Birmingham's KKK.

22   See, for instance, Kelly Weill's story, "Neo-Confederate League of the South Banned from Armed Protesting in Charlottesville," *Daily Beast*, March 27, 2018, which outlines the League's role in organizing the Charlottesville riot and shows how they armed racists.

23   William Keel, ""Wilson Ordered Blasts, Stokes Shouts"," *Tennessean*, March 29, 1955.

24   William Keel, "Wilson Actions 'Maniac's Work,' DA Tells Jury," *The Tennessean*, March 30, 1955.

25   "Eight Indicted by Grand Jury," *Nashville Banner*, February 10, 1936.

26   See Bentley Anderson's *Black, White, and Catholic*, for instance.

27   "Catholics Enroll Negro Students," *The Nashville Tennessean*, September 5, 1954.

28   FBI, *Pro-Southerners--SAC, Miami* (Miami, 1954).

29   In *Killing King: Racial Terrorists, James Earl Ray, and the Plot to Assassinate Martin Luther King Jr.*, Stuart Wexler and Larry Hancock spend a lot of time showing how big a role religion, particularly the Christian Identity movement, played in racial terrorism in the 1960s, specifically in King's murder. I think Kasper's close involvement with Stroud and other ministers indicates something similar going on here, but so little attention has been paid to Nashville's racial terrorists that it's hard to pinpoint their more obscure national influences.

30   Alec Marsh, *John Kasper and Ezra Pound: Saving the Republic* (London and New York: Bloomsbury Academic, 2015).

31   Marsh, *John Kasper and Ezra Pound: Saving the Republic*.

32   Asa Carter would go on to be a fairly successful novelist under the name Forrest Carter. He wrote *The Rebel Outlaw: Josie Wales* and, while pretending to be Cherokee, *The Education of Little Tree*. It's pretty easy to draw a straight line from "I was a racist agitator" to "I wrote a book about a Confederate who refused to accept Union victory." The line from "I'm a white supremacist and will go on to be George Wallace's speech writer" to "I'm passing myself off as a Cherokee" is less clear, but I think you could make the argument that, if you see his claims of being

Cherokee as a way of claiming some kind of pure, authentic belonging-to-the-land Southerness, a kind of Southerness that is being lost in the crush of modernity and federal intervention in Southerners' lives, he's actually got a very similar aesthetic project to Donald Davidson.

This may also suggest that Carter knew the Browns from Chattanooga well enough to know their family story. Even though they were the leaders of the Dixie Knights, Jack Brown's brother, Harry, applied to be on the Cherokee role, because they were descended from Cherokee leader Nancy Ward.

33   Read into that what you will.

34   "McCallie Student Gets Message from Nazi Radio Propagandist," *Chattanooga Times*, May 28, 1940.

35   1940 was the height of the Nazis' T-4 program, in which sick and disabled children were killed, many in gas chambers. This program was overseen and carried out by well-regarded German doctors. Though the program was "secret," it was an open secret. Lord Haw Haw would have known. I think Stoner regarded Haw Haw's offer as legitimate, but I also think it very likely that it would have resonated differently in Germany, which is both chilling and hilarious.

36   This raises another question I haven't been able to answer: How and why did the Memphis police know so much about networks of racial terrorists in 1958?

37   "Kasper Planning Session with Klan, White Council," *Tennessean*, August 1, 1957.

38   Garry Fullerton, "Kasper Halted at Park Rally," *Tennessean*,

August 5, 1957.

39   Fullerton, "Kasper Halted at Park Rally.""

40   FBI, "John Kasper File--Knoxville," (1957), Archive.org.

41   FBI, "John Kasper File," (1957), Archive.org.

42   William Keel, "Study Continues on Integration," *Tennessean*, August 9, 1957.

43   Nashville Public Schools. "School Board Minutes," (Nashville, August 8 1957).

44   If you've seen pictures of the "real" Rosie the Riveters—women building aircrafts during the War—most of those photos were taken at Vultee.

45   Carrie Wray, "Letter to Governor Frank Clement," in *Frank Goad Clement (First and Second Terms) Papers, 1953-1959* (Nashville, TN: Tennessee State Library and Archives, August 1957).

46   Just as an interesting side note, along with being continually outraged about rock 'n' roll, Nashville racists (and others, I assume) were apoplectic with rage at Frank Sinatra for his 1958 film, *Kings Go Forth*. I would have to guess that the reason they hated the movie, and Sinatra, was that it made clear that Sinatra's regard for Black people wasn't just kindness toward his Black friends, but was, in fact, his worldview. The coolest man alive and he's for everything you're against. Ouch.

47   "Carter Returns to Kasper Fold," *Tennessean*, August 26, 1957.

48   "Carter Returns to Kasper Fold."

49   FBI, *Hattie Cotton Elementary School Bombing file* (1957).

50   Wallace Westfeldt, "1st Grade Register Off 43%," *Tennessean*, August 28, 1957.

51   Westfeldt, "1st Grade Register Off 43%."

52   Westfeldt, "1st Grade Register Off 43%."

53   Westfeldt, "1st Grade Register Off 43%."

54   "United Press," *Daily New-Journal*, August 29, 1957.

55   FBI, *Hattie Cotton Elementary School Bombing file*.

56   FBI, *Hattie Cotton Elementary School Bombing file*.

57   "Kasper Returns, To Try Boycott," *Tennessean*, September 6, 1957.

58   Sorry, I know I said that we were going to launch into a recounting of the facts as we know them, but it's worth taking a moment to worry this notion of "violence" a little. Here's Norvell, who was so alarmed by what he heard on August 27 that he called the FBI and reported on Kasper. Now, a week later, he's saying Kasper never advocated violence. Those two things don't make any sense together. And Norvell isn't Kasper's buddy. He's not trying to save Kasper from FBI trouble. He's the one that brought Kasper back to the attention of the FBI.

But this idea of violence that is somehow more real and more alarming than regular violence is not unfamiliar in this crowd. J.B. Stoner was kicked out of Chattanooga Klavern 317 for being too violent. Later, the whole of Klavern 317 was kicked out of the Klan for being too violent. Gladys Girgenti, who we'll talk about in more detail later, was kicked out of the Klan for being too violent.

How in the hell can you be too violent for the Klan? The Klan's whole purpose is to use violence and intimidation to terrorize Black people.

I have, and I suspect you may have, just assumed that when someone was "too violent for the Klan," it meant that they were too unstable, unpredictable, and uncontrollable for the Klan, that their presence in the Klan was bringing too much unfriendly attention. But what Stoner, Klavern 317, and Gladys Girgenti all had in common was that they perpetrated violence against white people.

If you go back and add an unspoken "against white people" to what Norvell told the FBI, it actually becomes really easy to understand what shook Norvell enough to go to the authorities. Norvell "has never heard Kasper make any statement indicating that he adheres to violence [against white people] in connection with the radical situation ... Kasper has always made statements ... that he is opposed to violence [against white people]. Norvell stated that some of the people who have been at the Kasper meetings have talked of possible violence [against white people]." That certainly could shake a segregationist enough that he would go to the FBI.

But who knows if that's the subtext the FBI heard? If they were thinking of violence as any violent act against anyone (even people the FBI disagreed with), then Norvell would have seemed to them like a lunatic, telling them about Kasper giving a fiery speech talking about shotguns and dynamite, then claiming he never heard Kasper advocating for violence.

59   FBI, *Hattie Cotton Elementary School Bombing file*.

60   You'll sometimes see the Parents' Preference committee treated as a fourth group opposed to integration, in addition to Kasper's mob, the Klan, and the TFCG, but Kershaw gives away the game here. It was a branch of the TFCG. Nellie Kenyon, "12 1st Graders to Enter White Schools Monday," *Tennessean*, September 7, 1957.

61   We'll get into this more in a second, but suffice to say, this is probably "four quart fruit jars"; in the end, Reed says it was a quart fruit jar.

62   FBI, "John Kasper File."

63   FBI, *Hattie Cotton Elementary School Bombing file*.

64   FBI, *Hattie Cotton Elementary School Bombing file*.

65   Wallace Westfeldt, "Attendance Off by 25-30 Pct," *Tennessean*, September 10, 1957.

66   John Egerton, "Walking into History: The Beginning of School Desegregation in Nashville," *Southern Spaces* (2009). https://southern spaces.org/2009/walking-history-beginning-school-desegregation-nashville.

67   William Keel, "Kasper: 'Certain People' Talked School Dynamiting," *Tennessean*, September 13, 1957.

68   FBI, "John Kasper File."

69   Egerton, "Walking into History: The Beginning of School Desegregation in Nashville."

70   "6 Questioned in School Blast," *Tennessean*, September 11, 1957.

71   It's not clear they ever told Nashville police about Norvell.

72   FBI, "John Kasper File."

73   FBI, "John Kasper File."

74   FBI, "John Kasper File."

75   FBI, "John Kasper File."

76   FBI, "John Kasper File."

77   FBI, *Hattie Cotton Elementary School Bombing file.*

78   FBI, *Hattie Cotton Elementary School Bombing file.*

79   In order to make a long-distance call in the 1950s, you had to use the operator, who then had to set the call up through a series of other operators. The sound quality was often very poor, and the calls left an extensive paper trail (to make sure the caller was properly billed) as well as a trail of witnesses in the operators who connected the call. This Dalton may have been from Chattanooga, but he was in Nashville when he made that call, or it could have been easily traced.

80   FBI, *Hattie Cotton Elementary School Bombing file.*

81   FBI, *Christian Anti Jewish Party J.B. Stoner file* (1952).

82   "6 Questioned in School Blast."

83   Interesting fact: Reed had also been driving around town in a car with KKK on the side.

84   "6 Questioned in School Blast."

85   For many years, experts thought the Melungeons were an Appalachian tri-racial isolate group—white, black, and Native American. But recent DNA results suggest they may just be a bi-racial isolate group. Also, the term "Melungeon" is seen by some as a racial slur (though others have been reclaiming the term). There's not another word that so clearly identifies the families that make up this particular isolate group so I'm using it, but with the caveat that, unless you belong to the group, you shouldn't use it casually. For more information, see the Melungeon Heritage Association website, melungeon.org.

86   Larry Brinton, "Interview at Bellvue Starbucks," ed. Betsy Phillips (August 3, 2017).

87   FBI, *Hattie Cotton Elementary School Bombing file*.

88   I can't prove this, but it doesn't seem like the Nashville Klan had any Catholics in it until Cathedral and Father Ryan desegregated.

89   "Earlier Return of Kasper Seen," *Tennessean*, September 20, 1957.

90   "Court Delays Dynamite Cases," *Tennessean*, September 21, 1957.

91   I'm not saying he would have been found guilty—this was the South in the '50s, after all. But Nashville would have happily jacked him around in the legal system for a while if it feasibly could have.

92   Again, I didn't get into the religious beliefs of these men as much as I would have liked to, but there is a lot of important work that could be done here. It's clear that Christian Identity leader Wesley Swift's racist theology was known to many of the segregationists, and I can't help but wonder if Mercurio was the conduit by which Nashville racists came to be aware of Swift, who also hailed from the west coast.

93   FBI, *Hattie Cotton Elementary School Bombing file.*

94   FBI, *Hattie Cotton Elementary School Bombing file.*

95   FBI, *Hattie Cotton Elementary School Bombing file.*

96   Frank Houchin, Testimony, ed. O.O. Lee (Nashville, January 10 1958).

97   Houchin, Testimony.

98   His first name, not a title. He was a handyman.

99   Frank Houchin, Testimony, ed. O.O. Lee (Nashville, January 10 1958).

100   FBI, 62-116395.

101   See, for example, Chris Gavaler's article in the *Journal of Graphic Novels and Comics*, Volume 4, Issue 2, "The Ku Klux Klan and the Birth of the Superhero" for discussion.

102   Wayne Whitt, "Ku Klux Leader Admits Klavern in Nashville," *Tennessean*, April 13, 1950.

103   Don Whitehead, "Florida KKK Recruiting During Wave of Terrorism," *Tampa Tribune*, January 6, 1952.

104   "Recent Crackdowns Lead to Disunity in Klan Ranks," *Tampa Bay Times*, August 20, 1952.

105   "Hendrix Gets Evangelist's License," *Pensacola News Journal*, June 23, 1953.

106   Yes, Klan is in the name twice. I can only assume whoever was in charge of naming Klans was also the first person to use the term ATM machine.

107   Will Muller, "Ku Klux Klan Reins Held by Auto Painter," *Star Press*, September 5, 1955.

108   Shelton rose to power in a time when the Alabama Klan was also a viper's nest of infighting groups. You had the Gulf Coast Klan, the Alabama Knights of the Ku Klux Klan, and Asa Carter's Ku Klux Klan of the Confederacy all billing themselves as alternatives to a Klan that was too worried about being respectable. Shelton's gift, such as it was, was in straddling the line between seeming respectable enough for the comfort of some Klan members while being violent enough for others.

109   FBI, *Pro-Southerners--SAC, Miami*.

110   Mims is on the eastern coast of Florida.

111   John Fleming, "The Death of Willie Brewster: Guns, bombs and Kenneth Adams," *The Anniston Star*, March 24, 2009.

112   Dan Carter, "The violent life of Kenneth Adams: A story of

justice delayed," *The Anniston Star*, May 14, 2021.

113   The 5 looks like a 3, but I think that's a typo since Liuzzo died in 1965.

114   FBI, *62-116395*.

115   Yes, that's right. Hoover was bragging to the attorney general about the FBI's work helping to solve a murder an FBI informant was involved in, while protecting that informant from any repercussions.

116   Howell Raines, "Police Given Data on Boast by Rowe," *New York Times*, July 14, 1978.

117   FBI, *62-116395*.

118   FBI, *62-116395*.

119   David J. Garrow, "The Troubling Legacy of Martin Luther King Jr.," *Standpoint*, June, 2019.

120   Aimee Horton, "Letter to the Journal," *The Knoxville Journal*, August 1, 1963.

121   Aimee Horton, "Letter to the Journal," *The Knoxville Journal*, August 1, 1963.

122   "Tennessee Topics—Re-Election Glow Lights McKinnis' Political Star," *The Commercial Appeal*, August 22, 1965.

123   "State Klan Centered in Knox, E-T Area," *The Knoxville News-Sentinel*, October 19, 1965.

124   "House to Bypass State Klansmen," *The Commercial Appeal,* February 5, 1966.

125   "State Klan Clamps Secrecy on why Grand Dragon Quit," *The Commercial Appeal,* February 5, 1967.

126   FBI, *62-116395.*

127   Michael Newton, who literally wrote the book on the National States Rights Party, *The National States Rights Party,* says that the party wasn't founded until mid-1958. I agree, but I also think it's clear that there was some pre-party floundering where the people who would eventually settle on organizing the NSRP tried to decide what they wanted to do now that they had all these angry white people looking for ways to oppose integration. That floundering toward the NSRP seems to have started in earnest in November 1957.

128   Part of the confusion comes from the fact that the clearest information we have about how these Klans were set up at the time comes from the HUAC testimony of James Venable, a Klan leader who fought with both Jack Brown and Robert Shelton and had reason to lump them together and accuse them of being worse than him. Venable was also good friends with J.B. Stoner; they shared a law office—Venable was also a lawyer—in Georgia. Suffice to say that in 1958, Klan allegiances were shifting and new terrorist networks that crossed Klan groups and incorporated the NSRP were forming. J.B. Stoner sat at the nexus of those networks.

129   House Un-American Activities Committee, "Activities of Ku Klux Klan Organizations in the United States," in *Hearings Before the Committee on Un-American Activities House of Representatives, Eighty-Ninth Congress, Second Session* (February 1-4, 7-11 1966).

130   If you were trying to trace, say, how dynamite of a brand available in East Tennessee came to be used in so many bombings in Alabama where it was not sold, it's probably pretty important to realize that every time you see a mention in the history books of "Anniston Klan leader Kenneth Adams," what you're really seeing is "Anniston Dixie Knight leader Kenneth Adams." Once you know that Kenneth Adams and Jack Brown were in the same group, the mystery of how East Tennessee dynamite got into Alabama clears up easier than a Scooby-Doo mystery.

131   The FBI says they destroyed the file on the Mattie Green bombing in 2005. Much of what we know about that bombing then comes from a redacted copy of the file that the Southern Poverty Law Center got before then. The two men suspected in her murder were Klansmen brothers, Lester and W. E. Waters.

132   And, as Wexler and Hancock discovered, ten years later, Jack Brown's friend and likely Dixie Knight, Joseph Milteer, was instrumental in paying for King's assassination. Even if the group's importance dwindled—and who knows if that's actually true?—the individuals involved in the early years of the Dixie Knights remained prominent, active, and dangerous.

133   FBI, *J.B. Stoner File.*

134   FBI, "Bombings and Attempted Bombings," in *Racial Matters* (1958), Archive.org.

135   FBI, Bombings and Attempted Bombings.

136   David J. Meyer, "Fighting Segregation, Threats, and Dynamite: Rabbi William B. Silverman's Nashville Battle," *American Jewish*

Archives Journal (2008).

137   Donald Davidson, "Correspondence—Outgoing, July 21, 1957 - June 29, 1958," in *Donald Davidson Papers* (Vanderbilt University Special Collections).

138   "2 More Questioned in Center Dynamiting," *Tennessean*, April 17, 1958.

139   Remember, he went to federal prison at the beginning of 1958 as a result of his actions in Clinton in 1956. Then, once he got out of federal prison, he came back to Nashville in order to be a giant douche and to face charges resulting from his activities here in 1957.

140   See, for instance, Donald Davidson.

141   I'll be honest, I don't know enough about Christian Identity —nor do I care to learn—to know if the folks who would go on to be recognized as the leaders of the movement were already saying this explicitly, but this was the thought-train they were riding.

142   FBI, Bombings and Attempted Bombings.

143   FBI, Bombings and Attempted Bombings.

144   "Bethel Church Bombing and Temple Beth-El Bombing," in *Birmingham, Ala. Police Department Surveillance Files* (Birmingham Public Library, Department of Archive and Manuscripts).

145   AP, "Birmingham Reports Break on Bombing," *Tennessean*, May 2, 1958.

146   NSRP file (1959).

147   Though Fields had a number of mistresses and NSRP folks regularly complained about how Stoner's womanizing kept him away from party business—so, hey, finally bisexuals have some noted villains in their ranks.

148   *Jacksonville Conference on Bombings*, State of Florida (1958).

149   Maury County.

150   *Jacksonville Conference on Bombings*, State of Florida (1958).

151   Dublin, Georgia

152   *Jacksonville Conference on Bombings*, State of Florida (1958).

153   FBI, *J.B. Stoner File*.

154   FBI, *J.B. Stoner File*.

155   Until I read this in Stoner's file, I hadn't ever heard about the Confederate Underground taking credit for this bombing, but this is firm proof that the Confederate Underground wasn't only anti-Semitic. They were also plain old anti-Black racist. The bombings of Jewish buildings were a part of wider segregationist goals.

156   FBI, *NSRP file*.

157   FBI, *NSRP file*.

158   Gladys Girgenti told me that so many Klan leaders became FBI

informants because the money the FBI paid them was tax-free. I don't know for how long this has been true, but according to the IRS's website, it is indeed true.

159   FBI, *NSRP file.*

160   Though let me be clear: all we can know from the materials still available is that *someone* was in both Miami and Nashville on the same day. Morris is saying Stoner was in both cities for both bombings. But the fact that *anyone* was in both cities for both bombings is a fact only the attendees of the Southern Conference on Bombings knew. Morris seems to know that and who that person was.

161   FBI, *J.B. Stoner File.*

162   FBI, *John Kasper File.*

163   The ticket the NSRP ended up actually running in 1960 was segregationist hero, Arkansas governor Orval Faubus for president and Crommelin for vice-president, but in August 1958, the ticket they were toying with was Crommelin for president and possibly Kasper for VP.

164   FBI, *John Kasper File.*

165   FBI, *John Kasper File.*

166   FBI, *NSRP file.*

167   FBI, *John Kasper File.*

168   Rachel Louise Martin, *A Most Tolerant Little Town: The Explosive Beginning of School Desegregation* (Simon & Schuster, 2023).

169   FBI, *John Kasper File*.

170   FBI, *Robert Wray* (1958).

171   UPI, "Ku Klux Klan Trial Set for Today," *Tampa Bay Times*, June 30.

172   The Archives of the State of Florida has the materials from this June 1958 hearing. The whole hearing is in Series S1486, Box 4, folders 20–23. Sherrill's testimony is covered in folders 22 and 23.

173   *Tampa Tribune.* "Contempt Action Voted for Sheriff of Suwannee." June 27, 1958.

174   AP, "Undercover Man for FBI Testifies: Orlando Klan Blamed for Fatal Bombing," News-Press, June 28, 1958.

175   FBI, *John Kasper File*.

176   Stoner worked for the State Farm Insurance company at the time.

177   FBI, *J.B. Stoner File*.

178   Digging through the Birmingham police files and seeing how often Stoner's name and 16th Street Baptist Church bomber Robert Chambliss's name come up together, it does lead me to wonder if Stoner's Birmingham guy wasn't old' Dynamite Bob himself.

179   "FOIPA Requestion No.: 1372396-00 Subject: Z. Alexander Looby Bombing (April 19, 1960)," in FBI correspondence (May 1, 2017).

180   Talley, "Negroes Boycott Downtown Firms," *Tennessean*, April 5, 1960.

181   Mac Harris, "Kasper to Dissolve Own Citizens Council," *Tennessean*, April 17, 1960.

182   *Tennessean*. "King's Speech Location Moved to Fisk University." April 19, 1960.

183   Pat Anderson, "Looby Bombing Reward Voted," *Tennessean*, April 20, 1960.

184   In the 1958 city directory, Smith's home address is 1229 Caldwell Avenue. This is two blocks away from where the letter threatening Looby was found under a burning cross. This is just an odd coincidence, though. In 1951, he and his family were living on 22nd Avenue North.

185   Fisk Night Watchman interview transcript, ed. Ben West (April 19 1960).

186   Fisk Night Watchman interview transcript.

187   This is obviously Morena Street.

188   Fisk Night Watchman interview transcript.

189   Churchwell, Robert. "Fisk Guard Retires from 20-Year Walk." *Nashville Banner*, December 11, 1962.

190   Old folks may remember that Looby had a Black political rival named Neely. This is not him. This Neely was white.

191   "Confession of Bombing Discounted," *Banner*, April 22, 1960.

192   Looby, Z. Alexander. *The Civil Rights Documentation Project.* Interview by John Britton, 1967.

193   "Church Group Pushes Looby Fund Drive," *Tennessean*, May 21, 1960.

194   Debbie Elliott, "Blaming Victims for Mail Bombs Carries Echoes of Civil Rights Bombings," NPR.org (2018).

195   And getting beat up by Black inmates. He really hated that part.

196   I mention his middle name because there are a ton of Gentrys in the area and at least one other Robert Gentry our Robert's age who was running around getting into ordinary young person trouble, like speeding and such, who was not connected to racial terrorism.

197   Nancy Bradford, "Lawmen Wept During Arrests: Ex-Klansman," Tennessean, October 20, 1965.

198   House Un-American Activities Committee, "1965 Ku Klux Klan Investigation," in *Records Relating to the Investigation of Members of the KKK* (National Archives, 1965).

199   David M. Hardy, "FOIPA Request No.: 1374017-00 Subject: GENTRY, ROBERT PITTMAN," in FBI correspondence (June 27 2017).

200   Donal Godfrey and his mother.

201   I'm certain this is clear to you, but just in case, this quote is the

investigator's own words typifying Gentry's information, not a direct quote from Gentry.

202   Committee, Activities of Ku Klux Klan Organizations in the United States.

203   Committee, Activities of Ku Klux Klan Organizations in the United States.

204   Meaning, yes, she was in the Klan before our bombings.

205   Fun fact: Bill Wilkinson was an FBI informant. It's like Eastern Promises but with no naked fighting. That we know of.

206   Thompson, Jerry. "Klanswoman Leader in '80 Rally." *Tennessean*, May 26, 1981.

207   This is almost certainly not true. Emmett Carr might have let Catholics in his Klan, but no Klan at that time was going to let Catholic Italians in.

208   Remember, he might have been one of the early members of the Dixie Knights.

209   She regularly spoke at their gatherings, but Girgenti says she was never a member.

210   According to Girgenti, this was true.

211   King says 20. Girgenti says 30.

212   Jerry Thompson and Robert Sherborn, "New Klan Group Takes

on Name of 'Vigilantes'," *Tennessean*, May 27, 1981.

213   Girgenti says that the FBI raided her house after this bombing, accused Nick of being one of the bombers, and then stole Nick's wall crucifix. At the least, I think we can take this to mean the FBI suspected someone in the Girgenti household was tied to that bombing.

214   "Judge: Drop 1 of 5 Bomb Plot Counts," *Tennessean*, August 4, 1981.

215   Gladys Girgenti, Gladys Girgenti at her apartment, ed. Betsy Phillips (August 4 2018).

216   It should go without saying, but we can't assume this is true for all family members or for these family members all of the time.

217   See, for instance, Kelly Weill's story, "Neo-Confederate League of the South Banned from Armed Protesting in Charlottesville," *The Daily Beast*, March 27, 2018, which outlines the League's role in organizing the Charlottesville riot and shows how they armed the Klan.

218   *Jackson Sun*. "Blast Damages House of Negro Attorney." July 24, 1957.

219   Both Stoner and Kershaw represented James Earl Ray right after King's assassination.

220   Venable once shared office space with Stoner.

221   Stuart and Hancock Wexler, Larry, *Killing King: Racial Terrorists, James Earl Ray, and the Plot to Assassinate Martin Luther King Jr.*

(Berkeley: Counterpoint).

222 Kennedy

223 The 16th Street Baptist Church

224 Harold Weisberg, Joseph Milteer, The Weisberg Archive, Beneficial-Hodson Library, Hood College.

225 FBI, Dixie Knights.

226 We didn't have any racist killings in Tennessee during the reign of the Dixie Knights, to my knowledge, but if anyone has an unsolved murder of a Black person from the late '50s, early '60s, maybe look into these guys.

227 Dixie Knights, Knights of the Ku Klux Klan. Yes, two "Knights," right in a row. You'd think a social movement with so many poets in it could have come up with another K word that would work, but there was a lot of infighting.

228 FBI, Dixie Knights.

229 Harold Weisberg, Joseph Milteer, The Weisberg Archive, Beneficial-Hodson Library, Hood College.

230 FBI, Dixie Knights.

231 Harold Weisberg, Joseph Milteer, The Weisberg Archive, Beneficial-Hodson Library, Hood College.

232 And you can't explode C4 with a flame fuse, but that's kind

of irrelevant, since we don't know for sure that's what Somersett is talking about.

233   Keating, Robert, and Barry Michael Cooper. "Atlanta Child Murders: Our 1986 Feature, 'A Question of Justice.'" Spin.Com, December 29, 2015.

234   Keating and Cooper

235   Keating and Cooper

236   After King's assassination, Stoner was one of James Earl Ray's attorneys and Ray's brother worked for Stoner.

237   Federal Bureau of Investigation, "157-HQ-203," n.d.

238   Federal Bureau of Investigation, "John Kasper File—WFO, SAC," 1958.

239   It's actually more complicated and interesting than this, but suffice to say, since Reconstruction this is when the first Black officers joined the force. For more information on Reconstruction-era Black police officers in Nashville, see Justin Farr's "'The Mongrel Regime!:' The Untold Story of Tennessee's African American Policemen During the New South and Jim Crow Eras, 1867-1930," his honors thesis from Middle Tennessee State University in 2016.

240   "Police Trainer Urged for the City," *Tennessean*, January 30, 1960.

241   According to third-generation African American Nashville police officer Sergeant Gary Smith who has an encyclopedic knowledge of the

history of the Nashville police and whose grandfather was one of those first Black officers to join the force, Bailey wasn't a detective yet when the bombing happened.

242   LS T-2 designates a Louisville confidential informant.

243   Federal Bureau of Investigation, "157-HQ-203."

Image Index

Men protesting outside of Glenn School in East Nashville on the first day of school, September 9, 1957. The flyers they're holding are very similar to flyers John Kasper distributed in other Southern cities. *Nashville Public Library, Special Collections, Nashville Banner Photos*

September 23, 1963: Jack Cash (seated), Ralph Lewandowski, Edward Fields (with Confederate battle flag), and Gerald Dutton. Note the date. This is a week after the 16th Street Baptist Church bombing, and the brother of one of the bombers, Herman Cash, is in a room with Stoner's partner, Ed Fields. This photo was taken the day after they were all federally indicted for interfering in Birmingham's school desegregation. *AP Photo*

From left to right, Rev. James Lawson, Z. Alexander Looby, and Rev. Martin Luther King Jr. during the talk King gave at Fisk University on April 20, 1960. Looby's house was bombed the day before. I suspect the hat peaking out from behind Councilman Looby belongs to his wife, Grafta. *Nashville Public Library, Special Collections, Nashville Banner Photo*

Handwritten on the back of this photo is "1 Robert Stewart 2 Kenneth Castleman 3 Charles Hale 4 Emmett Carr." The sign they're placing on the car is a common Pro-Southerners slogan. Carr was the Pro-Southerners leader in Nashville in 1956, when this photo was taken. *Nashville Public Library, Special Collections, Nashville Banner Photos*

This photo was taken in Birmingham, Alabama, on September 13, 1956, when John Kasper (right) visited with Asa Carter (left). Carter and Kasper were both regularly involved with anti-integration activities in Tennessee; the implication of this photo is that they coordinated their efforts. For our purposes, let me be clear: this shows that Alabama racists were coordinating with Tennessee segregationists by 1956. And visa versa. *AP Photo*

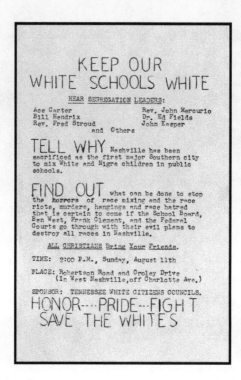

KEEP OUR
WHITE SCHOOLS WHITE

HEAR SEGREGATION LEADERS:

Ace Carter   Rev. John Mercurio
Bill Hendrix   Dr. Ed Fields
Rev. Fred Stroud   John Kasper
            and Others

TELL WHY Nashville has been
sacrificed as the first major Southern city
to mix White and Nigra children in public
schools.

FIND OUT what can be done to stop
the horrors of race mixing and the race
riots, murders, hangings and race hatred
that is certain to come if the School Board,
Ben West, Frank Clement, and the Federal
Courts go through with their evil plans to
destroy all races in Nashville.

ALL CHRISTIANS Bring Your Friends.

TIME: 2:00 P.M., Sunday, August 11th

PLACE: Robertson Road and Croley Drive
       (In West Nashville,off Charlotte Ave.)

SPONSOR: TENNESSEE WHITE CITIZENS COUNCILS.

HONOR----PRIDE---FIGHT
SAVE THE WHITES

Consider how the author of this flyer (most likely John Kasper himself) uses the term *race*. The most common usage of *race* in the 1950s was to mean "Black." Think of "race records" or "race man" or even how we use the term today when there's a "race riot." See how it creates room for white people to see themselves as the victims of desegregation; if it happens, there will be "race mixing," "race riots," and "race hatred." The implication is that Black people will mix with whites, Black people will riot against whites, Black people will hate whites. *Courtesy of the Tennessee State Library and Archives*

The whole east wing of Hattie Cotton was rendered unusable in the blast. Note Mayor West in the middle of the two police officers, examining the scene. *Nashville Public Library, Special Collections, Nashville Banner Photos*

Two of the suspects in the Hattie Cotton bombing, James Harris (left, with the American Flag) and Vincent Crimmons (right, with the Confederate flag). Note that Harris has a prosthetic leg. *Nashville Public Library, Special Collections, Nashville Banner Photos*

The Rider-Justin garage, still standing as of late 2022. *Photo by Betsy Phillips*

Protests outside of Glenn School in East Nashville on the first day of school, September 9, 1957. Look at the guy in the hat standing next to Rev. Fred Stroud. (Stroud's the one holding the "Communist" sign.) Look at the guy's right hand. You can imagine how much I hoped to talk to the family or friends of a man who looks like he might have had a dynamite mishap or two in his life, but I was never able to identify him. Could this man be Slim Thompson? *Nashville Public Library, Special Collections, Nashville Banner Photos*

Members of the Christian Anti-Jewish Party on the steps of the Chattanooga courthouse in 1954. This picture appeared in *LIFE* magazine in 1958, after Richard and Robert Bowling were arrested in the Atlanta Temple bombing. They're identified with arrows. *Photo by W.C. King, used with permission of the Chattanooga Times-Free Press*

November 6, 1946: Emory Burke. *Atlanta Journal-Constitution via AP*

November 2, 1961: Kenneth Adams. *AP Photo/Horace Court*

Atlanta Temple Bombing suspects, October 17, 1958: George Bright (front right, in glasses), Wallace Allen (front left), Luther King Corley (in shirtsleeves behind Allen), and Robert Bowling (stepping down from the wagon). *AP Photo/Horace Court*

The Jewish Community Center bombing was dramatic and scary, but the damage done to the building was mostly superficial. *Nashville Public Library, Special Collections, Nashville Banner Photos*

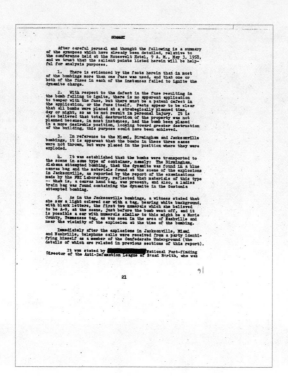

What's left of the materials from the Southern Conference on Bombing suggests attendees were openly naming and discussing suspected bombers throughout the South. *The Archives of the State of Florida*

Z. Alexander Looby's home in the wake of the bombing. Note the original wood siding of the house under the brick. *Nashville Public Library, Special Collections, Nashville Banner Photos*

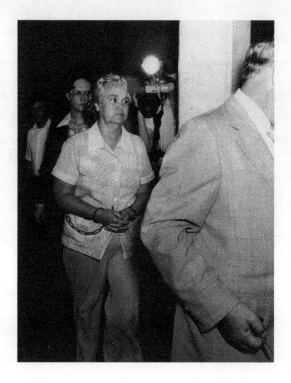

Gladys Girgenti after her arrest for trying to bomb The Temple in Belle Meade. *Nashville Public Library, Special Collections, Nashville Banner Photos*

Z. Alexander Looby's house. Look at how difficult he made it for bombers to target his house again. Gone is the big front window. There's no longer a front porch. Anyone who was going to bomb this house couldn't attempt it from the street. *Photo by Betsy Phillips*

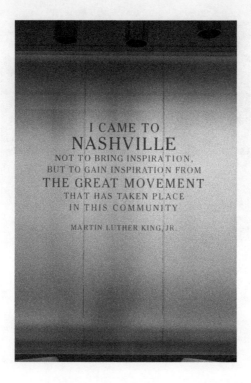

This quote hangs over the Civil Rights Room at the Downtown Nashville Library. *Photo by Andrew Najarian*

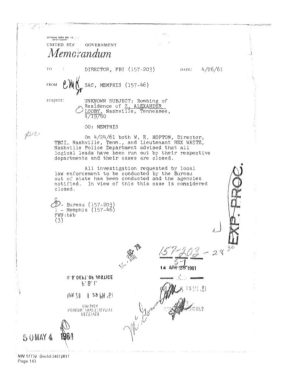

The last page of the FBI's file on the Looby bombing.

Jack Kershaw's Nathan Bedford Forrest statue, which was destroyed in 2021. *Photo by Eric England, Nashville Scene*

Bibliography

"1965 Ku Klux Klan Investigation." National Archives, 1965.

"2 More Questioned in Center Dynamiting," *Tennessean*, April 17, 1958.

"Activities of Ku Klux Klan Organizations in the United States," February 1, 1966.

Anderson, Pat. "Looby Bombing Reward Voted." *Tennessean*, April 20, 1960.

AP. "Birmingham Reports Break on Bombing." *Tennessean*, May 2, 1958.
———. "Undercover Man for FBI Testifies: Orlando Klan Blamed for Fatal Bombing." *Fort Myers News-Press*, June 28, 1958.

"Bethel Church Bombing and Temple Beth-El Bombing." Birmingham, Ala. Police Department Surveillance Files, n.d.

"Blaming Victims for Mail Bombs Carries Echoes of Civil Rights Bombings." *NPR.org*, October 27, 2018.

Bradford, Nancy. "Lawmen Wept During Arrests: Ex-Klansman." *Tennessean*, October 20, 1965.

Brinton, Larry. Interview at Bellvue Starbucks. Interview by Betsy Phillips, August 3, 2017.

Carey, Bill. "The Roger Williams Legacy." *The Tennessee Magazine*, July 2012.

Carter, Dan. "The Violent Life of Kenneth Adams: A Story of Justice Delayed." *Anniston Star*, May 14, 2021.

Chattanooga Times. "McCallie Student Gets Message from Nazi Radio Propagandist." May 28, 1940.

Churchwell, Robert. "Fisk Guard Retires from 20-Year Walk." *Nashville Banner*, December 11, 1962.

Commercial Appeal. "House to Bypass State Klansmen." February 5, 1966.

Commercial Appeal. "Klan Meeting Snubbed." July 17, 1965.

Commercial Appeal. "State Klan Clamps Secrecy on Why Grand Dragon Quit." February 5, 1967.

Commercial Appeal. "Tennessee Topics—Re-Election Glow Lights McKinnis' Political Star," August 22, 1965.

Daily New-Journal. "United Press." August 29, 1957.

Davidson, Donald. "Correspondence—Outgoing, July 21, 1957 – June 29, 1958," 1958.

Dawson, Lem. Fisk Night Watchman interview transcript. Interview by Ben West, April 19, 1960.

DeGregory, Crystal A. "Nashville's Clandestine Black Schools." *The New York Times*, February 17, 2015.

Delmez, Katherine E. *We Shall Overcome: Press Photographs of*

Nashville during the Civil Rights Era. Nashville: Vanderbilt University Press, 2018.

Dickson Herald. "Jack Kershaw Obituary." September 24, 2010.

Egerton, John. "Walking into History: The Beginning of School Desegregation in Nashville." *Southern Spaces*, May 4, 2009.

Federal Bureau of Investigation. "62-116395," n.d.
———. "157-HQ-203," n.d.
———. "Bombing of Atlanta Temple 1958-Chicago-1," 1958.
———. "Bombings and Attempted Bombings." Racial Matters, 1958.
———. "Christian Anti Jewish Party J.B. Stoner File," 1952.
———. "Dixie Knights," n.d.
———. "Hattie Cotton Elementary School Bombing File," 1957.
———. "J.B. Stoner File," n.d.
———. "John Kasper File," 1957.
———. "John Kasper File—Knoxville," 1957.
———. "John Kasper File—WFO, SAC," 1958.
———. "NSRP File," 1959.
———. "Pro-Southerners—SAC, Miami," 1954.
———. "Robert Wray," 1958.

Fleming, John. "The Death of Willie Brewster: Guns, Bombs and Kenneth Adams." *Anniston Star*, March 24, 2009.

Fullerton, Garry. "Kasper Halted at Park Rally." *Tennessean*, August 5, 1957.

Garrow, David J. "The Troubling Legacy of Martin Luther King Jr." *Standpoint*, June 2019.

Girgenti, Gladys. Gladys Girgenti at her apartment. Interview by Betsy Phillips, August 4, 2018.

Hall, Alan. "KKK Said Training SWAT Teams for War." *Tennessean*, October 4, 1980.

Hardy, David M. "FOIPA Request No.: 1374017-00 Subject: GENTRY, ROBERT PITTMAN," June 27, 2017.
———. "FOIPA Requestion No.: 1372396-00 Subject: Z. Alexander Looby Bombing (April 19, 1960)," May 1, 2017.

Harris, Mac. "Kasper to Dissolve Own Citizens Council." *Tennessean*, April 17, 1960.

Horton, Aimee. "Letter to the Journal." *Knoxville Journal*, August 1, 1963.

Houchin, Frank. Testimony. Interview by O. O. Lee, January 10, 1958.

Jackson Sun. "Blast Damages House of Negro Attorney." July 24, 1957.

"Jacksonville Conference on Bombings." State of Florida, 1958.

Keating, Robert, and Barry Michael Cooper. "Atlanta Child Murders: Our 1986 Feature, 'A Question of Justice.'" *Spin.com*, December 29, 2015.

Keel, William. "Kasper: 'Certain People' Talked School Dynamiting." *Tennessean*, September 13, 1957.
———. "Study Continues on Integration." *Tennessean*, August 9, 1957.
———. "Wilson Actions 'Maniac's Work,' DA Tells Jury." *Tennessean*, March 30, 1955.

————. "Wilson Ordered Blasts, Stokes Shouts." *Tennessean*, March 29, 1955.

Kenyon, Nellie. "12 1st Graders to Enter White Schools Monday." *Tennessean*, September 7, 1957.

Knoxville News-Sentinel. "State Klan Centered in Knox, E-T Area." October 19, 1965.

Looby, Z. Alexander. The Civil Rights Documentation Project. Interview by John Britton, 1967.

Marsh, Alec. *John Kasper and Ezra Pound: Saving the Republic*. London and New York: Bloomsbury Academic, 2015.

Martin, Rachel Louise. *A Most Tolerant Little Town: The Explosive Beginning of School Desegregation*. Simon & Schuster, 2023.

Meyer, David J. "Fighting Segregation, Threats, and Dynamite: Rabbi William B. Silverman's Nashville Battle." *American Jewish Archives Journal*, 2008, 99–113.

Muller, Will. "Ku Klux Klan Reins Held by Auto Painter." *Star Press*, September 5, 1955.

Murphy, Paul V. "Agrarians." In *Tennessee Encyclopedia*, September 4, 2017.
————. "Donald Davidson." In *Tennessee Encyclopedia*, January 1, 2010.

Nashville Banner. "Confession of Bombing Discounted." April 22, 1960.

Nashville Banner. "Eight Indicted by Grand Jury." February 10, 1936.

Nashville Public Schools. "School Board Minutes," August 8, 1957.

Newton, Michael. *The National States Rights Party: A History*. Jefferson, North Carolina: McFarland & Company, Inc., 2017.

Pensacola News Journal. "Hendrix Gets Evangelist's License." June 23, 1953.

Raines, Howell. "Police Given Data on Boast by Rowe." *The New York Times*, July 14, 1978.

Squires, James. *Secrets of the Hopewell Box: Stolen Elections, Southern Politics, and a City's Coming of Age*. New York: Crown Publishing Group, 1996.

Talley, James. "Negroes Boycott Downtown Firms." *Tennessean*, April 5, 1960.

Tampa Bay Times. "Recent Crackdowns Lead to Disunity in Klan Ranks." August 20, 1952.

Tampa Tribune. "Contempt Action Voted for Sheriff of Suwannee." June 27, 1958.

Tampa Tribune. "One Klansman Raps Another." January 6, 1950.

Tennessean. "6 Questioned in School Blast." September 11, 1957.

Tennessean. "Burning Cross Found Near Acklen, Grove." March 29, 1951.

Tennessean. "Carter Returns to Kasper Fold." August 26, 1957.

Tennessean. "Catholics Enroll Negro Students." September 5, 1954.

Tennessean. "Church Group Pushes Looby Fund Drive." May 21, 1960.

Tennessean. "Court Delays Dynamite Cases." September 21, 1957.

Tennessean. "Earlier Return of Kasper Seen." September 20, 1957.

Tennessean. "Judge: Drop 1 of 5 Bomb Plot Counts." August 4, 1981.

Tennessean. "Kasper Planning Session with Klan, White Council." August 1, 1957.

Tennessean. "Kasper Returns, To Try Boycott." September 6, 1957.

Tennessean. "King's Speech Location Moved to Fisk University." April 19, 1960.

Tennessean. "Nashville Man Quizzed in Blast." April 16, 1958.

Tennessean. "Police Trainer Urged for the City." January 30, 1960.

"Tennessee Federation for Constitutional Government Roster and Newsletter." *University of Tennessee, Chattanooga, Digital Collections,* October 1, 1955.

Thompson, Jerry. "Klanswoman Leader in '80 Rally." *Tennessean,* May 26, 1981.

Thompson, Jerry, and Robert Sherborn. "New Klan Group Takes on Name of 'Vigilantes.'" *Tennessean,* May 27, 1981.

"Transcript of Milteer-Somersett Tape." Mary Ferrell Foundation, November 9, 1963.

UPI. "Ku Klux Klan Trial Set for Today." *Tampa Bay Times*, June 30, 1964.

Weisberg, Harold. "Joseph Milteer." The Weisberg Archive, Beneficial-Hodson Library, Hood College, n.d.

Westfeldt, Wallace. "1st Grade Register Off 43%." *Tennessean*, August 28, 1957.
———. "Attendance Off by 25-30 Pct." *Tennessean*, September 10, 1957.

Wexler, Stuart and Hancock. *Killing King: Racial Terrorists, James Earl Ray, and the Plot to Assassinate Martin Luther King Jr.* Berkeley: Counterpoint, 2018.

Whitehead, Don. "Florida KKK Recruiting During Wave of Terrorism." *Tampa Tribune*, January 6, 1952.

Whitt, Wayne. "Ku Klux Leader Admits Klavern in Nashville." *Tennessean*, April 13, 1950.

Winchell, Mark Royden. *Where No Flag Flies: Donald Davidson and the Southern Resistance*. University of Missouri Press, 2000.

Wood, E. Thomas. "Nashville Now and Then: Banner Days Gone By." *Nashville Post*, February 15, 2008. https://www.nashvillepost.com/home/nashville-now-and-then-banner-days-gone-by/article_418f-c2fb-5478-5369-93b6-f4c6309be858.html.

Wray, Carrie. "Letter to Governor Frank Clement." Tennessee State Library and Archives, August 1957.

Printed in the USA
CPSIA information can be obtained
at www.ICGtesting.com
JSHW021719010824
67426JS00006B/131

9 798986 614571